Praise for Diana Ensign's *The Freedom to Be*

"Diana Ensign has done it again! She has generated an amazing book that encourages us to listen, to learn, and to love. I have grown tremendously from reading these stories. They have moved my heart and will move me to action." —**Franklin Oliver, History Instructor, Poet, Host of WhoDeannyPod Podcast https://whodeannypod.org/**

"*The Freedom to Be* highlights the amazing strength of LGBTQ+ people. Stories like these allow the youth at Indiana Youth Group (IYG) to know that life does get better, and they too can lead full, inspiring lives." —**Chris Paulson, Executive Director of Indiana Youth Group (IYG) www.indianayouthgroup.org**

"Diana Ensign has captured the voice and experience of youth and adults who need and deserve to have their voices heard. As an educator, I believe *The Freedom to Be* could help begin informed, positive conversations between parents, teachers, and other adults with trans and nonbinary youth in their lives." —**Dawn Merrill, Humanities & Technology (k-12) Teacher**

"This book is a great glimpse into several lives of transgender people and those close to them. The candid discussions help you feel connected to the individuals and serve to bring out our compassion. Each and every individual is unique, and these stories show that variety. As a parent to a transgender child, I recommend *The Freedom to Be* to family members, friends, and community members who want ideas on how to best support transgender individuals." —**Steph B., Parent**

"To be loved, valued, and accepted are basic human needs, but unfortunately all too rare for gender nonconforming and transgender people. As a clinical social worker, I've learned that society's binary idea of gender is a fabrication that limits our individual creativity and potential. As *The Freedom to Be* shows, these are human beings who just want to live their lives in peace and without threat so they can realize their full potential. My hope is that the human race will evolve to the point where differences in gender expression are no longer feared and demonized but rather enhanced, embraced, and celebrated." —**Tina Wiesert, Clinical Social Worker, LCSW**

"The telling of human stories is always a timeless, brilliant venture. The act of writing these stories into human history begins to capture our truth. Sharing your own story authentically during this time in history is brave and bold. They cannot erase our being! May we all continue to be brave enough to share and bold enough to listen." —**Kris Wise MSW, LCSW, Ally Counseling & Consulting**

"This book is *perfect* for anyone wanting to better understand those who are transgender, nonbinary, and/or gender nonconforming. Instead of focusing on abstract concepts and statistics, Diana Ensign brings us face-to-face with real people who share the power of their personal experience. Open your heart, and let God speak to you through these *amazing stories*." —**Rev. Jeff Miner, LifeJourney Church, Indianapolis.**

"Diana Ensign has lovingly and poignantly documented the lives of people who have faced obstacles because of who they are or because of who they love. Each account moved me in different ways as she has managed to provide an array of perspectives and voices. As an educator for 32 years, I appreciate that each portrait powerfully taught a different lesson." —**William Gulde, Educator (*retired*), Author**

"As we begin the process of understanding who we are within the LGBTQ+ community, most of us are incredibly vulnerable, uncertain of our futures, and hoping to find compassion. In those beginnings, we rely on the willingness of others to share their stories with us, honestly and humbly, so we can become who we were always meant to be. The foundation of our community rests in the courage and the raw honesty of people like those in *The Freedom to Be* who are bravely living their truth of being queer." —**Chris Handberg, Executive Director of Indy Pride, Inc. www.indypride.org**

Also by Diana J. Ensign, JD
Heart Guide: *True Stories of Grief and Healing*
Traveling Spirit: *Daily Tools for Your Life's Journey*
Available on the Author's Website: **www.dianaensign.com.**
Books also available on Amazon & Kindle

THE FREEDOM
TO BE

THE FREEDOM TO BE

*Stories from Transgender Youth,
Adults, and Their Families*

Diana J. Ensign, JD

Book photo image by Mark A. Lee, Great Exposures and used with permission. www.greatexposures.net
Book cover design by Arcane Book Cover Designs. www.arcanebookcovers.com

Published by SpiritHawk Life Publications.
Indianapolis, IN, USA

Library of Congress Control Number: 2019917996

Ensign, Diana
Title: The Freedom to Be: stories from transgender youth, adults, and their families / Diana J. Ensign
—1st edition
p. cm.

ISBN: 978-0-9883-320-10 (paperback)

1. Transgender people — United States 2. Transgender youth — United States 3. Transgenderism — United States 4. Families — United States 5. SOCIAL SCIENCE / Gender Studies 7. FAMILY & RELATIONSHIPS / Parenting / General 8. Gender Identity

Printed in the United States of America

Dedicated to:

The courageous individuals who shared their stories.
All the people bravely living their truth.
Freedom Fighters everywhere who remind us to care for one another.

FOREWORD

BY JENNI WHITE, EXECUTIVE DIRECTOR OF TRINITY
HAVEN, INDIANA'S FIRST TRANSITIONAL HOUSING
PROGRAM FOR LGBTQ YOUTH WHO ARE AT RISK
OF HOMELESSNESS (www.trinityhavenindy.org).

I have known Diana Ensign for almost 15 years, and I appreciate more than anything her compassionate heart, her desire to make a difference in the world, and her willingness to listen, learn, and love. Over the years, we have laughed together, cried together, broken bread together, prayed and meditated together, played games together, spent quiet time together, and made crafty projects together. In all that time, what I have learned about Diana is that she is kind. Thoughtful. Contemplative. Compassionate. And motivated.

When she reached out to me in my new position as founding executive director of Trinity Haven, letting me know she was writing a book to support trans folx, I knew without question that she had taken the time to consider all the reasons why she should...or shouldn't...pursue this project. I knew that she had prayed and meditated on it. That she had heard a call to action and that she was taking steps toward that end. When I then learned she was going to listen, first and foremost, to each person's story and compile them as they were shared with her and then share them with the world, I understood that she knew her role was to be a conduit, through which these powerful stories could be shared with others.

I am thankful for Diana: For her drive to make a difference in the world. For her ability to listen without judgment and with an open and compassionate heart. For her willingness to listen – to herself, to others, and to the spirit which calls her to a higher purpose. May you learn these things about Diana as you explore the offering in *The Freedom to Be*, and may you learn a bit more about our trans friends, family, strangers and neighbors.

May your heart be as open as hers to learning more about others and about yourself.

—*Jenni White, Executive Director of Trinity Haven*
She/Her/Hers

CONTENTS

"We have one job: to love and support our children."
—Karen, From *The Freedom to Be*

"Communities and our country benefit when we have a wider array of citizens. Our differences don't make us evil. They just make us different."
—Addison J. Smith, From *The Freedom to Be*

INTRODUCTION

Years ago, I stumbled upon a play showing at the Phoenix Theater in Indianapolis called, *The Laramie Project*. The play told the story of Matthew Shepard, a 21-year-old, openly gay young man living in Laramie, Wyoming, who was brutally murdered. Matthew's horrific death and the harrowing stories from people in his hometown helped to raise pubic awareness of the need for hate crime legislation to protect LGBT individuals. It also broke open my heart.

Today, the rampant hate, bigotry, and violence against transgender people calls not only for our urgent awareness and compassion but also for our collective action. Transgender individuals, particularity transgender women of color, risk deadly violence merely for existing and for being who they are.

Along with violence, transgender individuals often experience rejection from their families and overt discrimination in housing and employment, all of which leads to increased homelessness. Just in daily living, transgender individuals are forced to navigate obstacles that cisgender people (people whose gender identity aligns with the sex assigned at birth) may not even think about, such as restroom access, being misgendered, social stigma, and laws and policies that create inequalities based on gender identity and/or gender expression. Please note that the term transgender in this context is an umbrella term that includes the beautiful, vast spectrum of gender identities and expressions. A glossary of terms is found at the back.

Such widespread and pervasive transphobia also puts transgender people at risk for suicide. According to a recent American Academy of

Pediatrics study, transgender and nonbinary youth have alarming rates of suicide attempts. In many states, there are no statewide legal protections for transgender people against discrimination in their schools, employment, housing accommodations, medical services, and other aspects of their lives.

As Destinee Salinas says, "The harassment of trans people needs to stop."

There is no excuse for hatred, and *under no circumstance* should violence (verbal, physical, or emotional violence) be tolerated: not in the form of jokes, not on social media, not in the workplace, not in schools, not in our neighborhoods, not in our places of worship, and most importantly not in our families.

Instead, we can each lift up, support, advocate, and care for people who are transgender. More than that, we can embrace and celebrate the unique contributions from the *numerous* intelligent and talented individuals living in our communities: humans who happen to be transgender, nonbinary, and/or gender nonconforming.

We can ensure that people feel safe and feel loved.

Where do we begin?

In doing social justice work, whether in the United States or across the globe, it's important to ask people what they need *and then to listen.* People are the experts on *their* life experiences. Anyone trying to "help" likely has a tremendous amount to learn from those they wish to serve.

For instance, in addition to their roles as parents, students, spouses, artists, musicians, employees, advocates, and so forth, the transgender and nonbinary individuals in this book recognize better than most people the negative and harmful impacts of social conditioning. Their lives frequently necessitate outside-the-box thinking, creative problem solving, perseverance, and courage, along with an ability to overcome perceived limitations and direct experience of personal transformation. Why would anyone *not want* that incredible skill set in schools, businesses, government, and community organizations?

As Matty Slaydon explains, "We have something to contribute too, and we're just people."

We would all do well to learn how to listen to the hearts of others, without judgment and without trying to "fix" or change someone else.

To that end, this book is first and foremost about listening.

For me, listening is a sacred practice as a spiritual person on this planet. Listening to one another, from the heart, is how we learn and grow. It is how we understand more about our shared humanity: our common hopes, dreams, fears, losses, desires, and triumphs. Desmond Tutu reminds us, "Differences are not intended to separate, to alienate. We are different precisely in order to realize our need of one another."

While listening to one another is not always easy, it is necessary if we want to build bridges of compassion that allow us to join together to create a more loving world. Author Huston Smith, a scholar of religious studies, aptly noted, "Daily the world grows smaller, leaving understanding the only place where peace can find a home. Those who listen work for peace, a peace built not on religious or political hegemonies, but on mutual awareness and concern. For understanding brings respect, and respect prepares the way for a higher capacity, which is love."

In this book, I asked transgender youth, parents of transgender individuals, and transgender adults doing advocacy work in their communities the following questions:

What do people need to know to be better allies? How can our communities be more supportive?

Each person interviewed provides crucial insights on how to build healthy, safe, and caring communities. This book is intended to amplify their voices, not mine. A friend recently described my role as "a story catcher." The people I encounter in my work as a writer are always my teachers, which is both humbling and also extremely gratifying. I believe we are *all* each other's teachers, ideally with learning that continues throughout our entire lives. Regrettably, I thought we (as a society) had made more progress. Current attempts to legislate hate tell us otherwise. As someone pointed out to me, when we are not living day in and day out with oppression, our privilege can make us complacent.

This book is my effort to speak out as an ally. When someone asks me, "Why this book?" My question back is, "Why isn't *everyone* doing something to bring these issues front and center?" If we have learned anything from history, it is that we have a moral imperative to do our part when we see situations of injustice or when we witness harm toward our fellow humans. The famous quote by Martin Niemoller (German theologian) reminds us: "First they came for the socialists, and I did not speak out—because I was not a socialist. Then they came for the trade unionists, and I did not speak out—because I was not a trade unionist. Then they came for the Jews, and I did not speak out—because I was not a Jew. Then they came for me—and there was no one left to speak for me." Always, we are stronger when we stand united in the struggle for justice and equality.

A portion of this book's profits will go to support LGBTQ+ organizations doing the challenging work of saving lives. Trinity Haven (service and housing provider for LGBTQ youth at risk of homelessness) and Sa'hara Miller's work in her Sophisticated Divas program at BU Wellness are two organizations I wish to support. A list of Community Resources is included at the end of the book for anyone who wants to do more to help. I am also setting up a GoFundMe™ campaign to provide book copies free of charge for rural libraries, schools, small nonprofit organizations, and/or low-income individuals. (The funds will be used *solely* to produce book copies for distribution to those in need. None of the funds will go to me).

We all have something we can add to the effort of bringing greater compassion to humanity. Our contributions might be creative, educational, financial, advocacy, or daily acts of kindness. Whatever our individual offering, we cannot simply ignore the hateful memes against transgender individuals on social media or the disparaging remarks by people who should know better. Everything we do (or fail to do) has ripple effects. These are smart, talented, creative individuals—just being who they are in this world. No one should *ever* feel like the world is against them. Transgender and nonbinary individuals, as well as their families, deserve respect, acceptance, and love. Moreover, joy and freedom should be the birthright of *every human* on this planet!

Two precepts from Buddhist monk Thich Nhat Hanh that guide not only my writing but also my life are: "Have the courage to speak out about situations of injustice, even when doing so will threaten your own safety. Live in a way that will create a better future for our children." I try to use my writing to advocate for people I care about deeply. Writing is my way to raise awareness whenever people are judged, stigmatized, and not fully supported by the community. (My book *Heart Guide*, for instance, addresses the stigma around deaths related to substance misuse, heroin overdose, mental health issues, suicide, and sexual violence).

For transgender and nonbinary individuals struggling simply to make it through the day, it is imperative that we do everything in our power to share a universal message that conveys: *You are worthy. You are loved. You matter!*

Certainly, we can all find reasons to care for one another and reasons to act for the betterment of humanity. Research indicates that transgender youth who are rejected by their families face a higher risk of homelessness and suicide. Additionally, we may know individuals who are not openly living their authentic lives because they are terrified of being fired from their jobs, or they are afraid of losing family and friends, or they are scared of becoming victims of physical and verbal cruelty. These are legitimate fears. Even many of the people who willingly shared their stories in this book express anguish over employment discrimination and recount incidents of verbal or physical violence. In fact, some people did not feel safe sharing their stories here, and others who shared their stories did not feel safe using their names. All of that *must* change.

A quote I read recently from Rev. Masando Hirako (*Science of Mind* columnist) sums it up well, "If we have the ability to disengage, it may mean we have been lucky enough to have a life that does not have to live with these kinds of daily struggles."

The individuals I interviewed are primarily (but not exclusively) from the "*Hoosier Hospitality*" state of Indiana. The Midwest is known as America's Heartland. It is made up of people who are often identified as hardworking and industrious. People in America's Heartland are known for their willingness to lend a hand to help out their neighbors. With that in mind, we cannot permit hate or acts of violence and discrimination against transgender individuals in our communities—or anywhere in the world!

What we can do is work together to create places where *all* families are valued. As Pauli Murray (activist, lawyer, Episcopal priest, author) declared decades ago: "True community is based upon equality, mutuality, and reciprocity. It affirms the richness of individual diversity as well as the common human ties that bind us together."

We must learn to expand our hearts and extend our friendliness and kindness to everyone, whether their gender identity and/or gender expression is the same or different from our own.

I wish to add a few words about *what this book is not.* It is not intended to portray the rich, full, and varied lives of transgender people. Myriad books, YouTube™ videos, and artistic expressions depict the unique life journeys of transgender men and women. Several individuals interviewed here reference some of those materials. LGBTQ organization websites list abundant resources as well. Check out that wealth of material to learn more. Dive in!

Next, this book is not merely about tolerance and diversity. Members of a community may express some tolerance of diversity: consider the varying levels of acceptance (or non-acceptance) towards age, race, religion, disability, sexual orientation, national origin, gender, gender identity, and gender expression. (Individuals may also occupy more than one category simultaneously). However, tolerance alone is not enough.

In life, we are not necessarily cognizant of our own blinders (areas where *we don't know that we don't know*). For instance, if I present a workshop and someone who is hearing impaired attends, there may be a lot of things about the workshop that I (as someone who hears) never took into consideration. Am I speaking while adjusting the lights? (The person can't read my lips if my back is turned). Have I brought in a sign language interpreter? Is my language inclusive or does it make reference to waking from the sound of chirping birds and *assume* that is the norm for everyone? In other words, I may have tolerance for differences and not consider myself prejudiced, but I don't have much actual knowledge. A lack of understanding can result in not making the needed changes in my presentation. Worse than that, it can communicate a message that some people are more worthy than other people.

Even with tolerance for all types of diversity, cisgender people might not *know* anything about the transgender individuals living in their community, and they may not have any friends who are transgender. As Rose Peck (recent college graduate) explains, "A lot of people who end up bigoted have never met a trans person or met a gay person and know nothing about it. If you just met a couple of us, we're very nice." This book encourages everyone to form friendships with people in the transgender community. Get to know each other! That's how we break down misconceptions and hate, for those who are willing to make the effort.

Vivian Edwards says, "We are just normal people. We have the same sort of dreams and goals, and we just want to live our own lives."

This book is also not about limiting the voice, through the use of copyright, of those who were interviewed. Copyright is a way to ensure that this book is not reproduced or sold without permission of the author. It also protects the profits that are intended to go to LGBTQ organizations. Nothing in the copyright prevents *anyone* interviewed from telling their story or from writing a book about their personal journey. Just the opposite, I fully support and encourage any of those interviewed herein to contact a publisher, show an excerpt from this book, and perhaps receive a contract to write their life story. In my experience, creative artistic people try to help other creative people in pursuing their dreams.

Finally, this book is a starting point, not an endpoint. The starting point is getting to know one another and learning how to be effective allies. Joining our efforts, we then continue each day the ongoing, difficult task of eliminating bigotry, discrimination, hostility, and violence against transgender individuals—in every segment of society.

As Mike, a parent of a transgender son, emphasizes, "Discrimination against transgender people is discrimination against the entire family. It's anti-family."

Jordan, a transgender college student, states, "If I take my brother out, I always make sure I have my cell phone with me, fully charged and everything, so I can call for help. I don't want to be in a situation where he sees a hate crime happening involving me. He doesn't need to see that. He's only 8 years old."

At the back of this book are *Practical Action Steps for Allies* to aid everyone in collectively engaging in meaningful, affirming actions going forward. The action steps were written in conversation with Kit Malone, who works on behalf of the transgender community in various capacities at the ACLU of Indiana and as a Board Member of Trinity Haven.

A useful mantra that may guide our efforts to be helpful is: *Listen. Learn. Act.*

Allies can be powerful advocates in their communities. As Ryan Smith says, "The whole point of being an ally is a verb. It's the essence of being and doing. And it really transfers into being an advocate."

Allies can work toward equal rights and legal protections that provide the necessary safeguards for transgender individuals to receive education, housing, healthcare, and employment opportunities—ALL without discrimination based on gender identity or gender expression. It should never be the burden of a transgender person (or individuals in any marginalized group) to solve ignorance and end hatred. That responsibility rests firmly in the larger society: from each person responsible for hiring and promoting employees, educating students, raising children, preaching from the pulpit, providing healthcare services, enacting laws, organizing community events, and creating works of art . . . to those private, personal and intimate conversations we have with family and loved ones.

Ultimately, humans want more than equal rights. As Kimberly Acoff voices in her reflections, people need the freedom to live their authentic lives. They need the freedom to be who they are: freedom to work, freedom to pursue dreams, freedom to worship, and freedom to love one another.

As she says, *"It's about recognizing humanity and ensuring that every person is given what the constitution guarantees: the right to freedom and the right to liberty and justice for all."*

May it be so.

Peace, Love, & Solidarity,
Diana J. Ensign
She/Her/Hers

Part 1

AWESOME YOUNG ADULTS

Andru Lanning

Student – Performer, Singer, Actor
He/Him/His
18 years old

> *"We're all people, and we're all here for a reason . . ..*
> *and the best way to get things done is to just do it with love."*

I was born in Hemlock, Indiana, in the middle of nowhere, with a population of like 11 people. It's a very small town, the size of a block. It's near Greentown, on the outskirts of Kokomo, which is where I grew up. I have a pet in Kokomo named Nummy. It's the first word I knew how to say. (Laughs). It's a big kitty!

I just graduated from North Central High School in Indianapolis. I'm a business major in the ASAP program, which is an 11-month associate degree program, and then I'll be attending further college, probably Ball State University, but I'm also looking at Columbia. I got into the BFA theater program at Ball State University, but it cost too much money. I'm either going into performance theater or I am going to law school. So, either acting or law school. (Laughs). A very big contrast!

What are your favorite foods, movies, or books?

My favorite food is Macaroni and Cheese. My favorite movie is *"La Cage aux Follies,"* which was a French Broadway show. *The Birdcage* movie (starring Robin Williams) was based off of the performance. It's a wonderful, wonderful show.

RuPaul is my favorite author, and she came out with a book, *GuRu*, talking a lot about her self-discovery, her journey, and she actually put some pieces in there from her journal when she was young, and it's helped me a lot with accepting who I am. You know, "We're Proud," but every single day is a journey with self-love. That book helped me feel like I am here, and I am noticed, and I am valid. That's something I say a lot: I am valid.

What are your hobbies and interests?

I really enjoy writing, and I love any artistic outlet: dancing, singing, and playing piano, painting, photography, and acting. I am performing this Saturday. It's an open stage event for youth, 21 and under. I will be doing a drag queen performance. I love performing and doing drag is kind of everything I love to do in one selective thing. It's playing an influential character that can engage an audience in four minutes. My goal is to make them feel every emotion and give them a full Broadway Show.

Gender identity and gender expression are two different things. So, when I do drag, I can still see myself as a man, but externally present differently than how I feel. For me, drag is a character. It's acting. It's a performance. Drag to me is like me at my highest artistic power. I feel unstoppable whenever I am in full drag and performing.

What do you like to do in your spare time?

I am always busy. I don't have spare time. Just when I think I have spare time, I get busy. I keep myself pretty occupied with art. My brain is always going a million miles an hour. Some people stay on 100. I stay on 150! (Laughs). I'm always finding outlets to express how I am feeling, and I love just making people happy.

Tell me a little about your journey.

I came out as transgender when I was 13, which is really young. It was the summer before I entered my high school freshman year. I had always struggled with my gender identity from a really young age, and it never fully made sense to me. I don't even remember how I came across the term transgender. But it was probably a Lush YouTube™ video where the fact that I was trans just kind of clicked. So, when I was 13, I stayed up all night constructing this video I had made, with my little note cards. After I had stayed up all night and brought it down to the fine details and looked through everything, around 9 AM I posted it on Facebook. I came out to everybody as trans at the same time. (Laughs).

That's when things started getting complicated. Not long after I came out on social media, I came out to my father. My mother was not in the picture and was never in my life up until recently. It was just me and my dad, and he did not understand it and was not accepting of the realization I'd had. His immediate response was to push it away; and so, he pushed me away. I ended up moving out because of my dad not being accepting of me, and I moved in with my grandmother.

For the next few years, I would move between my grandma's home and my dad's home. But every time I went back to my dad's, it got worse because I was now more comfortable in my skin and started standing up for myself. Everything up until like age 17 is kind of a blur. I think I was 15 or 16, and I had moved in with my dad again. At that time, my grandmother didn't have her own place, which is why I had moved back in with my dad, and me and my dad got into it, and he kicked me out of the house because I told him that I wanted to transition. At 15 or 16 you're eligible to start taking hormones. I'm pretty sure that's why that argument arose. I was trying to start hormones.

So, I was homeless.

I was young, and I was sleeping at friend's houses, and I used to sleep at this park called Foster or pretty much anywhere I could go. That was the start of my high school. Through the first two years of my high school life, my freshman and sophomore year at Kokomo High School, since I didn't have a home I spent a lot of my time at school. I was a really good student. I got good grades. I couldn't really go home, so I was always there. I got super involved in drama club and also the debate team. My sophomore year I was involved in show choir. The drama club, debate team, and show choir took a lot of my time. I stayed at school until 8 PM or 9 PM every single day. My outlet was acting because it brought me away from what my reality was.

Junior year, I ended up moving in with my grandmother again. My dad was not in my life at this point. She lived out in the middle of nowhere, by Taylor High School. At that time, she was staying with my uncle, upstairs. It was just me and her in this little room: a one-bedroom with a bathroom, that we also made into a little kitchen, a living room, and then like this little closet area, which is where I slept. We made it the best that we could. I attended Taylor High School, and there was no drama club or show choir there.

At Taylor High School, I was not involved in anything and, honestly, junior year was such a waste of time. I didn't make any friends. I just kind of went back home to my cornfield and stayed there. But it gave me a lot of time to reflect on who I am, what I want for myself, and where I was and also, how much I loved my grandma, a lot! I realized she was there for me, and we talked about what had happened. I got really close with her. When there's two people trapped in a little box upstairs in the middle of nowhere, you get close. It also meant I got to know her more like a person, rather than just my grandma.

All through high school, both at Kokomo and Taylor, I faced bullying: emotional and physical. There's this one time at Kokomo, I was with my friend—there were only two trans people at the school that I knew of—and me and him were passing out trans buttons to people. Once the bell ring, I stayed out there a little bit longer. I think I had homeroom next or something. I was passing out buttons in the hallway while kids were going to class, and a guy came up to me and grabbed my chest and shoved me into the women's restroom. I don't remember what he said, but he called me faggot or something. Kokomo was not the best place to be out.

At Taylor High School, a similar incident happened where I was walking in the hallway and a kid walked past me and slapped my books out of my hands and said, "Move Faggot." Taylor was very Republican and had something like a Drag Your Tractor to school day. It was not a fun experience. Everywhere I walked, everybody stared. I just felt like I was always on spot at Taylor, like a constant show. I didn't even need a show choir or drama club to be the center of attention there.

End of my junior year, I was living with my grandma and I was dating this boy in Indianapolis. I had talked to him about wanting to move to Indianapolis because my grandma was sick. She could no longer take care of me. It was too much, and I just needed to leave. He started reaching out to people to try to see what we could do. I also came to Indianapolis on the weekends to see him. Every single weekend I was with him. He was my best friend, and he attended North Central High School. He graduated the year before me, and he was in show choir and the performing arts.

This girl Cora and her mom decided to help me try to figure out how to get out of Kokomo. My friend's mother is an artist, and she's good at networking. She started trying to figure out if I could stay with a family. She had me make this little biography of my story, about why I wanted to leave. I wanted stability. I wanted to go to a good school. I loved show choir, and I really wanted to be in Counterpoints at North Central. I just needed a good environment to be in, and she posted that on social media asking if there were any Washington Township families that would be willing to have me stay with them for my senior year.

One of the students at North Central High School, Grace, saw the post and told her parents. I think they were on vacation in Canada at the time. But this one day they called me and said they were willing to let me stay with them and told me when they would be back. When they called, I had locked myself in the bathroom, sitting on the floor while I was on the phone talking with them. I was *so* happy! My grandmother didn't want me to leave, but she knew that it was what was best for me, and she wanted me to be successful and happy. She wanted me to do what I thought was best for myself.

This was right before school started. I think it was July 31 when I got to their place, and they got back from their trip. I had all my stuff packed in the little trunk of my grandmother's car, and we drive down to Indianapolis and got my stuff unpacked, and I moved in. Two days later, I enrolled and started at North Central. I love North Central, a lot! I auditioned for Counterpoints Show Choir and made it in. That's where I realized I want to be a performer. Counterpoints is a Varsity Show Choir. It is a nationally winning show choir and very much a family. Once a Counterpoint, always a Counterpoint. I made really good friends there and probably some are lifelong friends. I had a good outlet and good support system.

I also got involved in theater at North Central. I was too nervous to audition for parts in the beginning of the year, so I started doing costume crew because that was the side of theater I'd never navigated before. I did costume crew and tech all the way up until the last show. The last show I did a drag performance. The only show I did was in full drag! (Laughs). It was really fun, and I enjoyed it. That's pretty much all I did. Show choir took up a lot of my life and being in Counterpoints was a dream of mine. I remember being in the Kokomo show choir and going to show choir competitions and seeing them perform, and I would be like, "Oh, I wish I could do that!" So, it was very much a dream this past year being in Counterpoints and going to North Central and having these friends. It was the best year of my life so far.

I just graduated. They weren't going to let me have my name announced at commencement. (Andru does not go by his birth name). I called up an attorney who filed a legal court case. My attorney went in and spoke to them about the legalities. The case settled. Eventually, I was able to have my name announced at commencement. I also changed the rules at North Central to where other trans kids now can have their name announced in commencement as well. So, I had my name announced at commencement, and I wore full-face hot pink makeup and the men's gown. I did hot pink makeup because society would tell me that I can't. And I graduated. I am staying with a friend right now. She's a senior and still in high school.

What are your future hopes and dreams?

The biggest thing for me would be the discovery of me, of who I am. I have started my transition. I'm on hormones. I have taken three hormone shots so far, and my fourth one will be on Monday. I'm also documenting all of that as well, posting videos and voice singing updates. Something I was really worried about, and am still worried about, is losing my singing voice. I document everything and do drag shows. It's been a lot of self-discovery over this summer.

Do you have any thoughts on what our communities could do to better support transgender individuals?

There need to be more outlets, everywhere. Places where youth can go to make friends and feel like they belong. A lot of the time we feel like we don't fit in anywhere. Just having more connections for younger youth and also for older youth as well. I don't know of any places for LGBTQ young adults to go other than bars. Just having something for them, like a weekly hang out or maybe go somewhere on a trip. We do have IYG

(Indiana Youth Group), which is really good for people under 21. I think we just need to be noticed more.

What would be helpful for people to know?

For more people to be accepting and to understand better that we can't change who we are, just like you can't change who you are. At the end of the day, we're all people, and we're all here for a reason. You never get anything done with hate. I just always say, "I do me and you do you." I am me, and you are you, and the best way to get things done is to just do it with love. That's what I would say.

What is your long-term future dream?

To make the world not easier, but a happier place. It's really simple. I know I will end up doing what I love to do. I would like to be an activist for homeless and LGBTQ youth and work in my community. By night be a drag performer, and I don't know, maybe law school. But if I do go to law school, I want to be an attorney for transgender youth to help them get their records changed. Right now, I'm shooting for the stars and that's performance: singing and dancing. That's where my heart is.

Jordan

Student – Artist, Illustrator, Writer
He/Him/His
20 years old

> *"Every trans person is different, and everyone's*
> *background is going to be different."*

There are five in my family: my mom, my dad, my sister who is 17, my younger brother, and me. I'm the oldest. The only pets we have are two hermit crabs. Honestly, I have no idea why my sister wanted hermit crabs! (Laughs). She just came home one day with two hermit crabs.

I attended Plainfield High School on the west side of town. I just graduated from Ivy Tech, and I'll be heading off to study at an art school. I'm going to major in Fine Arts: Drawing and Illustrations. I want to write and illustrate children's books and graphic novels for middle-age children. My favorite authors are J.K. Rowling, who writes the *Harry Potter* books, and Rick Riordan, who writes the Percy Jackson books. (Jordan has an old, worn copy of *Harry Potter* on the table beside him). I love the storylines, the plot, the character interactions, and the illustrations—either on the covers or the actual illustrations inside the books. I also love Indy Folk music. One of my favorites bands is *Mumford &*
Sons (a popular British band).

What do you do for fun?

If I have time, I like to binge-watch "Brooklyn Nine-Nine," a police TV show. I like hanging out with my brother. I'll take him out to the park or the pool. He likes to play games, and he loves Legos. We'll stay up to rent and watch movies. When I get my own place, I want to have him come over and take him out more and go visit places.

Can you share a little about your journey?

Probably around age 5 or 6 years old, I didn't want to be called by my birth name or be called she. I started to realize I was different when I was in elementary school. I didn't like to be identified as a girl, and I didn't like anyone using she pronouns. It just bugged me. As I started to get older, I kind of kept to myself. Around my sophomore year of high school, I started looking at terms in the LGBTQ community. At first, I started identifying as gender-fluid because I wasn't sure. But then, I looked up trans and something clicked with me: *Yes, this is what I feel.* I felt relief when I figured out what it was. I am a transgender man. A trans man is someone who is born in the wrong body, in terms of what they identify with versus what they are perceived as by society. So, I was perceived born female.

I was afraid to come out to my parents at first because you don't know what it is going to be like. We were living in Ohio at that time, for my dad's job. I wasn't near any other family. If something did happen in Ohio, I would have no place to stay if it didn't turn out good. I was really nervous. The first person who knew in my family was my sister. I came out a couple of times. The first time, I don't think my parents understood the terms and stuff. I don't think they got it. I was in high school. The second time, I told them again, and I think they finally understood what I was talking about. They accepted me right away, but I think they are still trying to learn the terms and things like that. It's a learning process for them, but they are getting better with using Jordan and he pronouns.

I started going by Jordan during my junior year of high school. Only very few teachers knew in high school when I started coming out. When I was announced at my high school graduation, it was deadnaming. Deadnaming is when someone doesn't use a trans or a nonbinary person's name and instead uses a birth name they don't go by anymore.

When I graduated from Ivy Tech, they used my name: Jordan. I was talking to Stephanie Robertson, who was my professor, my work-study boss, and my mentor. She was talking to me at the end of my portfolio class, and she asked me if I wanted her to talk to people in charge to make sure they had Jordan on the graduation announcement list. She was able to get them to say Jordan for the graduation and on my diploma. The only documents that won't have Jordan are my transcript and any other legal document because my name hasn't been legally changed yet.

Have people been supportive?

My friends are big-time supportive. Right after I told them, they were like, "Awesome!" My friends and my college professors are actually more supportive than half my family. I'm out to my whole family. When some of the family was not going to support me, one of my aunts supported me right then and there. She is the one who actually took me to get measured for my chest binder. A chest binder is, you could think of it like a corset; but instead of just stopping at your ribs, it goes up to your chest and binds your chest to help me pass as a trans man or just a man. My mom and dad are really supportive. We're actually in the process, once everything slows down, we're going to work on changing my name legally.

My classmates at school are supportive. I've only had a couple incidents at school. One incident is where someone tried to drag me into her verbal fight with the professor, by making a comment that was not appropriate. During their fight, she turned and pointed at me, saying, "I demand respect like that person keeps demanding respect." Pointing at me. It was around the time I had just come out as trans. She was a straight person, and she was using that card to try to win her fight.

I also had someone ask me transphobic questions. I was by myself in the art studios at that time. She kept asking for my birth name, which I said, "No," multiple times. And she was asking me questions about how I look, like what makes my body trans. So, for instance, everyone assumes that trans guys look a certain way, with flat chests or whatever. I just told her she was asking me inappropriate questions. Ugh!

How can people in the community be more supportive?

Every trans person is different. Not all of them are going to be the same. Not everyone wants to have the surgery or do the hormones. For me personally, I don't feel comfortable doing the hormones yet because there are a lot of "what ifs" and moneywise it's expensive. I would want the surgery, just the top, hopefully. But as I said, every trans person is different, and everyone's background is going to be different.

People have to understand it's not going to affect the other person's life. When someone comes out as trans, nothing has changed about them on the inside. They just realize who they are. So yeah, just give them the same respect as you should anyway. Support them as much as you can, just using the right pronoun or the right name. That little bit can actually help that trans person a lot.

One of the things I don't feel comfortable with is shopping. I shop in the men's section. I had a couple of times where creepy guys followed me. There are times where I don't look like I'm passing. Like, I'll be walking around looking at jean sizes and clothes and then I'm being followed. There were a couple of times where I had to just stay with the group to make sure they weren't continuing to follow me.

I've had dirty looks given to me. One time, I was getting a suit for my high school graduation and my mom was with me, helping me get it the right size and everything, and every time I came out of the dressing room, this old couple kept getting this dirty look. No words. Just dirty looks. It was uncomfortable. Haircuts too, every time I get a trim. There was this one incident with this lady who was waiting for her turn, and she just kept looking at me, giving me this weird-ass look. My mom had to keep starring at her to make sure she didn't keep looking at me.

The area I live in is conservative. Right now, it's more divided. I don't feel comfortable a lot. Politics is a big thing and if you're not Christian, you're going to get shunned. I saw this incident where this Muslim family was leaving the library and one of the library workers was giving them dirty looks. In my neighborhood, if you tell someone that you're not Christian, they will give you a dirty look and just ignore you afterwards. My spirituality is paganism. I am more focused on the nature aspects of life. I don't let a book lead my life. So, there are a lot of issues at times.

I always try to stay with the group if I'm going out. I always make sure I have a couple of people with me. If I take my brother out, I always make sure I have my cell phone with me, fully charged and everything, so I can call for help. I don't want to be in a situation where he sees a hate crime happening involving me. He doesn't need to see that. He's only 8 years old.

What are your future hopes and dreams?

My major is Drawing and Illustration so I can write and illustrate books. Hopefully, I will have at least one book published, maybe two. I would like to have a space for my artwork. I started out working with a lot of pen work, but then I started adding watercolor. I want to get my hands on some equipment and work a bit on digital art. Eventually, I want to travel outside the country.

What are your hopes for the community?

Honestly, I am hoping they get their act together and pass laws that protect LGBTQ people in general. Make it affordable for people to get the surgery and make it easier with the hormones and also have more doctors trained in that area. There should be more coming out support systems too and ways to help the kids who come out when they're younger. Sometimes it's hard for them to find a place if they get kicked out because a lot of people will deny them just because they're trans.

Rose Peck

Macedon Technologies Consultant
She/Her/Hers
21 years old

"Humans basically all want the same stuff. We want love, we want agency in our lives, and we want enough money to be financially secure."

My family moved to Naperville, just outside Chicago, when I was one. I lived in Illinois until I was 18 and then went to college in Rochester, New York. My major is a Bachelors of Science in Computer Science and a minor in Mathematics. I start work next week as a consultant for Macedon Technologies, a software technology company. I will be 22 in four days.

What are your hobbies and interests?

I like tabletop board games, Dungeon & Dragons, video games, and I play piano. I also like watching people on Twitch, which is a video game live streaming website.

What would you like to share about your journey?

I am a trans woman. A question I get with some frequency is, "How did you know?" To which I answer, "Define what you mean by *know*." At some level, I believe I knew ever since I was a very little I kid. I didn't necessarily have the words or the means to express or explore it. Until puberty, it wasn't really a concern. My family is liberal and traditional gender roles were not something that was stressed. To me, gender was mostly a non-issue. Then puberty happens, around age 14, and you have a sexual identity; and suddenly, lines of gender and sexuality became, not more important but much more in your face: like, how do we define the types of people that we desire? I am bisexual, to put that in some context.

Puberty was probably when I started having some thoughts of: I think I would be happier if I was different and what types of sexual activities I might enjoy. That's something you think a lot about in puberty! (Laughs). So, I would think, I might enjoy this more, quote, "if I were a girl," which is somewhat problematic phrasing, but that is how I talked to myself back then. Throughout this entire time, there were very large amounts of denial. I was thinking, you know, this doesn't mean I'm "trans."

By the time I got into college, I was aware at some level I would be happier if I were different. But, there are two major hurdles. The first hurdle is coming out to yourself and understanding, "I am this way, and I would be happier if I changed myself," which was in high school. The second major hurdle, which was in college, is overcoming the fear enough to actually start doing it. Because it's scary, right? Making any change to yourself is going to be scary, especially one which is usually of considerable breadth. You're changing a lot of things about yourself that traditionally are somewhat drastic. It's not a change like, "Oh, I want to exercise more." So that makes it scarier. Also, it's not exactly taboo, but a lot of people in society are not cool about it and that makes it more difficult.

One of the fears I had, which is really common, is: What is the current state of medical technology? And this fear that if I start transitioning and can't, quote, "go all the way," I will end up less happy than where I started. Like, maybe you will end up somewhere halfway between two things, and you will be unhappy. That thinking is totally false. But that's a preconception I definitely had to overcome and that many people have to overcome.

The first few years of college were getting over that and accepting: "If there was a magic button I could push to change me to be a cis girl (assigned female at birth and identifies as a woman), I would press it in a heartbeat. But that button doesn't exist and so I guess I'll just be sad forever." In college, I met some other trans women, which I credit as a source for what eventually got me to start transitioning. Meeting other trans women, seeing what their lives are like, having their perspective on transitioning, and having someone I could go to when I needed help, was very helpful.

Right before my senior year of college, I came out to my small circle of trans friends. I was like, "Hi, I'm trans." And they were like, "Yeah. We knew." (Laughs). A month later, I came out to my social circles and family as a whole. Actually, I came out officially to all my friends and on social media and to my family on my birthday. I talked to one of my trans friends and she said, "Well, if you do it today then your girlthday will be the same day as your birthday." Girlthday is like a pun on Birthday. Often, people come out and announce it in stages, but a girlthday is some notable coming out day, a significant marker that says, "I'm a girl now."

That was a year ago. I changed my name. I go by Rose now. I use she/her pronouns. I use they/them, which is relatively new. I have been on hormones almost a year. I dress differently. I style my hair differently. I rarely wear makeup only because I'm lazy. That first couple of months were a time of experimentation and trying different things.

I mentioned earlier the fallacy of, "going all the way," which is born of a misconception of what this thing is and how this thing works. Essentially, that mentality is coming from the idea that transitioning is a linear process. So many things in life are a linear process: You do one thing and then the next thing and then you're done. But this is not a linear process. It's easy to think that it is because a lot of things in life are, and this may be something not many people are aware of. In addition to not being linear, as a computer scientist I can say with some confidence that this takes on more of a graph or tree (non-linear data structure). When you're first starting out, there are different things you can try and different things you can do, and you might try one of them or there are a whole bunch of other things you might try, and you can try different things concurrently, in parallel. There is not necessarily a set end goal, because it is not a goal but a process. It is the process of finding a place where you are happier and more comfortable with yourself. Once you understand that, it becomes obvious that this idea of, "What if I only get halfway rather than all the way and I'm sad?" And the answer is, "There is no all the way." All the way is wherever you are.

The ingredients of this reinforcement learning process are quite friendly in that they tend to have a single maximum. From a less technical standpoint, that means the steps in the correct direction will feel better, regardless of how big those steps are. There are a lot of processes where you need to start going in a certain direction, and at first, you feel worse. But you need to keep going and eventually, you feel better. Exercise is like that. When you start exercising, you feel terrible. But if you stick with it, you start to feel really good. In my experience, transitioning is not like that. When you start going in the right direction, you will know you are going in the right direction because you will start to feel better. And then, you just feel better and better the further you go, which helps alleviate that worry of, "Oh, what if I end up in a well," so to speak, "and can't get out the other side?" That is not really a thing that happens.

What do you think is important for allies to know to be more helpful?

The answer to how allies can be helpful depends on the context. There are lots of ways! You could know a lot of resources and then if someone is coming out, refer them to these thousands of resources. You can just provide emotional support. You can be more generally aware. There are a lot of ways things can be improved.

General awareness around this topic is really low. Most people don't know any trans people and really don't know anything about it. Which is tricky for a couple of reasons. It makes it harder to empathize and to help when somebody you know is starting to go through this. It's harder to be careful around eggs if you don't even know what I mean when I say the word "egg." So, an egg refers to a trans person who hasn't realized that they're trans. The idea is that you're an egg, and at some point, you will hatch into whoever you are meant to be. Trans people will usually spot eggs, and there are certain ways you should be careful around eggs. You want to help them go in the right direction by nudging them gently but not obviously.

Also, the lack of general knowledge about what this is and how it works makes it much easier for uninformed people to form misconceptions. A lot of people who end up bigoted have never met a trans person or met a gay person and know nothing about it. If you just met a couple of us, we're very nice. I just like playing board games. I'm not trying to take over the world here.

Being better informed is a good thing. But as human beings, we have a tendency to care about things that affect us, and we have a tendency not to care about things that don't affect us, just because there's too much stuff in the world to care about everything. It's hard to be knowledgeable about *everything* and if you try, your brain will explode. (Laughs).

You can see this tendency in friends and family. My mother knew very little about trans people and about what transitions are like. I came out as trans, and rather suddenly, she did a lot more reading and became well versed and did more trans activism. I am not faulting her. That happens a lot. It doesn't become important to people until it affects them, which is just how people are, which is why it's so difficult to do anything actionable because if you try to make people more informed, they only care so much to listen.

Another way people can be helpful is when constructing spaces, be mindful of what trans people go through and what you should be more sensitive to. That will help make spaces more welcoming. For example, people talk about making their spaces welcoming to minorities. In my experience, it is not nearly as active a process as people think. For instance, the solution for making your space welcoming is not necessarily to advertise yourself, which is something people talk about a lot. It's more the much less sexy and much more positive solution of just make the space in such a way that is friendly to people of minorities and then there is a snowball effect. However, even with the nicest cis people (people who identify with the sex assigned at birth) in the world and the best allies in the world, I will generally feel more comfortable around trans people because we're the same, and that is just a human tribalism thing.

More concretely, when constructing spaces, common things I see organizers mess up by not knowing any better—I also see this on the Internet all the time—is having to sign up for things with your legal name. I can understand why you might need to use your legal name for various things, such as software that helps an employer manage paychecks. You have to get the paychecks in the legal name that match the bank account. But then, there are custom greeting messages on websites that just pull your legal name. Well, people may not like their legal name. It's a really common and simple mistake if you're just not aware of it. The solution is so easy: just add a field for a preferred name. If you don't want to say preferred name, then use nickname.

Having pronoun tags on everything is best. One of my personal crusades is just more pronoun tags on more things because it is a useful thing and good to know and is super easy to do. And call people by their proper name.

What are your future hopes and dreams?

I describe myself as a realist, although I hate describing myself that way because most of the people who are realists are assholes. But I am an actual realist in that I believe in science, and I believe in data. One of the things I firmly believe to be true, which is realistic but not necessarily comforting, is that most of your macro life goals are going to be basically the same as everybody else's.

Humans basically all want the same stuff. We want love, we want agency in our lives, and we want enough money to be financially secure. People have calculated that if you make any amount above a certain threshold, it adds no additional happiness to your life. So, for my macro goals in life, I need to work a job that I don't despise. I prefer to work a job where I have flexible hours and where I have lots of free time to do what I want to do. I am the type of person that has personal side projects I like to work on. I like to have time to do that. Being able to construct a working environment where I can make enough money to live and also have freedom is important to me in the long term.

I would eventually like to marry someone because committed romantic relationships are important to me.

I would like to see and live in a world where people such as myself are more accepted, better supported, and there isn't as much discrimination. Those are huge goals in my circle of concern but not necessarily in my circle of influence. There is very little I can do about making society at large better just because society is huge, and I'm just one person.

On a more personal level, I plan to keep taking hormones and letting things develop the way they are. Usually, the two-year mark is when things settle down. I'm at the one-year mark, and so we will see how things go this next year. There are some procedures I thought about, but I'm not willing to say with any real commitment that I plan on doing them.

I want pretty much the same things everybody wants, which is love and agency. Psychologists learned the secret to happiness in the '70s, and they told everybody, but everyone keeps making cringy self-help books anyway even though the secret is obvious: It's love and work. Agency is a term that encompasses work. Specifically, agency is the feeling that your choices matter, which is very closely tied to feelings of accomplishment. Like, you are getting things done. The choices you make and the things that you do are having some impact. You have agency over your life, such as I can make choices that affect how my life is, and the work that I'm doing has a tangible benefit to society. Obviously, the hard part is how do you achieve those things in your life? Which is a very long way to say: I want the same things that everybody wants.

What are your hopes for the community?

I hope that discrimination goes down. Who doesn't? I hope this community gets bigger because I think there are a lot of people who don't necessarily realize they're trans or they realize very late in life. As the trans community gets larger that will get better.

There is a concept in marginalized groups and similar groups of this idea of open spaces and closed spaces. For those who aren't familiar, in an open space anybody who wants can be in it, and closed spaces are restricted to only people that are within the group. I think those are important and both serve different purposes, and it's good to have both of them. An example of this is in AA (Alcoholics Anonymous), which has open meetings and also has closed meetings only for people in the program.

In my experience, the queer community has not been great about having open spaces. There is a lot of reason for that, such as the history of discrimination and not wanting to be out in an open space because you could get fired from your job or beat up. I understand why this is the way that it is. But that doesn't mean I like it. I feel the queer community could be doing a lot more to have open spaces. As I mentioned, both types of spaces serve important purposes. There are often a fair amount of closed spaces, but not so many open spaces.

The biggest benefit to the queer community by having open spaces, in my opinion, is that it is a place for questioning people to go where they feel safe to question themselves. You're not committing to coming out as anything, and you're not committing to even saying that you're not cis-gender or not heterosexual. You're not committing to anything. But it's a place where you could meet other queer people and learn their perspectives and learn their stories and sort of get involved in that community without necessarily having to out yourself in any way. The other benefit to open space is that it's a good way to educate people who otherwise would not know anyone who is trans and would not know any better in their beliefs.

Was there anything you wanted to talk about that I didn't ask you?

I have things that I wish someone had told me when I was 18. Number one is that steps in the right direction will feel good, and you don't need to worry about what if I get halfway there and am less happy than where I started. That is not a problem that occurs by and large. If you are going in the right direction for yourself, you will feel better every step of the way. Making changes that are good for you will feel good.

I also wish I had known that the first three months of hormone therapy are reversible. By the time you are at the three-month mark, you will know if it's a good idea for you. So, I'm not going to screw myself forever if this is the wrong decision. Like, you can try this for three whole months. You can feel safe to experiment.

The last thing is getting to know people by having a trans community of friends. I had people I could go to before I was out. That is really, really useful and important. There are two people I met in college who I credit as being no small factor to what led to me coming out and transitioning, and I am very grateful for that.

My other piece of advice: You can just try shit. Nothing is stopping you from trying shit and this is a process where you can just try shit. You try things, and if they feel good, you keep doing them. If they don't feel right, you can just try other things. This is a nonlinear process, and it's going to involve a lot of experimentation because everyone is different. Everyone's transition is different. Everyone's experience of trans-ness is different. So, it's okay to just try things. The only way you will know for certain if this is right for you and if you are trans is if you try it and it feels good, which is tied to finding people within that community because it's a space where you can experiment safely.

Anything else that is helpful for people to know?

The idea of tribalism, where we tend to think in black and white—not in terms of race but groups—and want to have clean divisions between groups, is totally true. Tribalism is something that affects us all. We tend to think in terms of in-groups and out-groups. That is a side effect of the same type of tribalism that allowed humans to do teamwork and become extremely successful. A trait that makes us work as teams and work together is also the trait that makes us want to work against people who are different from us and reduce things into very simple, "Us versus Them." If there was a way to have the teamwork without the nasty parts of tribalism—like if I had access to the Universe button—that is something I would love to change. But just being aware that is a tendency people have is the best solution.

You should always be careful trying to ascribe simple models to real-world situations. If I were to describe two groups of people where everyone falls cleanly into one group or the other, that would be a very simple model of how something could manifest. In general, you should be careful of ascribing those types of models. As a scientist, I can say it is important to recognize that your models will almost certainly need to be changed and updated as more evidence comes in. Being willing to change how you view the world based on the evidence you find is a really important skill that is *really, really* hard to do.

Vivian Edwards

Community Volunteer, Counterculture, Political Activist
She/Her/Hers
24 years old

> *"We are just normal people. We have the same sort of*
> *dreams and goals, and we just want to live our own lives."*

I was born in Elkhart, Indiana, and grew up in Bristol, a town just outside Elkhart. I have not yet completed college and am currently not attending (for private reasons). Right now, I am a delivery driver for Jimmy Johns.

What are your hobbies and interests?

I play bass guitar. I like the Pellinor books. It is a young adult series by author Allison Croggon. I watch, "Miraculous Ladybug" and "She-Ra and the Princesses of Power," which are animated TV shows. I also read tarot cards and practice chaos magick and Hellenic Polytheism, which refers to the ancient Greek theology. I don't like the term Greek "mythology" because what is mythology except a religion that people don't believe in anymore?

Is Hellenic Polytheism your spirituality?

Yes. Specifically, I worship the Goddess Hekate, originally from Asia Minor, who is a goddess of liminal spaces: in a sense, transitional space. In the original myth of Persephone being kidnapped by Hades, Hekate is the one who helps Demeter find where Persephone is and accompanies Persephone in and out of the Underworld. In later theology, she becomes associated with being a psychopomp: one who guides souls from this world to the next, and she is associated with the souls of people who are trapped on this plane, like ghosts. Hekate is the goddess of the crossroads, which in ancient times was considered a liminal space. So, you know, as a genderqueer person, as a trans person, I inherently inhabit a liminal space within society. I would say I am a binary trans woman, but I don't really get caught up in labels too much anymore.

Is there anything you want to share about your journey?

I knew I was always different from all the other boys. For example, when I was a kid, I would ask female friends of the family, like 14-year-old girls, to put makeup on me and put me in a dress. I was probably around 7 or 8 years old. Once I put on the dresses, I acted like I hated it, but I actually didn't. I'm part of that last generation of transgender people who did not have that term growing up. It wasn't within my conception of like even within the realm of possibilities that I could be a girl. The term transgender wasn't in the mainstream then the way it is now.

In middle school, I would carry my books clutched to my chest, and I remember boys telling me off and telling me to carry my books at my side because I was carrying my books in a feminine way. Before puberty, it wasn't that big of an issue because there's not as much difference between boys and girls. Once I got past that point in my life and got into high school, I just didn't get along with men as well as I did with women. I had more close female friends than I did male friends. Around the time I was 17, I had a female friend that I asked to buy me panties. That was really the start of exploring my gender.

Also, there was this person in high school who was genderqueer. I don't know exactly what their gender identity was, but they were some form of gender nonconforming and that introduced me to the concept in high school. I would not have come out in high school because that person was terribly bullied! Even associating with that person would have been a problem. But, it was definitely on my mind. This was in Elkhart, which is as far north as you can go before you hit Michigan.

That's when I started to question whether I was supposed to be a girl. It was not going to work out though because there were people I did confide in and all of them said, "Do not come out. Do not do this. This is going to be really bad. Don't even think about it!" So, I didn't.

I remember I tested it out with my dad. I made fun of that trans girl with my dad to gauge his reaction, and he also made fun of her. That was the point where I knew I really couldn't come out. I came from a pretty conservative family. My family was very, very churchgoing and very devout Christianity. My grandpa was not exactly fundamentalist, but in that vein of things.

I just suppressed all of this. And then I attended college at Ball State University, and I think that's when I genuinely started to explore those kinds of feelings. One of my friends ended up being a theater major or a dance major and that introduced me to the queer scene and that's how I was introduced to the concept.

Around age 20 or 21, I started exploring the idea of being trans, but then I realized how difficult passing was and so I ended up going back in the closet. It just didn't work out. Then, about a year after that, I did a bunch of political activism on campus. Being into political activism significantly changed my life. The confidence I got from political activism helped me in that regard. With that, I just came to this realization that I'm going to die one day, and I need to live my life in a way that makes me happy.

Through political activism, I accepted that I was trans and that I needed to transition. This was in 2016, the "dumpster fire" year. All that term means is a situation that's just an absolute mess, a wreck. Facebook was a dumpster fire and people were at each other's throats because of the election. There was a Pride parade in Turkey that the government shutdown through tear gas and pepper spray. They are not allowed to have Pride parades in Turkey. There was this woman who was a trans prostitute who was at the front line of that protest and that Pride parade, basically like a Turkish Sylvia Rivera (Latinx American Transgender Activist). She was found dead and lit on fire the next day. I remember seeing this article on Facebook and wanting to respond to it and finding I was unable to comment or say anything about it. That emotional reaction made me realize that I was trans because I was empathizing with it on a level that was too deep to be anything else.

What would be helpful for allies to know to be more supportive of the transgender community?

Listening.
Don't get me wrong. There is a lot of vitriol in the trans community and in the queer community toward allies that is just so undeserved. There was a doctor here who had done so much for our community and gone so far out of their way to help us and they accidentally said, "brothers and sisters" in a speech instead of "siblings" and people basically tried to run them out of town—despite all of the work they had done for our community. One thing to keep in mind is that trans people themselves need to work with our allies and not throw them under the bus, because there's this very real attitude within the trans community of this term social capital.

To explain that, basically, there is this idea of a callout culture, which isn't in and of itself bad. It was originally about calling out people who have power and an opportunity to do something about a situation. What it has degraded into is people crucifying each other over minute differences in rhetoric in order to make themselves look better. So, instead of addressing an ally in a calm and peaceable manner and trying to get them to see why something is hurtful or why we don't agree with it, it just immediately becomes jumping down another person's throat so that you can be the most woke person in the room. Something that really annoys me as a trans person is that crucifying our allies is somehow seen as just as important as dealing with the people that genuinely hate us. A big problem we have in this community, as trans people, is prioritizing what the actual threat is.

For allies, the big issue is listening. I have often seen and experienced myself that when I bring up something that is hurtful, people try to rationalize why it wasn't hurtful. You know, I don't want an excuse. I don't want you to come up with a reason for why what you said wasn't an issue. I just want you to change your behavior. That's what I'm asking for. Believe us when we tell you something is hurtful.

Stand up for us when we're not around. Again, a lot of the issues I see come down to being performative allies. People want to look good instead of actually doing good.

I have spearheaded the East Central Indiana (ECI) Transgender Alliance Clothing Drive, which is for trans people. I don't have time to spearhead it right now. But trans people are disproportionately poor and so a lot of people just don't have the money to completely replace a wardrobe and this is us getting clothing so we can give them away to people who need them.

What are your hopes and dreams for your life?

That's a difficult question. I'm not, as far as goals are concerned, I'm not the kind of person who wants to have kids and like a normal career and buy a home and settle down and do that sort of stuff. I've kind of accepted that I'm beyond the periphery of our culture, a counterculture person or in the counterculture, and I'm okay with that.

What are your hopes for the community?

I've been really focused on local politics in general because national politics seem so impossible to do anything about.

I was born in Indiana, and I lived here my entire life. I don't know anywhere else, at all. And it feels like I'm not welcome in this state. It feels like what they want is for me to leave. A lot of people in the city and in the state are like, "Well, if you don't like it here, you should just move to the West Coast." But I don't know anywhere else. So, I guess, I just hope that Indiana becomes a more welcoming and understanding place.

I do have a lot of hope in that regards because Indiana is one of the best red states (Republican) to live in. For example, to change your gender marker in Kentucky, they want proof that I got bottom surgery, which not everyone wants. If I lived in Ohio, I would not be able to change my birth certificate at all. In Indiana, we have nonbinary drivers licenses, which is pretty shocking. They did ice out trans people in the hate crimes bill in Indiana. The hate crimes legislation was intentionally meant to ice out trans people.

Indiana is definitely a conservative place, but people just seem more concerned about the conservative aspects of finance than they do about conservative religion. I mean, it's definitely an element here, but it's not nearly as strong as it could be compared to other places, especially since RFRA (Religious Freedom Restoration Act, a law signed by Mike Pence that put LGBTQ+ people at risk of discrimination). People here are very afraid to knuckle down on religious conservatism now.

Being trans has pushed me to the far, far left. I have no faith in capitalism and no real respect for authority anymore. I do vote Democrat, but I don't expect them to have our best interests in mind or to be working "for the people." I was really into politics at one point but, honestly, I have disconnected from it and become rather cynical. But I feel pushed into political action. It's not so much that I am madly in love with political action. It's just I don't really have a choice. It's self-defense.

Is your family supportive?

My family is sort of supportive. It's been very difficult for my dad and for my grandparents. My mom and I are estranged from each for reasons completely unrelated to queer issues. I went on the offensive in a sense, and I told my family: "You either accept this or I'm not going to be a part of your life," kind of talk. I was very nervous and took a very aggressive stance on it. But, for example, when I went to Thanksgiving last year, my dad made it clear to the rest of the family that they would not be welcome in his house if they disrespected me for being trans. It was a long road, but he accepts me.

Was there anything you wanted to talk about that I didn't ask you?

I mean, we're just people. There is this weaponized rhetoric against us that says we are this force of evil or that we have some end goal that is evil. But we are just normal people. We have the same sort of dreams and goals, and we just want to live our own lives.

Ryan Smith

IYG Activity Center Coordinator, Musician
They/Them
23 years old

"Being an ally means also showing up when things are hard."

I graduated from college this past summer as a Religious Studies major. During my major, I focused on multiculturalism, and during my time at IUPUI [Indiana University-Purdue University Indianapolis], I worked at the Multicultural Center doing diversity work. I really wanted to serve youth. It's definitely my passion.

At Indiana Youth Group (IYG), we relate to the youth that come there, providing services to them. In my job, I facilitate programming and create youth-centered events for LGBTQ+ youth, ages 12 through 20, as well as for their allies. We have a Youth Summit Conference every year. We also have a Holiday Party, Volunteer Appreciation, Pride events, a Youth Night, a Prom, and so forth.

What are your hobbies and interests?

I'm very interested in music. I write music. I play the piano. I sing, and I really like theater. For my music, I write a mix, somewhere between alternative and hip-hop and a little classical. Whatever I like transfers into my music, and I try not to limit myself to a certain sound.

I like to watch "Queer Eye," and I watch "The Real Housewives of Atlanta." (Laughs). Interestingly, I also really like the Helen Keller book that she wrote. I think the writing is beautiful. And I watch this television show called, "Steven Universe," which is a cartoon. I like it for the story, but it's also cool to have this universe where there is this boy who is half alien and half human, and there's a lot of queer and trans representation. Anybody can like anybody, and nobody's canonically defined. There is a woman who likes women, and there are people who go by they/them on the show. It's not necessarily an educational thing. It's more that they just exist in this world.

Can you share some of your personal journey?

Yes. I was very young when I realized I was queer. A friend asked me randomly, "Do you like boys?" and I said, "Yes." And she said, "Do you like girls?" and I said, "Yeah, I think I do." And she said, "Me too." (Laughs). I was young, around 6 years old. So, she was like my first "girlfriend." Not like as adults, but more like we'd watch movies together as straight people and pretend to be the homeowners: "Hi honey, I'm home." (Laughs).

My mom found out I was bi (bisexual) when I was 12. I was on this Bi-Christian forum, and I left the browser open. (Laughs). My mom saw it and when I came home, my mom was like, "What is this Ryan?" I was denying it. I told her, "Oh, you know, I'm not gay. I was just on it pretending to be gay to help the people who are gay because their lives are hard." She said, "No, I don't really care about all that. I loved you yesterday, and I am going to love you today. But you're not going to be talking to people online. That's not what's happening." So, she has known since I was very young.

I identify as genderqueer and pansexual. I personally don't mind if someone uses the term bisexual, but for me pansexual means that my heart can reach and extend to all. And by all, I mean genders. It is inclusive to nonbinary folks as well. Genderqueer is being able to express my gender based on how I feel and not limiting myself to femininity. Sometimes I feel masculine and want to affirm myself in that way, and sometimes I feel feminine, or it may be neither or both.

My dad is a very traditional Baptist Christian. There's nothing wrong with that. It's just my personal experience that all of that is a little daunting for my dad. However, now I am 23 years old, and he is reaching out to me because he doesn't want to lose his daughter. He wants me in his life. Even though he doesn't understand my identities or who I love, he wants to be a part of my life and supporting me is part of that. As of right now, my family is supportive.

What do you think is important for allies to know?

It's important for allies to know that showing up itself really means a lot. Not just being there for when the fun things happen. Pride parade is beautiful, and I am so glad to have met so many people who are LGBTQ+ allies who show up to the Pride parade and say, "I am here. I want to be supportive." That's fun, being at the festivals. But being an ally means also showing up when things are hard. So, when these legislative bills are being passed that minimize the rights of trans people and their healthcare, make sure allies are there and are well versed on the issue. And tell other allies about it, and let them know what is happening as well.

Also, reach out to the specific people who need support rather than just sharing sad stories on Facebook. Showing up means a lot to me. The whole point of being an ally is a verb. It's the essence of being and doing. And it really transfers into being an advocate. Another example is showing up for Trans Day of Remembrance. That's when we have a ceremony for all of our trans who have passed, specifically those who have been murdered. It's usually in November. Indiana Youth Group (IYG) has more information on the website.

With regard to Facebook, it's not just posting about dramatic things. As an LGBTQ+ person and as a black person myself, it is traumatic. It needs to be talked about, but it also doesn't feel like the social media post is for me. It's for other allies or other people who may not be allies to understand this is what's happening and this is a problem. I feel like reaching out to the people who need to know that information is helpful, but also take into consideration the possibility of re-traumatizing people as well. There's nothing wrong with posting articles, but reach out to the people who are directly impacted, rather than only posting something.

What are your future goals and dreams for your life?

I want to stay and develop myself here in Indianapolis. But, eventually, I would love to get my master's degree and maybe a Ph.D. abroad. Maybe I can stay out of the country for a while and really be in multicultural work. As a Religious Studies major, I would love to get my master's in Religious Studies and stay in another culture or multiple ones. Maybe write a book in the future. Outside of the logistical, career-driven things, I want to work on my music. I have played piano since I was 6, and I sing. Even if I don't become a celebrity, just using music to express myself in front of people would be great, and that's something I want to do.

What are your hopes for the community?

I would like to see more affirmation in our general society. To be specific, making resources for people to affirm themselves more accessible would be great. I am trans nonbinary, and I just happen to have a nonbinary name, and I happen to be able to dress the way I want. But I know a transmasculine person and for him to get his name changed is expensive and to get top surgery is expensive, and it's not accessible. It is very hard for some people who might want certain things to get to those resources.

Also, job security. I would really like to see people be able to express themselves while also feeling secure in their job. LGBTQ+ homelessness is rapid. I would like to see those numbers, hopefully, vanish and more resources made available for those people who need them as well. My hope is for the people after me to have more resources and less chance of being a statistic.

The homelessness numbers are caused by a multitude of things. My experience working with youth at Indiana Youth Group (IYG) is that some of it is non-acceptance at home. Maybe the parents don't want them over because they are LGBTQ+ and they don't want that around their family. Some queer and trans youth may also use drugs and that might be smoking cigarettes or marijuana, but like all youth, it can also be opioids. Homelessness can also be job insecurity as well. The Trevor Project (LGBTQ suicide prevention organization) puts out some good resources on this topic.

What can communities do to be more supportive and accepting of LGBTQ+ youth to help with the homelessness numbers?

The only thing I can think of right now is creating the resources. It does become harder because it's the third party thing: You have to be at least receptive for it to be effective. For instance, resources won't work with a parent who says, "I don't want anything to do with this!" Verses a parent who says, "I don't like it, but I'm willing to try to understand." We have a Parent Program at Indiana Youth Group (IYG), and it goes toward people who are affirming and want to know what else they can do. It helps people who need more resources for their children or for the youth they are watching over.

Based on my experience, the more at-risk people are trans women, particularly trans women of color, who are at risk not only for homelessness but also for violence. There is research about that risk. When

I go through sexual violence and assault trainings, we talk about who is at high risk and it's often trans women of color and black trans women specifically. It is a very big risk group and the numbers show that by how many losses there are and how many cases there are—and not all cases are reported.

As for the people who want nothing to do with their child who is LGBTQ+, I'm not sure how to reach them. More housing would be helpful for the kids who do have parents on the far end of the spectrum and end up homeless. Helpful resources for parents include programs, books, social media links, information, and then in-person meetings. But we need more resources that are easily accessible.

Part 2

STRONG FAMILY ALLIES

Rebecca (Becky) Troyer

Mother – Massage Therapist
She/Her/Hers
48 years old

> *"Your kid is your kid. If you are okay with letting your child go,*
> *I guess that's your choice. I'll be there to love them."*

I was born in Oklahoma. I have lived in Indiana since I was 2 years old. We have a pet cat and a lizard. Do you want a lizard? (Laughs). I have one child, age 20, who identifies as nonbinary and uses they/them pronouns. That means they don't identify as strictly female or strictly male.

What is your favorite thing about your child or their strength?

There are so many things. My kid is amazing. They never give up. They are always pushing forward. There have been a lot of obstacles in their path, and still are, and they just keep finding a way to move forward in life. I don't know if I would have done as well without some serious propping up from other people. But my child is amazing: very talented artistically, a freedom fighter, and smart.

Currently, they are going through vision therapy and enrolled in on-line college starting in October. They've tried two different schools, but the vision issues got in the way. They have Convergence Insufficiency, which means that when they look at print, the words overlap with each other. It's a neurological and muscular issue. So reading is very difficult for any period of time. Right now, they're working at Starbucks and are on a Management Training track but would also very much like to be the next Ruth Bader Ginsburg.

What would you feel comfortable sharing about your journey with your child?

In middle school, they told me, "Hey mom, I think I'm gay or bi." I said, "Okay, do your homework." Then in high school, they were dating a trans girl, and I think somewhere in that relationship, probably around age 15 or 16, they told me they were nonbinary. I said, "Okay." Now, the nonbinary has just become more so.

Around age 15 or 16, my child got active in Indiana Youth Group (IYG), and my kid was just my kid. I didn't ever have expectations of anything for my child in terms of what their life would look like. To me, it was okay for them to just be who they are and develop into who they are being. None of it has been that big of a deal. Whatever pronoun is best to use, I do my best. They/Them was next to impossible for me for a couple years. But, it's made me grow.

Did you and your child have family support?

You know, my child will have a different perspective than I do on this. My side of the family is supportive. When I grew up, there were gay friends in the family my whole life. My mother lives with a family friend who is gay and HIV positive, and I've known him since I was little. And so to my family, sexuality is not a concern. The other side of the family is a totally different story. My kid's aunt has been great, but some other family members have not been as supportive. We have another trans man in the family, a relative who is of my kid's generation, and that person got to break everybody in.

What would you say to families who are struggling?

I would say: "This is your child. This is the same child that you held, that you played with, that you loved, and that you helped through everything they've been through. They just have a different pronoun now."

I've had to be very supportive to other kids whose families were not supportive. I understand that these families struggle. For many of them, it's a religious thing. But this is your child. It's the same kid. You loved them before. Why don't you love them now?

What are your hopes and dreams for the community?

To me it's simple: Why does anybody care what somebody else's gender is? It just doesn't matter. I've had some people argue with me that it is a mental illness. There are kids who are transgender or nonbinary who suffer from issues like depression and anxiety, but I think that often comes more from the way society treats them than from anything inherent within them. I think that if they were accepted and didn't have to live in fear, their anxiety would go down and their depression would go down. So yeah, you try living their life: being afraid of being beaten up wherever you go and even your own family is not safe for you a lot of times.

In elementary school, my child became friends with every kid who had any gender dysphoria (incongruence between assigned sex and gender identity) from as early as kindergarten! So, I've watched a lot of kids on their journeys. They really are joyful the day they start their hormone therapy or get their surgeries. They finally feel like they're being who they are. Gender dysphoria is when they look in the mirror and their brain tells them they are male or female, but it doesn't match their bodies. It's when your insides don't match your outsides. My kid's boyfriend is trans, and he recently shared on Instagram®, so it's okay for the world to know this, he is a junior in college and super bright and finally has the confidence to speak up in class because his voice matches what it should be in his head. He had dysphoria when he looked in the mirror and when he spoke. Finally, he feels like he can participate in classes again, confidently. He is doing great in school!

How can our communities be more supportive to transgender individuals and their families?

Everybody could chill out about the bathrooms. For the trans community, the bathrooms are one of the biggest physical barriers. Also, people could ask for pronouns rather than making assumptions.

In general, I would say that people are more accepting than not. It's just those who are not are really loud. I think people have a lot easier time accepting something when it's not their own child because you do not have as much invested in *your dreams* of your little girl getting married in a white dress someday, and it doesn't happen that way. Since my kid is nonbinary and will accept female pronouns in pubic if needed, there is not as much bias. I've seen more bias against their trans friends. I worry about all of their safety when they are out. I don't stay awake at night worrying about it. But, it occurs to me that they're not always safe if they're out, in terms of someone attacking them. As anybody goes through transition, it's not always safe for them.

At the Pride parade, I did the Free Mom Hugs, and there was a trans woman, probably 40 or 50, who dressed as a woman but did not look particularly feminine by society's standards. I gave her a hug, and she just held on. I could feel all the pain and the non-acceptance from decades and that one just about did me in. She just cried, and I thought, "Oh my gosh, honey." I think of myself as being here for the kids, but some of the kids are the ones who are having it easier. My kid's circle of friends are the theater kids, and there was never any non-acceptance within that core group of friends. My kid was part of Young Actors Theater, which is just awesome.

What is Free Mom Hugs?

It's a group of moms who realized that many kids don't have support-ive families, and so we put on our Free Mom Hugs T-shirts and go to Pride parades and other LGBTQ events and give hugs to people who want them. It seems so simple. My kid said, "Oh my God mom, you're being such an activist." My kid said that is actually one of the most radical acts of activism within the LGBTQ+ community. I thought, "Okay, well, that's pretty easy." There are trans kids who are friends with my child, and I may take them to dinner occasionally or invite them over on holi-day. They come over usually after spending time with their family, just to decompress.

Probably, the most heartbreaking phone call I have ever gotten was from my child's ex-girlfriend, who is trans. One night I got a call, and she is just crying uncontrollably, and I am thinking, "Oh my God, what's go-ing on?" And she said, "Thank you for always accepting me." I thought, "That's the most heartbreaking thing I've ever had to hear." To her, it was supposed to be a positive phone call, to say thank you. But to me, that was the saddest thing ever: that somebody treating her as a human being was special. I did nothing other than say, "Hey, do you want to stay for dinner?" You know. I just saw a kid who could use some parental love. To me, that's not a big deal. But apparently, buying a kid a meal, saying nice words, and listening to them is radical activism. And *it's not*. I'm not storming the restrooms saying, "You will let people use it!" I am just nice.

So, Free Mom Hugs took place at one Pride event and moms all over the country were like, *"Hell, yes!"* I posted about it on Facebook, and I got responses from so many people who said they are doing that next year. I feel like there's more support than not, maybe not in your nuclear fam-ily, but everybody I know seems to know a kid who falls in the LGBTQ spectrum: a niece or a nephew or a cousin. The first article I saw about the Free Mom Hugs was at a church. At the Pride event, they had Free

Mom Hugs, Free Pastor Hugs, and Free Dad Hugs. So, Free Mom Hugs are just moms who say, "We could be nice to people."

Was there anything you wanted to talk about that I didn't ask you?

My kid went to a high school where the people are radically accepting. There were not barriers there. So, we did not have the same experience that many people have had. The high school can make a big difference. The person who called me up crying went to a school that had to have a big meeting about including sexual orientation and gender identity in their non-discrimination clause. It took the whole community protesting for them just to include those few words. My kid was never hassled on a bus and had radically different experiences. The school system can make a difference, elementary through high school.

Most of the kids I know probably didn't decide to transition until high school. But I know there are kids who do as early as elementary school. There are a lot of elementary schools pushing back against the bathroom issue. It seems like the bathrooms are the biggest deal, which is just interesting to me. I know that schools are already designed the way they're designed, and you can't always go back and change it all. But, I've seen elementary school bathrooms where they have all these stalls and the sinks elsewhere. You just use the stalls, and it doesn't matter. A theater I went to in Chicago had non-gendered bathrooms: unisex bathrooms with urinals and unisex bathrooms without urinals. Things like that can make it easier. I think that's where people get the most freaked out about transgender issues.

I grew up in a small town, two stoplights in that town now. Some of the people who stayed there and never left, their world stayed small and their minds stayed small. They might say, "I don't really care about transgender, but don't you dare go in the bathroom with my daughter or my son." And I say, "If people are going into a stall to use the bathroom, you aren't going to know." Or maybe you'll question, but nothing is going to happen. It seems like that is just a sticking point. These people would not be unkind to a trans person if they saw them walking down the street. But they are going to get real tribal if that person goes to the bathroom, which is so unnecessary.

I have had some hard chats now and then and a couple of people are willing to listen to me and think about what I say. I generally approach it very kindly and not too in their face. I try to just move the dial one notch. That's what I learned in SURJ (Showing Up for Racial Justice). SURJ has a lot of great trainings. They talk about changing bias and that it's like a speedometer: way over here is racism and way over there is anti-racism. It's important to keep notching the needle towards the anti-racist side. It's the same thing with any bias.

Any thoughts on what helps move the needle toward acceptance of transgender individuals?

Staying calm. Using relatable personal stories. Don't call somebody a bigot. It's really hard some days. I would like to say that facts and figures work. They don't. I'm happy to share articles that show the trans brain is wired to the gender they feel they are, but that doesn't necessarily change minds. I like science and so I'm always saying, "Look at what the science says." But it doesn't always help people understand.

I just say, "If it was your kid, what would you do? Would you really kick your kid to the curb," which some people do. I might say, "Would you disown your child because they wanted to be a writer instead of a physicist or whatever your dream was for them? Would you really cut them out? No. So, why would you for a transgender child?"

But it's not so easy for people to just let it go, especially since the Bible has been misinterpreted. If you go back to the way it was written, it doesn't actually say anything about homosexuality. It's just the way people chose to interpret that passage, which is really talking about how you can't be a pedophile. I will show people research, and they'll just tell me I'm wrong.

Any other suggestions for parents whose kids are transgender or nonbinary?

I didn't attach a lot of ideas about how my child would be. Khalil Gibran, says, "Your child comes through you. They are not of you." It's true. You also have to think: Did you do exactly what your parents wanted you to do? Would you have been happy if you'd done everything exactly as your parents wanted you to do and be? And if you did, are you happy? Just look at it from your kid's point of view. It's not easy. It's not like they chose it. I mean, who would ever say: "I know what I'm going to do. I'm going to make my life as hard as possible and be rejected by society and my family and possibly, you know, get killed." Why would you choose that? No one would choose that. It has to be an incredible internal struggle to transition.

My kid is accepted and loved and still had to have friends there when they told me they were gay and then again when they told me they were nonbinary. My kid knew there would be acceptance. They still wanted support there just in case maybe possibly there wasn't support. Even in that situation, where we are fine with it, my kid still felt the need for friends who already knew to be there.

With all these terms, I had to grow a lot because in my day it was gay or straight and male or female and now it's all on a continuum, which makes sense. I don't care. But my mind had to be expanded and say okay to all kinds of terms I didn't know. I could see if you were not open to that, it could be very overwhelming. IYG (Indiana Youth Group) has classes for parents.

One of my child's friends was in lots of therapy. The family knew there were issues, and the mother forced a confession that the child is trans. The family is very, very conservatively Catholic and that kid's truth was unacceptable to the family. The father accepted it somewhat okay, but the mother kind of lost it and took away the child's phone, computer, and rides to school. The mother decided that the child was trans because of forces on the Internet and musical influences.

My child was very concerned because the kid who had just been outed had suicidal ideation from time to time. So, we drove to this kid's house because there was no way to call. I wanted to speak to the mother, but the mother wouldn't come to the door. So, I spoke with this child at the door and just asked if she was okay, if she was safe, and if she thought she might hurt herself. I told her to call me if she needed anything, and I gave her younger sister, who had a cell phone, my telephone number. I said that if she needed to come with me right now, she could stay at our house. The mother heard every word I said. I said, "If it becomes unsafe, please have your sister call me."

My child was in the car waiting, and we drove away and before we got out of the neighborhood, my kid's phone rang and it was this child saying, "Hey, I got my phone back. Can you come over?" And my child sat down with the mother and helped the mom come to terms with it. The mother is not great at getting the gender pronouns right. The mother has accepted it but does not embrace it. So, it can be challenging for family gatherings.

You can't pray away the gay. You can't. If you want your child in your life, you're going to have to work through it. Your kid is your kid. If you are okay with letting your child go, I guess that's your choice. I'll be there to love them. To me, that's not hard.

Linda Helmick

Mother – *Professor of Art Education, Artist*
She/Her/Hers
64 years old

> *"Be supportive in the way the transgender person asks you to be*
> *supportive, and not in the way you think you should be supportive."*

I was born and raised in Ohio. I have five children. Destinee is my middle child. I moved to Indiana when my youngest was in kindergarten.

I am a Professor of Art Education. That's cool to say. (Smiles). I officially received my doctorate from Indiana University in Bloomington last month. It stills feels weird to say, "Doctor Helmick." I recently accepted a job as Professor of Art Education at the University of Missouri.

I taught art at a private Catholic school until I came to Bloomington (Ind.) for the Ph.D. program. The year the school noted in my file that I was gay was the year I decided to leave. It was already a frightening occupation because as a teacher, you work one-year contracts. Every April and May everyone is super stressed all the time wondering if they're going to be offered a contract for the next year. Having it officially noted that I am gay was nerve-racking, especially given everything that happened in Indiana with the Catholic high schools firing teachers or counselors for being gay. So, it was a good move because in Bloomington I didn't have to hide who I am. I could just be me.

Can you tell me about your journey, in terms of being Destinee's parent?

Destinee is my third child, right in the middle. She attended Lawrence North High School. She didn't tell me until later in high school that she actually identified as a girl. But I always knew. I knew when she was 3 years old and collected troll dolls. I knew in elementary school when all of her best friends were girls. I knew in the sixth grade when she fought to be the first boy cheerleader. She was such good friends with all the other cheerleaders and their parents that they embraced her, and she became a cheerleader that year. She has always been the bravest person I have ever known. I couldn't do anything other than just support everything she wanted to do. In high school, she really never dated anyone. She just had lots of great girlfriends.

After high school, she slowly transitioned into fully being a woman, 24/7 (twenty-four hours seven days a week).

She had gotten to know several drag queens she met through friends. They introduced her to the drag world, and after high school, she performed as a drag queen. As she was performing, she gradually went from performing as a drag queen to beginning to dress and be female during the day.

After she moved to Minneapolis, she told me she felt freer to be who she was. She went to court and officially got her name changed because, as you can imagine, looking for a job identifying and dressing as a woman when your driver's license has a male name would be difficult. So, she went through that process about seven years ago.

What is your favorite thing about Destinee or her strength?

Her ability to be herself, no matter what that means or looks like to other people. She seems to have no fear, and I admire that in her because

I don't always have that myself. She works in a hospital to help people with HIV and AIDS get the services they need, and she's a Medical Case Manager now.

How might allies be more supportive of transgender individuals and their families?

To listen, without judgment. Also, to be supportive in the way the transgender person asks you to be supportive, and not in the way *you think* you should be supportive. Does that make sense? Because what we want and what we feel is right is not always helpful.

So many people are under the impression that this is a choice, and it isn't. If people really believe that God created us, then he created everyone exactly as they are and this is how they were born. This is how Destinee was born. She was born to be this person. That's *really* important, to be able to accept and to know this is who this person is.

What is your hope or wish for the community?

My wish is for there to be more visible support. Destinee told me that when she moved to Minneapolis, she instantly felt freer to be who she is and to walk through the mall holding the hands of her boyfriend, in a way that she never felt free to do in Indiana. So, I would wish for more visibility and more open conversations and supportive groups that are easier to find.

I have a friend who just found out last summer, by accident, that her child is transgender, and this mom didn't have anyone to talk to about it. She didn't know how to navigate all of this and neither does her child, except for online searches, which is not ideal. There are too many websites out there that are not ethical and not good places to get reliable information. I believe her child didn't feel safe enough to confide in her mom even though the mom always felt like they had a very open and trusting relationship. I'm not sure how we bridge that gap because we can inadvertently say or do things that make our children feel like we might be judging them for this or that, and they might not feel free to talk to us.

I think it helped that I came out as a lesbian 25 years ago. Doing that and living that probably helped Destinee talk to me and be more open. That would be an unusual situation for some people.

When children see us being judgmental toward others, and we gossip with our friends and say things about people and our children are there, they are going to feel like they might be judged if they are a little different, even though that's certainly not what we mean to happen. It's hard to know.

Are family members supportive of Destinee?

My mom and dad are conservative, but Destinee is their granddaughter. So yes, they are supportive. I don't know how they were able to become supportive, but my mom got really upset when one of my cousins got kicked out of their church for being gay. It feels like when it's happening with family and people they love, it's different than society at large. I don't talk religion or politics with some of my family, but yes, they are supportive. They may not agree or they may not wish that for one of their children or grandchildren, but they're supportive.

I know from listening to other people's stories that it's not always as slow a process as it was for Destinee. This probably would have happened faster for Destinee if she had been born twenty years later. She is 37. It was a gradual process for her. First, performing as a drag queen, then living as a woman, and then going to court to officially have her name and gender changed. She dates men. She takes hormones. She is in every way a woman. She is who she was always meant to be, and I think if that had happened now, it would have happened faster.

I don't know if it's because I'm in a university setting and we talk about this a lot, but I feel like it's more open now, and it's definitely talked about in high schools and even in middle schools and elementary schools sometimes. There are kids out there who know in elementary school, which blows my mind and is amazing at the same time.

Is there anything else you wanted to share that I didn't ask you?

It would take forever to tell you everything. But there were milestones and those are strongest in my memory: like in the sixth grade when Destinee fought to be a cheerleader and then in high school going to prom with her best friends, which were girls, and making the decision to perform as a drag queen, and then making that decision to identify as a woman all the time, and now working with others who go through that process. It was all just a process that grew with her.

Do you have a favorite memory of Destinee?

Well, there were five children, so there was never *anything* I did with just one of them! (Laughs). We enjoyed doing things outdoors.

My favorite memories involve her bravery to be herself. We talk every single day. I see my other children more than I see her because she lives far away, but she and I talk every day. I'm the one she comes to for advice, and I go to her for advice. Now, she is the person, the daughter, who has become my girlfriend.

Philip B.

Father – Physician (OBGYN)
He/Him/His
71 years old

> *"The people who thrive are the ones who are accepted in
> the workplace, in their homes, in their places of worship,
> and in their educational environments."*

I was born in Des Moines, Iowa, and grew up in Madison County, of *The
Bridges of Madison County* movie fame. I was in the Army in Germany.
I went to Colorado for undergraduate school and back to Des Moines
to go to medical school. I did an internship and residency in Denver and
practiced as a family doctor at a little town in the prairie for ten years in
Colorado. I went back in the Army and did an OB (Obstetrics) residency
in El Paso, Texas, and then did a service tour in Panama City, Panama,
for three years.

I have lived in Indiana now for close to thirty years. I am an OBGYN
and have a medical practice with my wife, who is a family practice physician. We have four children. We each have one child by a previous mar-
riage and then we adopted two children. To protect the identity of our
oldest adopted child, I will call her Gale (not her real name).

Panama is kind of the crux of this story.

My wife and I married when we were a bit past our peak reproduc-
tive years, but we both felt we had something to offer as parents. We were

living in Panama, and we said, "Let's adopt a couple of babies." We adopted a baby who was born at the Gorgas Army Hospital in Panama City, Panama. I was Chief of OB (Obstetrics) and was able to arrange for my wife to room in with the baby. At the time, the baby was given a male birth name. Then, we adopted another baby a year and a half later. So, we had these two babies while we were in Panama. We immigrated them to the United States where they became citizens about four years later. We always thought that our child, Gale, was going to come out as gay.

What are your favorite things about Gale or Gale's strengths?

She is an incredibly caring individual with a really good heart. She appreciates nature and spirituality. She is very kind. She doesn't smoke cigarettes. She doesn't drink alcohol. She doesn't do drugs. She has some learning challenges, but she is in college out west, part-time, getting decent grades and progressing toward a certificate in computer coding. She has a passion for coding and a passion for cooking. She's just a really kind individual.

One of the other things we noticed early on was her ability to negotiate the world. At 2 or 3 years of age, we would go into a store, and she would be talking to the salespeople, asking where things were located and telling them what we were looking for. She's always been able to do that, be an advocate for herself and be curious about her surroundings.

Can you tell me a little about your journey as Gale's parent?

We were living in Panama for a couple of years when Gale was born. In Panama, you have house help. We had a nanny for the kids and a housekeeper. Even on army pay, we had a fulltime live-in maid and a gardener. So, you can imagine what life was like there for the kids, pretty laid-back. We and the kids were able to enjoy some of the finer things about society, including travel and the beauty of the tropics. Gale has a deep appreciation for nature. In fact, she and her mom are taking a road trip next month to Northern California to see the redwoods. That's the kind of thing that Gale really, really appreciates. The kids were raised as Unitarian Universalists, and they took OWL (Our Whole Lives) classes, and they have a deep appreciation of the inherent worth and dignity of every person. Gale keeps a small altar in her bedroom that is reflective of her spirituality, which is earth-based.

After Panama, we moved to San Antonio, Texas, and I was on the faculty for the OB residency program there. My wife worked in a family practice, and the kids continued to have Spanish-speaking day help. Then we moved to Indiana, and we really couldn't find anyone to be a Spanish mentor for them. The kids were raised in Montessori schools and private schools that focused on children with learning challenges. Finally, we found an Au Pair, who has remained like family to us. She was from Spain and we thought, "This is great. We will have a Spanish speaker helping take care of the kids." But Spanish was not her first language. She spoke Catalan, and it was actually easier for her to communicate in English with the kids than in Spanish, which is pretty funny. She became like a family member to all of us. Last Christmas, we took the family and visited her in Barcelona and spent time with her and her family up in the remote areas, and it was a really rewarding experience.

Gale had special skills as a figure skater and became nationally ranked as a singles figure skater in a highly competitive environment. At age 15, she publically came out as a transgender female, and that made figure skating difficult because in figure skating, biological women mature early and become quite adept at the craft by the time they are 12 or 13 years of age. By 15 years of age, it is national and international competitions. Gale was 15 and was too old to compete against women and too frustrated with the transition process to be identified as trans and gave up a promising skating career. You can imagine the challenges you would be faced with when struggling with not only, "I am actually a girl," but also with the non-acceptance in the figure skating community. She kind of withdrew from society and tried to be her authentic self without having had any surgery and just trying to do the social transformation. It was a rough time. She dropped out of school and went through an educational exchange where they prepare kids to take the GED (Graduate Equivalency Degree).

We were worried about her not only because she's a mixed-race individual but being transgender and mixed-race is a pretty dangerous existence for that individual in society. Every time the phone would ring, we would be on edge about whether it was going to be bad news. That went on for a few years. Finally, when she 17, we were able to arrange the surgical transformation in Thailand.

Gale and her mother went to Thailand for a month for the surgery and for the recovery time. In trying to find a doctor, we looked at a variety of things. We wanted someone with a good reputation and someone that we could afford. As it turns out, the guy with the best reputation at that time was in Thailand. Keep in mind this was back in 2010, and only a handful of doctors in the states were doing gender-confirming surgery. There were doctors in training, but many were not yet practicing. Also, the age of consent in the United States was 18 and Gale was only 17. In Thailand, the age of consent was 16. Surgery was a difficult decision. We were trying to weigh emotional maturity with the knowledge of body morphology because the longer you wait the more difficult the physical transformation process becomes. My wife took a leave of absence from work and took Gale to Thailand and spent a month there and then came home, and we helped Gale with everything while she recovered.

What would be helpful for people to know to be better allies to transgender individuals and their families?

I have what I call my corollary to the Golden Rule. The Golden Rule supposedly says, "Do unto others as you would have them to do unto you." I think that's selfish. My corollary to the Golden Rule is, "Do unto others as *they* would have you do unto them." That is my advice to anybody about anything. It's not about you. It's about them. What is *their* need? Not, what do *you* think they need. Begin by asking if there is anything you can do for them in this relationship. We overlook that in a lot of ways and in a lot of relationships. This relationship includes me, but just like with a partner, you ask: *What is it that they need that you can provide?* That's what sustains a relationship.

What is your hope for the community?

As with a lot of racially charged things right now, we tend to look at someone as "other," and we demonize, victimize, and criminalize them. As a Unitarian Universalist, that pains me greatly, whether it's someone who is Asian, African American, Hispanic, or Native American, we are all are just people. People might not look like you if you are Caucasian, but they're people, just like you and me. And gay people and transgender people are people just like you and me. Maybe there are differences in terms of how we partner up and relate to other people, but they have jobs, and they have families, and they have dreams and aspirations, just like the bricklayer and just like the postal carrier and just like the airplane pilot. They have a life and needs and dreams and deficiencies just like everybody else.

We would do society a great favor by saying, "Okay, I may not understand, but I'm going to accept people." That's really the bottom line. I accept. I may not understand what being a transgender person is because I can't live it. But I can be empathetic, and I can be compassionate. Nobody can expect to understand what it is like to be transgender because only the people who are transgender are the experts on that experience and the same with any other group of people. But we as a society can say, "Okay, well, that's your deal, and you are free to live your life and let me live mine." We could do society a huge service by treating everybody like that: live and let live. It doesn't make them right and me wrong, and it doesn't make me right and you wrong. We are all just people. Transgender people eat and sleep and poop and have whatever intimate lives that they have, and they use the roads and the schools and drink water and buy groceries: just like everybody else.

In my medical practice, I have been able to develop an appreciation for the transgender community. I am one of the few doctors in my area that takes care of the hormonal needs of transgender individuals, and at any given time, I have about a hundred transgender patients. So, I hear all these stories about acceptance and rejection and their intimate lives and their work and life in general. The people who thrive are the ones who are accepted in the workplace, in their homes, in their places of worship, and in their educational environments, and so forth.

So, that's all I have to say: Acceptance, whether you understand it fully or not. They are here. They occupy space. They are not hurting you. They do not expect you to change your religious beliefs because of them. They just want to be accepted as people. We would do society a huge favor by accepting them. That's my pitch.

Was there anything I didn't ask that you wanted to talk about?

Well, I will share my perspective as a dad. I had a bit of a struggle with it only because Gale was an accomplished skater, and I was an integral part of that process. My concern was not for me but for her, in having to give that up, because I knew it was a satisfying thing for her.

We have been really fortunate that we had the resources to help Gale's transition. A lot of people couldn't withstand that expense, but we did a lot of things to help make this happen. No regrets! We were happy to help Gale be Gale.

I want to share a quote from my wife's mother. Gale's grandmother was 88 years old. When we presented Gale after her transition to my wife's mother, she looked at Gale and she said, "Oh, this is wonderful! I've always wanted another granddaughter and now one has fallen out of all the sky." How cool is that? That set the tone in our family. Imagine that!

Amy

Mother – Learning & Development
She/Her/Hers
54 years old

Zander

High School Freshman
He/Him/His
14 years old

> _"As a society, we need to stop teaching the hate and
> just accept everyone for who they are."_

MOM: I have three children. The two older ones are cisgender female (gender identity matches sex assigned at birth). Zander (nickname Z) is the youngest. He is 14 years old and a freshman in high school. I work in Learning and Development at a pharmaceutical company. We have five cats and a dog.

What are Zander's gifts or strengths?

MOM: It's a combination of creativity and tenacity, and he is a problem solver, always has been. He is funny, smart, and compassionate.

Can you tell me a bit about your journey as a parent?

MOM: When he was 18 months old, I was watching him play, and I said to myself, after having raised his older siblings, I wonder if this is what transgender looks like? Watching him play, he never played like his sisters did. I didn't force gender roles. I never said, "You can't do that because you're a girl or you can't do that because you're a boy." Except football, I said no to that.

When he was 2 years old, we were at a Cracker Barrel restaurant with his grandparents. His grandpa said Zander could pick out whatever outfit he wanted. I went over to Z and told him, and he didn't even have to stop and think. He ran straight to the display of Sharp boy's T-shirts and shorts and that's what he wanted! I didn't say, "No, you need to buy something pink because that's what grandpa wants." (Laughs). I never forced it. But I hollered at him so many times, "Why are you so disgusting, stop that!" Had I known I was raising a boy, I would not have been so surprised because I had a brother. I knew how they were. (Laughs). It was more my disconnect from who he was to who I thought he was.

So, I kind of wasn't shocked when he came out to me at age 11. But at the same time, I didn't want that for him because I know how cruel the world can be, and I know what a hard journey it is. I was like, "Why can't you just be a boy at home and a girl in public," which was the wrong thing to say. (Laughs). But that's how I felt. But at age 11, he said, "I'm pretty sure I'm a boy."

ZANDER: No, I said, "I am a boy." And she said, "What makes you think that?" I knew when I was 6 or 7, but I had no words to put on it. My mom and my sister were talking in the car about my sister's classmate who had recently transitioned to female. And I was like, "Oh, you can do that!"

MOM: The daycare gave us picture albums and when we look back through pictures, the days when the smile was brightest was when he was dressed as a boy, and he always played with the boys.

ZANDER: My best friends in daycare were Nathan and Eli. One of my favorite pictures is where I am carrying a baby doll like a football with a backwards hat on it, and I have just the biggest smile in the world. I didn't start fully, socially transiting until I was 13 when I came out to my dad.

MOM: The thing is, life started getting real difficult in his third-grade class. That was when this click of girls who were really popular asked Z to join them. And Z was like, "No thank you." Then they started picking on him. That's when the bullying and the self-harm started.

From third grade to eighth grade, it was a constant struggle and under the care of a psychiatrist while trying to figure out how to help him be happy, and he was on antidepressants during those years. He got thrown out of school so many times for fighting and being combative. He was failing almost everything, and he has a very high IQ. All of that, I think, was more a function of him not being his true self and using up all his bandwidth to deal with that. It finally got so bad in the eighth grade that I pulled him out of school for six or seven weeks. I home-schooled him, and he socially transitioned. We swapped out the wardrobe, and that's when we told our friends and family.

The change has been absolutely incredible to watch. He is doing well in school, and he's making friends. He has a pleasant disposition, he is helpful, and he doesn't fight anymore. So, just that change of being okay with the transition helped.

Did Zander switch schools?

MOM: We didn't have to change schools. I just called the school and said, "Hey, he is coming back, and by the way, he prefers male pronouns and his name is Zander." They gave him a key to the bathroom.

ZANDER: I didn't like being separated at school and having my own bathroom. I wish they would have just let me use the guy's bathroom.

MOM: Weren't you afraid to use the guy's bathroom because you were afraid they would beat you up?

ZANDER: No, I wasn't afraid they would beat me up.

MOM: Okay, we were afraid they would beat him up. Things were not going well at that time with a particular group of boys. But, the school was a lot more accommodating than I thought they would be.

ZANDER: They weren't *that* accommodating. It was kind of here and there, a 50/50 chance whether it would be okay or not. Certain teachers were okay and some teachers were kind of okay, and a couple of teachers deadnamed me on purpose. (Used the wrong misgendered name). But being deadnamed doesn't really bother me because it just makes the other person look like a douche. That's not the best word, but you know what I mean.

MOM: I am in a Facebook group for parents of transgender children, and many of the parents are helpful for questions. It seems a lot of their children will have complete and total meltdowns if they get deadnamed. So, I was expecting more of that. But Z is very gracious when he is misgendered. I still occasionally deadname him because it's hard when I think back because I didn't know him as Zander back then. I knew him as someone else. When I talk about him from that earlier time, it is more difficult for my family too. My sister, the first time after she knew, stopped me mid-sentence and said, "Oh wait, how do I talk about him when he was little?" We didn't know what to do.

ZANDER: I told you guys! I told them, "I am he/him and Zander, even as a child." And my sister was like, "No, you were this other name back then." And I said, "That's *not* the point."

MOM: I get that now. In the beginning, it was a struggle. But he has always been this creative, fun person. What I call him has changed, but this person hasn't. I had to get my head around that so I could think of him as Zander when he was 2 years old.

When he first came out to me, I said I would support his pronouns and appearance, but I would never say okay to hormones. I am now three years there, and I am supporting hormones.

ZANDER: I didn't even know the difference between boy and girl until, I want to say kindergarten, but it was more like first grade.

MOM: Our daycare never gendered toys. They just had toys, and they would get out all the trucks and cars and that's what everyone would play with. Or they would get out all the kitchen stuff and that's what everyone would play with. They were never separated by gender.

ZANDER: They would separate us into lines to go to the bathroom. I didn't know which one to go in. I generally stood in the back and walked in the middle. I wanted to be on the guy's side, but I didn't want to get yelled at.

Anything you want people to know to be more supportive?

ZANDER: Don't ask, "What was your name before?" because it's not really need-to-know information. I get that people are curious and people are nosy, but it's a little humiliating. People will say, "So, what's your *real* name?" And I'm like, "Zander."

Is the high school supportive?

MOM: We moved to a different side of town, and we are at a charter school now. Oh yes! All the people and the teachers there are supportive. That school has been amazing with just allowing Zander to be who he is!

What should the community know to be more supportive?

MOM: There was a mother I contacted who was in the same school system, and we were both volunteers. I kind of knew who she was and that her child had transitioned. I reached out in messages and said, "Hey, could you help me work through a thing or two here?" She was from a very religious background, and she said, "You know, at the end of the day, you have to remember that you love your kid and that is the most important thing." For me, that helped a lot because I was worried about society in general and about religious family members who would never accept this. And as for my friends who are very conservative, well, I would rather have an alive child than a dead one.

For people who argue that transgender is a choice and God doesn't make mistakes, I wholeheartedly agree that God does not make mistakes. God made this amazing little human who happens to be transgender. They don't know why people are transgender, but they are and have been here throughout time. As for me, I would really prefer if people would take religion out of it. Because whether or not you believe it's a choice or you were born that way, they're humans, and they deserve compassion and support. That's the thing I want people to know.

What is your hope for the community?

MOM: I hope that society, as a whole, will get to the same level of acceptance as most children. When a young cousin of Zander's asked: "Are you a boy or a girl? Mom says you're a girl, but you look like a boy. I think you're a boy, and so I'm going to call you a boy." And that was it. Kids do not care. It's just another thing to them, and it's not a big deal. The parents teach the hate. As a society, we need to stop teaching the hate and just accept everyone for who they are.

It would also be great if we didn't have to fight the insurance to get the medical care of the physicians. Basically, WPATH (World Professional Association for Transgender Health) are the experts the insurance companies look to and are the ones that determine whether hormones or gender-confirming surgeries are medically necessary. The insurance company will say, "Well, WPATH says you can't start hormones until you are 16." Every physician and psychiatrist and therapist are all saying this child is 14 and can have testosterone so he can start puberty with his peers. The parents and medical community have to go to war with the insurance companies to eventually get approval, if they're lucky. It would be good for society to come far enough along that they could trust the physicians in charge of medical care.

Anything else you want to talk about that I didn't ask?

ZANDER: Gender and sexuality are different things

MOM: Exactly! I've heard it said, "Gender is who I go to sleep as. My sexuality is who I go to sleep with." (Laughs). I do think people get that confused a lot. Also, I think it would be great if people didn't ask about your child's genitalia. It's a rude question. It's none of anyone's business if my child is transgender or not. This child is a boy, so why would you ask, right? I don't ask you if your child is cisgender.

ZANDER: Of course, my answer to that is: *You want to find out?* (Laughs). So, usually you get a horrified look as a response, and they walk away! Shock factor.

MOM: I always feel a little uncomfortable sending him into boys' restrooms and boys' dressing rooms to try on clothes. I think it's just that for so many years I took him in with me. I probably would have gone through that with him around age 7, had I known, and I would have had that separation anxiety then. But I'm having it at an older age now.

ZANDER: Separation anxiety, wow! (Starring incredulously). I am not little.

MOM: Well, okay. One of the things I noticed in the schools is that they separate and categorize by male and female. You know, boys go to this gym and girls go to that one. For Z that was a painful thing, and I didn't know. I didn't know to advocate for him. The schools could just go by numbers: even on one side and odd numbers on the other and separate like that. It's not always easy to answer that gender question when you're 6 years old.

ZANDER: I knew my answer. I just didn't want to get made fun of or yelled at.

MOM: They could say, pick the right line or left line or just find another way. There are *so many* other ways to group people, rather than by gender.

Diana

Mother – Nonprofit Support Staff, Photographer
She/Her/Hers
52 years old

> _"Families can just love each other for fuck's sake._
> _Who cares what gender they are."_

I was born and raised in a small town. I am a part of the support staff for a nonprofit organization during the week, and I am a photographer for a local company, a small business, for 19 or 20 years. So, I have two jobs: my office job and my part-time job.

I have two biological kids, and I have a son-in-law. My youngest, Rigel, is 22. Rigel is transgender. My eldest, Freddy, is 26 and married to Jake, who is transgender. Freddy is nonbinary, and I supported them in their court case when they went to court to have their name legally changed and the gender marker changed on their driver's license.

What pronouns do your children use?

Rigel uses he.
Freddy uses they.

What are your favorite things about Rigel and Freddy?

One of the most favorite things I like about Rigel is he has a kind and generous heart. He has been working with a feral cat community on the east side—working on taming them and, eventually, going to get them spayed and neutered at a clinic. I call him the "Cat Whisperer" because when I pick him up for dinner or something like that, the cats know when he comes and goes, and they all sit on the front porch meowing for him to feed them. One time I took a picture after I dropped him off. It was cute. He was walking up the sidewalk, and there were three cats behind him like little baby ducks.

Rigel is working a part-time job at Whole Foods. He struggled a lot because he is Aspie (Asperger's) as well. So, he struggles with some stuff. But, he's really talented in art. He is a phenomenal artist. I believe he had one art show at a restaurant back when he was in high school. He's very talented and very generous and has a way with animals. All my kids do. I don't have grandchildren; I have "grand fur babies." (Laughs). Rigel has two cats. My eldest and their husband have two dogs and one cat.

With Freddy, it's how strong-willed they are and how passionate. They do an awesome job with makeup. They can rock a feminine look, and they can rock a scruffy look. There was one instance when they were experimenting. It was five or six years ago. I had worked 12 hours that day, and I was taking a bath, and Freddy texted to say, "Hey, do you mind if I stop over?" I said I might still be in the tub. I heard Freddy coming up the stairs and then Freddy came in and that was the first time I saw them with a beard. They were rocking a scruffy look, and they looked like their father so much that I gasped and covered up really fast! (Laughs). Yeah, I think that was the first time I saw them with their more masculine look.

Freddy can be a force to reckon with. All three of my kids try to make time to go to the protests and have their voices heard. I'm very proud of them, especially in a world where a lot of people, me as well, can be guilty of just going along to get along. Sometimes that can be easier than standing up for yourself, your beliefs, your love, your lifestyle, or your friend's race, gender, or nationality. There are racists and haters out there. But, my kids try to make the world a better place by being heard. The last protest they went to, I said, "Hey, can you make an extra sign for me because I can't be there. I have to be at work." I'm very proud of all three of them.

When you say all three, are you talking about your two kids and your son-in-law?

Yes, my youngest son, my eldest child, and my son-in-law. My son-in-law, Jake, bless his heart. He was really close to his mom, and I'm really proud of him. He had top surgery a couple of years ago, and his mom died of breast cancer. Just this past year, he got a really nice tattoo incorporating his top surgery scars and some symbolic images of his mother's favorite things. Jake is a sweetheart and is an awesome husband to my eldest. He is patient and kind and generous and so loving. The two of them together are cute as a bug.

Can you tell me a little about your journey as a parent?

It was probably Rigel's freshman year of high school that he came out to me and fully embraced and accepted, to himself, being transgender. Obviously, you know inside that you're different. I think he had the vocabulary—and could name his feelings and identify how he felt and why—when he started high school. It had been developing for years before that.

From my knowledge and experience, I believe it has only been in the recent past that the term nonbinary has been an option. My eldest has gone by Freddy and embraced being nonbinary and has used they pronouns for years. I have a crappy memory for time, and I am not sure of the exact timeframe.

I have tried to be their biggest proponent and cheerleader for them, especially because of a family member who refused to respect their preference for names or genders or pronouns. Their biological father basically said to Rigel, "You're my daughter. I've known you longer than you know yourself, and so I know you better than you do." Well, you do know yourself and, in my opinion, that's being an egotistical asshole.

Rigel and Freddy don't have much to do with the rest of their biological family.

Right now, I think they're just exhausted from correcting their grandparents. I feel like I'm in the middle because mom and dad will say, "We're trying, and we love them no matter what." However, there have been instances where they also say, "You're always going to be (x) to me" and then deadname them (use a misgendered name they do not go by). Or they say, "This is really hard for me to change." I don't think that way. So, I just don't think they put in enough effort. That is my opinion of their problems with it. They'll use the generational thing: "We're old. It's hard to change, and we've known you as x (deadname) for 26 years." Well, that is just lazy excuses. Rigel has gone through several evolutions of names. We didn't call him the first name on his birth certificate. We called him by his middle name. He also tried Kendran for a while but people kept saying Kendra. He tried something else too, and people kept turning that into a feminine name.

Did you have support for yourself and for your family?

No, not really. When they were younger, after the divorce, they had counseling. I encourage them to continue as far as finding their own support system and network. I have been in therapy for decades. (Laughs).

Schools weren't a big issue for Freddy because he publically "came out" after high school. For Rigel, it was a struggle.

My main thought is the bathroom use in school and how he struggled. Probably several UTIs (urinary track infections) have been attributed to the fact that Rigel preferred not to go to the bathroom at school just to avoid that issue and not peeing when he had to. It helped that as soon as school was over, he went to the library, which was a hundred feet from the high school. We lived two blocks from the school, and so that helped.

What has been the best or hardest part about being a mom of children who are transgender or nonbinary?

The best thing is learning from my kids and having them teach me to be more sensitive to others and to not assume. I have a journalism degree, and I was always taught they/them is plural. But I read something recently that said they/their/them was actually singular when it originated and was used to reference individuals.

A great thing about being a mom to kids on the gender spectrum is the generational learning from them.

The hardest part is the worry that they're going to face hostility, judgment, bigotry, and possibly violence. I worry about how others will interact with them. It's frustrating that society doesn't have gender-neutral and family unisex bathrooms. I took Rigel out to dinner at a burger restaurant, and he had to go to the bathroom. They didn't have gender-neutral bathrooms, and they didn't have a family bathroom, in a public restaurant!

Rigel hangs out at the library a lot, every day that he doesn't work, and the people there know him. But he has to go ask for a key to go to the family bathroom. The family bathrooms are in the kid's section on the second floor of the library. So, it feels like it's a kind of jail where you have to *ask* to go to the bathroom.

What do you think is important for allies to know to be more helpful or supportive to your family?

Educate yourself. Be an advocate for transgender families. Vote for fuck's sake. And don't be an asshole.

If you're out with trans friends, offer to go to the bathroom with them. Take a step above and beyond just friending them and help be an advocate regarding the bathrooms. I know this is all more than just bathrooms but our government leadership can be like Neanderthals. One thing everyone can do is ask for a gender-neutral bathroom. I love businesses, like Ruth's Café, where instead of a male or female on the bathroom, they have Star Trek characters and it says, "To Boldly Go." I'm a big nerd. (Laughs).

I want it to be more than just the bathroom issue and human hygiene. But in Maslow's *Hierarchy of Needs*, trans people do not even have basic needs accommodated. People should be more aware that it's just a bathroom: You go in and do your business and come out. If it is a one-person bathroom, what does it matter which gender is which? If there's a line for the women's restroom and there's no guys in the other one, I will go into the guy's restroom if it's a one stall. There's a door, and there's a stall. So what if there's a urinal in there? I've got privacy. I thought about this a couple weeks ago when there was a guy at my office fixing the bathroom paper towel dispenser. He said, "You can't come in here!" And I said, "Oh, it's closed?" I just had to pee, and there's a separate room with a stall and a door. He's like, "I'm in here!" It's a bathroom. You do your business. With the day I've had, it's the main thing I can think of right now.

Just educate yourself and think about other options because I know Rigel has gotten sick; and he doesn't drive, so he takes public transportation. If he had to run in someplace to use the bathroom, that would be a big ordeal for him! So, yeah, be more accepting and educate yourself.

I have been around people where they say, "That dude's wearing a dress." *Really?* Let them be, and let them express themselves however they want to express themselves. I'm actually bisexual and so what does my sexuality or their gender have to do with you? I want more open-minded people. It doesn't have to be a big deal but just say, "Hey, that was insensitive. What you said was rude." The younger generation is more, to use one of their terms, woke: to gender, to race, to nationalities, to religions, to sexuality. I loved having my kids teach me the differences between gender identity and sexuality, and it's not just black and white. It's not two choices. Although Christians will say, "There's Adam and Eve, there wasn't Steve." I say, "Why not? Why not Adam and Steve? Or Jane? Or whoever?"

What is your hope for the community?

Globally, the violence. I am trying to think of how eloquently to say it, but I don't do eloquent after a long day of work. But all the violence against transgender people in other countries and just the hate and the killings because people are different, and not restricted only to gender issues.

I've performed in *The Vagina Monologues* (a play by Eve Ensler) for about ten years. There is a trans piece in the monologues that still brings tears. The person is talking about schools and bullies and says, "He smashed my magic marker painted nails and punched my lipstick mouth." The piece goes on, "I just wanted to carry a purse to school, and they beat me up every day for it." (Pauses). "And they beat my boyfriend with a baseball bat, just for loving me."

So globally, end the violence and the targeting of trans people because it is so scary, especially for trans women of color. The statistics for trans women of color, it's just off the charts.

Statewide, the laws suck. As for community-wide efforts, there's so much we could be doing to advocate for acceptance and better facilities. Families could reach out. I would love to see more community outreach, not just with nonprofit LGBTQ+ organizations but outreach with *all groups.*

I tried going to a couple of meetings for LGBTQ families a while back, and I stopped going because some of the parents were more, "Woe is me. I've had to deal with this." They weren't solution orientated. It was, "I had to go through this and that and our family had to deal with my son being gay" and so on. And well, *so what?* Let people do themselves. They know themselves a lot better than you think. I have never said this to my children's father, but I want to say, "Fuck you. You haven't walked in their shoes! Just walk a mile in someone's shoes to see what all *they* have to go through before judging them." Be more sensitive to the feelings and needs of others.

Families can just love each other for fuck's sake. Who cares what gender they are? I also find these "gender reveal" baby showers annoying. I don't care what's in someone's diaper. And I don't give a crap about what's in someone's pants. I care about what's in their heart.

Mike and Karen

Parents – Founders of GEKCO (Gender Expansive Kids & Co.)
He/Him/His and *She/Her/Hers*
62 years old and 61 years old

"Your first job as a parent is to love your child and support your child."

KAREN: We have been married 36 years. We have five children. Our fourth child is transgender. We have a bunny rabbit as a pet.

MIKE: We use the name "Will" or "William" for our son because he does not want his real name used. ["Karen" and "Mike" are being used here to protect Will's privacy].

What are your favorite things about Will?

KAREN: His strength and courage in the face of adversity is amazing and is very inspirational to me. He has leadership qualities that can't help but rise to the surface.

MIKE: I would agree. His courage, and he is a very kind person and caring of others, very smart. He's a tenacious individual. In high school, Will was a straight-A student, a band drum major, a valued member of the theater department, French Club President, and winner of multiple academic awards.

Would you share a little about your family's journey?

MIKE: We went through a period in his junior year of high school that was difficult, cycles where he would be very anxious and depressed. We did counseling and were trying to diagnose the problem. One night, Sunday night, he was particularly devastated. We sat down and I said, "What's something we could do that would make you feel better right away?" And he said, "Nothing." It occurred to me that we could visit his older sister who had a 2-year-old child. I said, "Let's go visit your niece."

We went over to visit the next day, and it was a very nice day. We had a great time. His niece is a typical 2 year old, and who cannot be joyful with a toddler? (Laughs). He felt better during the visit, and as we're driving home, on the Interstate with trucks zinging past us at 70 miles per hour, all of a sudden, he asked me, "What do you think of the name William?" My ears perked up because I knew that was an odd question, and so I said, "Why do you ask? What do you mean?" And he said, "Well, that's my name." I kind of processed that for a minute and then said, "Tell me more about that." He said, "Well, you know, I'm really a boy, and my name is William." This is where one's experience as a lawyer pays off. When we get surprise information that we didn't anticipate, we learn: *Don't react. Just soak it in and ask lots of questions.*

He proceeded to tell me that he was transgender and really a boy, and he wanted me to know that. And then, like a lightning bolt, it all made sense for why he would seem to get better and then crash and burn because he was being assaulted, basically, with the fact that his assigned birth sex didn't match who he really was. We had a very good conversation on the drive back. I asked lots of questions. When we got home, I thanked him for telling me and said, "I really appreciate you telling me. You know I love you. From my perspective, this doesn't change anything, and I appreciate knowing." Then, I came in the house, and I told Karen.

KAREN: Well, we didn't know very much about what that meant. We assured him that we supported him and that we would learn and proceed together, forward. We had only heard of certain famous transgender adults in the news, but there wasn't much we knew about it. We didn't know what that meant for a kid. Besides being happy he told us, I was mostly afraid for his safety because I did know enough to know that society doesn't really accept or tolerate transgender people well. So, we did some research, and we did dive right into learning as much as we could as fast as we could. We talked to some professionals—therapists and doctors in town—to help him transition and with whatever else he needed.

What was most helpful for your journey as parents?

MIKE: It felt like, wow, after all the anxiety and depression, this was a helpful advance, and we were pleased that he was just able to tell us.

KAREN: In the beginning, there were few online resources and some of those seemed kind of sketchy. So, the most helpful thing for me at the beginning was a counseling program that had a group for parents of trans youth. It was for six weeks and part of it was learning more through education, and the second part was discussion with other parents. I found that extremely helpful. Before that, we didn't know anybody else in town with a transgender child, and we thought we were alone, and we felt very isolated. It was extremely helpful to get accurate information from professionals and go over aspects of the process with people who knew about it and also to connect with other parents.

MIKE: Fear for his safety was always at the forefront of my mind in terms of: Did him being able to live as his authentic self put him in danger? That seemed like a really unfair position for him to be in.

KARREN: We started a group with another couple, and it's a group for families who have trans kids. We meet monthly, and we have been meeting over three years now. Every week, we talk to parents about whatever it is they want to know. The organization acronym is GEKCO, and it stands for Gender Expansive Kids and Company. The family is "company." The whole family can come, including siblings, and we have crafts, group time, food and activities, and then the kids go off to other fun things, and the parents have a chance to share.

GEKCO encourages families and helps them find resources. The parents are supportive to begin with, but they may not know all the ways to be supportive. Or maybe they come just to bond with other supportive parents on their journey.

MIKE: As Karen says, it's important to meet parents where they are. There are lots of steps in this process. In terms of what is helpful for someone to share, you let them guide you based on where they are in their journey. We didn't have any trouble voicing what we wanted to know and even just saying, "We don't even know what we want to know." I think there are lots of different steps. Sometimes it is information, such as what do terms like transgender mean and how is gender identity different from expression and different from sexual attraction? There are all these different thoughts and feelings because you want to know how to best support who your child is. One of our first challenges was figuring out where he could go to the bathroom while we were traveling and finding the apps online that told you safe places, like single stalls. We had to find places that were safe for him to go to the bathroom.

KAREN: Our group provides not only camaraderie and shared personal experience but also resources and links to different LGBTQ+ organizations. We can tell families what to expect and who might help them in this situation or that situation. I'm constantly giving resources and links to help them with whatever issues arise. We also advocate at the city and state level and write and call our legislators to make ourselves heard.

For example, it became known that the BMV was going to allow a gender-neutral mark on the license instead of a male or female identifier. A lot of nonbinary people and trans people were very happy about that change. However, once news of that got out, the legislator took note and proposed a bill that would have removed the doctor's letter as appropriate legal documentation to have your identity marker changed. The doctor's letter had been sufficient for years, and now they were going to make it mandatory to have your birth certificate changed, which can be an extreme hardship for many people and impossible for others. You cannot change your birth certificate for any reason in Arizona, for example. So, those people would never be able to have their legal state ID match their identity. We got lots of people to call and write and that bill died. Advocating for those kinds of things helps.

We want to have a statewide nondiscrimination policy that includes gender identity. We keep advocating through GEKCO.

MIKE: Another example is high school athletic associations that require surgery for student-athletes when surgery is not something that is done by some children while in high school. We are working with them to form better policies because their requirements are against the standards of medical care.

KAREN: Those types of things are ongoing: legislation, policies, and laws.

MIKE: Whenever we interact with political people—such as congressmen, congresswomen, senators, and people active in politics—we are very open and direct on the fact that we have a transgender child and that discrimination against transgender people is discrimination against the entire family. It's anti-family. The notion that somehow this type of discrimination is religious freedom or pro-family, is just not correct.

A key thing we need is to make it illegal to discriminate against transgender people in employment and housing accommodations. That is particularly critical.

KAREN: There's a big problem with homelessness: One-quarter of youth are removed from their home in one way or another. Either they don't feel safe staying home, or their parents make them leave when they come out as LGBTQ+. We have quite a homeless problem here in the city and the numbers are much higher for transgender kids.

We need to work on helping families understand what LGBTQ+ is and how to love and support their children, even if they disagree in some way.

I've been on the board of IYG (Indiana Youth Group) for the past five years, and we saw that we were outgrowing the little house they had, and I was on the committee to raise money and bring about a new building; it is three stories plus a basement. It's awesome. We keep expanding our reach so we now reach more homeless and housing insecure youth. IYG opened a special night just for basic needs. Youth can shower there and get food.

MIKE: Currently, the homeless shelters don't have facilities for transgender people so some of the shelters are having fundraising campaigns in an effort to have single unit accommodations that would be appropriate for someone who is transgender.

KAREN: We need safe, accessible homeless shelters for youth and especially for LGBTQ+ youth. We also need transitional housing that will step in where parents have not and help these youth learn how to be an adult. Places where they can learn how to get an apartment, apply for jobs, get further education, and manage a bank account—all those basic personal finance skills, like how to get a car or navigate around the city. Even Trinity Haven, a housing and service provider for LGBTQ+ youth at risk for homelessness, will only be taking in a limited number of youth, and we need more help.

Your first job as a parent is to love your child and support your child, so kicking them out isn't part of that. We have one job: to love and support our children.

Did friends and family support you and your child?

KAREN: Yes. Our families are amazing. They all live elsewhere, so we notified them by letter, partly because it's a nice way to receive something and also you can look at it and take some time before you respond to the sender. A letter also gives you a chance to articulate it in exactly the way you want. We wrote it in conjunction with our son, and he definitely had input on the letter's content.

MIKE: Oftentimes, extended family reaction poses challenges and causes people to believe they are entitled to question your parenting and to ask totally inappropriate questions about your kid's genitals and whether they had surgery and things like that. Since when are my kid's genitals anyone else's business? Or my kid's healthcare!

If you could wave a magic wand, what would you like allies and the community to do better?

KAREN: First of all, we need to end gerrymandering. Then, we need to elect responsible, responsive people who will listen and learn what it means to be LGBTQ+ and enact fair laws that protect the most vulnerable. We need to teach parents and family members what that means and how to love someone, even if someone is different than what we might have learned while we were growing up. It was totally different from what I learned growing up. But we can learn, and we can learn how to support.

We can also go into churches and discuss these issues. Unfortunately, many churches are the problem, whether out of ignorance or misunderstanding or intractability. We need to be able to go in and have programs that discuss this in a reasonable way. Just educating people and having a nice discussion on what it means to be transgender and what it means to be lesbian, gay, bisexual, and all the gender diversity. There are many welcoming churches. Let's spread the word that brings about the family support and community support.

MIKE: We also need to recognize institutional bullying and call it what it is when institutions failed to call people by their name and proper pronouns and things of that nature. That's bullying and that is against Indiana law. Institutions are not allowed to bully, and we need to enforce those laws and educate people.

KAREN: That could be a state entity, a government entity, a church or a school. All those entities.

MIKE: Definitely, schools are a huge issue. In Hamilton Southeastern School District, there were comments at a meeting that the chairperson of the board concedes were completely inappropriate, comments that were stated in public and were very hurtful. Being a kid in school is already so dog-gone hard and to make it worse by institutional bullying by the school is just reprehensible. There ought to be clear state policies mandated for schools. Certainly, any school that gets public money must comply with those. Our son was in a high school that wasn't supportive, and so it was a very, very difficult senior year for him.

KAREN: They wouldn't call him by his legal name, *legal!* And they told teachers that if they did call him by his legal name, they would be fired, even if they were the most beloved, longest-tenured teacher of the school. We were told that if we created any incidents, we would be told to leave.

MIKE: There needs to be a uniform policy because school administrators get confronted by some parent, which is often a bystander parent that raises issues that are not actually present. There's been no disruption of anything at school, and no one else has a problem with it, but some parent goes in and complains to the administration and then they get scared and the school board gets scared of controversy. So, we need state policies so they can say, "This is what I'm required to do."

KAREN: Certainly, if you discriminate in that way you should not be getting public money. It should be treated the same way as any other form of discrimination.

MIKE: No one can control in your head whether you're a misogynist or a racist or homophobic or transphobic, even if you're President of the United States. But what we can do is say you can't legally act on those things, and you can't discriminate against someone because that is illegal.

KAREN: Just last night someone said their child had trouble on the first day of second grade. A teacher outing a child is detrimental to that child right off the bat.

Families could use more support. A large city often has a variety of support systems. But in many smaller towns, support is hard to come by. So, we need more support groups—online support and in-person support. We have some PFLAG chapters, which is a group that is an extended family of the LGBTQ+ community, providing families with education and support. We could also use funding for groups like GEKCO so families, counselors, medical people, and educators can all come together to learn more about how to support transgender individuals and families.

MIKE: The medical community is another area that needs improvement. In talking to parents, the one thing we all share in common is the difficulty of finding doctors with offices that are knowledgeable and capable of treating people who are transgender and also educating their staff on how to handle a transgender patient.

Every parent I know with a transgender kid, the kid lives in fear that every time they go to the doctor there will be some incident, or they will get called out in the waiting room with the wrong name that outs them or otherwise creates a problem. We've addressed one class at the IU medical school, and there are younger doctors in training and some younger doctors working who are more attuned to the issues. But there are a lot of healthcare providers who are not. The same is true on the mental health side of medical care.

KAREN: We need more welcoming offices, and they need to be better informed so they can better care for our kids.

MIKE: In our society, how many times are you asked if you are male or female when it's not relevant and there's no need to? How many times do you see a restroom that could be gender-neutral, a single stall, and they have a male or female symbol? All these issues are barriers if you're a transgender person trying to navigate the world.

KAREN: All those barriers make it harder for them to get a good education and finish their education and go on to post-secondary education and get a job. If people don't feel safe because they're perceived as different or odd or an anathema, they won't get hired, or they will get fired from their jobs for transitioning. Then, where do they live? On the margins of society. And that creates other problems on down the line, not only for them but also for society. We need to do a lot better job all along the way.

MIKE: One of my goals has always been to be transparent, pun intended. Right from the outset, I was very open with my colleagues at work and others. You probably can't spend too much time with me before I make sure you know I have a transgender kid. I will tell you our story with the notion that people need to understand that this is nothing to be freaked out about. It's just part of the human experience, and there's no need to feel threatened or worried about it. It's just letting people be who they are. When we let other people be who they are, we can be who we are, and it's more comfortable for all of us.

KAREN: It is part of the great beauty and variety of the human condition. Being human, we have lots of variety. At one point, it was looked down upon if you were left-handed or had red hair. We understand better now, and we understand better now about LGBTQ+ as the great variety of being human. Let's educate people about that.

Part 3

ADULT FREEDOM FIGHTERS

Sa'hara Miller

BU Wellness, Sophisticated Divas Program
Coordinator
She/Her/Hers
31 years old

"Just give our trans community their roses before it's too late."

I was born in Gary, Indiana. I graduated with a double major: Business Marketing and Theater and Dance. I started at Chicago University, and I finished at Vincennes University. I have a pet I just got. It's a Shih Tzu mixed with a Maltese, a very small, little lap dog.

I work for BU Wellness. We are the only black wellness agency in Indiana, and I am the Program Coordinator. I have a program I just started called Sophisticated Divas. We focus on trans and nonbinary individuals. For my trans population, we definitely can help with wellness. We have people from Eskenazi Health Hospital come in and help with hormone therapy. For nonbinary individuals, we help them feel more comfortable. You don't have to look like a woman to be classified as a woman for example. As far as trans individuals, we give them tips to help with getting a job. We have LGBTQ affirming doctors come in that will help them get on primary care. If you need care coordination, we do that. If you are high-risk HIV negative, we make sure you are put on PrEP, which is pre-exposure prophylaxis, and the pill for that is called Truvada.

Basically, we take care of the trans and nonbinary community in terms of health, wellness, and jobs. To sum it up, I would say we provide a safe space.

What are your favorite TV show or books?

I have a favorite TV show, which is "The Boondocks." I have two favorite books. In school it was *A Child Called It* because it was such an impactful book. I reread it and watched the movie, and it really gave me a soft spot for that child. The other favorite book would be *The Color Purple*.

What are your hobbies or interests?

Growing up, I was a dancer. I got on a very big, first-class championship dance team. We did hip-hop, contemporary, modern, jazz, ballet. I spent about 2½ years studying at Alvin Ailey American Dance Theater in New York City. I took a scholarship program there. Then, I came back and finished up my theater and dance studies at Vincennes University. So, one of my hobbies is dancing. A lot of my time is working full time, and so, I do not dance as much. I'm in the ballroom scene. If you ever watch the TV show "Pose," I am part of that and it focuses a lot on the trans women.

My second hobby is I am a Pageant Queen. I am the two-year running Miss Circle City Newcomer.

What would you like to share about your journey?

Some people say that when you transition you should do it early in life. But I spoke to many older trans women who said you should really take your time in transitioning. The reason I didn't do it early is because I was worried about what my family would say. To make a long story short, my family is pro, for it.

In the community now, you do see a lot of black trans women get killed. So, my parents do bond a little bit closer to me, and they make sure that I do have second options when I do go out. Right now, I am happy with my life because I can live the life that I always wanted to live. At first, my parents didn't accept it, but they still loved me. Now, we have gotten to a stage where they love me for who I am. As long as I have their support, then it really doesn't matter as far as anyone else.

What is important for allies to know so the community can better support transgender individuals?

The most important thing for allies to know, when it comes down to being who I am, is: Yes, it is LGBTQ, but as for the T and the Q, a lot of the allies forget that we're here. I see a lot of my black trans sisters getting killed. It takes a lot of courage to walk out of your house and become this person that you always wanted to be. Even if you are doing hormones, even if you have a female feminization, it takes a lot of courage because you always get the stares, and you always get the looks. For just a regular black gay male who isn't classified as feminine, he can walk outside and blend in with society. It's easier for him than someone like myself standing at 6 foot 3 inches, trying to blend into today's community.

What I like folks to realize is that we in the trans community, for many years, have had this stigma that if you are a black trans woman or if you are any type of trans or queer, that you jump into the sex industry. A lot of jobs don't like to see the look that we give in their businesses. That makes it hard to stay focused and try to have a good-paying job without someone always trying to stigmatize you.

I think allies need to learn that there are a lot of educated trans and queers out here, and you don't give people a chance because you might see their name that they were born with, but they might actually be something else. A lot of people still act like it's a joke because they don't understand some people's backgrounds.

Every trans individual, every gay person, has not been touched (mentally not competent). Me personally, I have never been touched in my life. This is just something I've always wanted to be, and I just had to wait because I wanted to make sure my parents were proud of me and of my education before I worried about the little things. But now, I know that the little things are really big to me.

Allies need to understand the background because every trans and queer individual has a background. All of us aren't born with a silver plate or gold spoon in our mouth. If you really get to know everyone's background, which you probably won't, but if you ever get a chance to know a lot of trans people, we're really just the same, and we have emotions and feelings too.

Tell me a little about your background.

My background growing up, like I said, I was always the feminine type. I always had female characteristics, from long hair to just, you know, I wasn't the type to be outside. I liked the Barbie™ dolls. I always felt as this person. Growing up in our house, being a black family in a rural area, education was so important. We always wanted to make our mother proud. Always, my parents' opinions came first. I was the baby of the family. I am the youngest of three. I didn't want my mother and father to feel like they didn't fulfill their job.

I grew up in the church. I still do love church. But one thing about churches nowadays, I see on social media that a lot of people will humiliate a gay or trans individual going into church. That's one thing I've never had to experience coming into the House of God. But I know my trans and gay brothers and sisters do experience that. Like I said, growing up I was in the church, and I was on a cheerleading team when I was younger. They knew that I was the little gay boy in the church and just the fact that

I wasn't out in the streets mattered. So, a lot of that impacted me for the journey I knew I was getting ready to do.

Then, I was educated, and I was talented. I didn't transition until I was 23 or 24. You can say gay or trans but put other things in front of those characteristics. Put a degree. Put a diploma. I am an Educated Black Trans Woman.

Do you currently have a church?

There is a LGBTQ church called Powerhouse Church that is led by Pastor Keith McQueen, and he is a very impactful pastor. It's very "come as you are." You still get the Word, and, yes, he is married to another male. But you still get the Word. I don't go to church every Sunday, but I will get up and play all my old-school gospels that my grandmother used to always play when we were younger. Sometimes I can make it to church and other times I can't. But I still know God, and I still know the Bible.

What are your future goals and dreams for your life?

I've accomplished one of my future goals and that's being a black trans woman alive after the age of 30. Our lifespan often ends before age 25. One of my goals is to just make it in this world and in this society. That's one of my major goals.

My second goal is to become an advocate for my community, which I currently am doing right now, and that's just giving back to the community and learning different things about health equities and all of this. So, that is my second goal.

My third goal is just to make sure that my parents are proud of me before their heads are cold.

What are your hopes and dreams for the community?

My biggest dream and hope is to end the epidemic of HIV and AIDS. So many of my friends are living with HIV and AIDS that I just pray. Even though from the epidemic in the early '90s and taking multiple pills to now where it is one pill a day, still I just hope that we can find an end to the epidemic.

When it comes to the community, it is a very touchy situation. I've seen so much in the news. I am proud that we do have Pride month, and I'm glad we do that. But I wish that Pride would last 365 days instead of one month. Just give our trans community their roses before it's too late. Give us a chance to show people that we're more than just escorts and professional hookers and all that. Give them more importance in these LGBTQ roles and in life in general.

Is there anything you wanted to talk about that I didn't ask you?

At this point in my life, I can say I'm blessed because I have a good-paying job that respects my pronouns, and I have coworkers who love me for who I am. I have friends that love me for who I am, and I just pray that every trans and nonbinary individual that comes behind me can have the same blessings I have.

I just really wish a lot of parents would stop thinking that just because my child became in this LGBTQ population that you failed. Because you didn't fail! All of us: You are blessed as a human.

Before we are who we are, we are humans. We might not all believe the same, our skin tones might be different, but like I said, feelings can always get hurt. I just hope before I'm gone that I impact many individuals, like me, who are scared to come out.

Being an advocate for my community is my main focus, and I'm just blessed for the opportunities I do have and upcoming opportunities.

Alex Erwin

River City Pride Secretary
He/Him/His
27 years old

*"My hope is to bring a more positive light to the transgender community.
It's something that is not very understood."*

I was born in Huntingburg, which is about 45 minutes outside Evansville (southern Indiana). I lived a majority of my life in Perry County (Ind.), and I moved to Crawford County (Ind.) while I was in high school. I have one dog. Her name Krissy, and she is a two-year-old German shorthaired pointer.

I went to Indiana University in Bloomington for a year. While I was in Bloomington, I was a Music major: Percussion, Composition, and Performance major. From there, I came to Evansville to attend Ivy Tech College where I studied Criminal Justice and Paramedics Science.

After Ivy Tech, I got offered a state job at the Branchville Correctional Facility in Perry County as a correctional officer. Now, I work at the Hilton DoubleTree.

What are your hobbies?

I dabble in photography. I definitely play music when I can. I play the guitar, the piano, the saxophone, and the trumpet. It depends on my mood that day. Most of my time is pretty consumed with the nonprofit organization, River City Pride, and I am working two jobs. On the weekends, I am a DJ at *Someplace Else Nightclub*, the only gay bar in Evansville. I have DJ'ed there for about four years.

What is River City Pride?

River City Pride is a new nonprofit organization in Evansville. We put on our first Pride event in June. I sit on the Board of Officers as the Secretary. My main job is to keep track of everything that keeps us legal—crossing all the t's and dotting all the i's—and keeping us in a positive light in the community.

Can you tell me about your personal journey?

I'm pretty open about it, especially at River City Pride, just to be an example for others who may be going through the same thing or struggling with some of the experiences that maybe I've had. I publically came out as a transgender male when I turned 23. I will have been fully transitioning for three years. I went through about a year of therapy prior to starting hormone replacement therapy.

The biggest part for me was making sure I understood why I was transitioning. I think that gets overlooked. People may not fully understand what they're going through, and they may think just starting hormones is the right answer. It's a 50/50 shot whether that is actually what your body needs. Not every transgender person needs hormones. There are different levels and different stages of being transgender. I just happen to be one that felt I needed to be on the hormones to live my life the way I wanted.

The hardest part was coming to terms with the fact that I was going to lose a giant support system in my life, which was with my family. I did end up losing a majority of them in my life. It definitely is a daily struggle that transgender individuals go through.

But the best thing is I ended up gaining a more supportive family than I had before just from people in the community.

I was going to ask you if your family is supportive.

We still speak off and on but not very frequently. They refuse to address me as a male or call me Alex. They still call me by my legal given name. So, that's hard. I try to be understanding of where they're at and know that as hard as it is for me, it is equally as hard for them. But, they're not supportive of it at all. I'm more supportive of the way they go about it than they are in supporting how I feel.

What would be important for people to know to be more supportive?

The biggest thing is understanding that every person is different. We all operate differently and what works for one person might not work for someone else. Like I said before, hormone replacement therapy is not for every transgender person. It is not always going to be the answer you need to feel the way you should. It's not always going to fix the problems you have going on. The only thing I can stress the most is make sure that you go to your therapy, and you continue with it. If you have questions, you need to make sure you ask them. That's why medical professionals are out there: to help us go through what we are going through.

Also, making sure each person is being supportive of the other person's process. That may be as simple as just listening to someone else talk and not saying anything.

For allies, I think it all comes down to education, making sure you're being educated on what you're talking about and who you're speaking to and understanding how you might come off in the wrong way. It's all about how we word things and who we're wording it to.

More educational outreaches will help things along. That's what

I would like to see happen more in schools. The schools don't address those things in terms of the school understanding who we are and how they can make things easier for us.

That's something River City Pride is working on. We're currently trying to start a Youth Group. We have to be established three years prior to doing that. We're just hitting our two-year mark, but we're already in the works to get a Youth Group together for those purposes.

What are your future hopes and dreams for your life?

I would like to see myself continue with River City Pride. We have things going in connection with Indianapolis that I would like to work on.

I would like to see myself move up within my career with Hilton DoubleTree, which is already in the works.

Once our term is up at River City Pride, we go on to the Board of Directors where we still oversee everything that goes to the organization, and then we have a group of officers that work under us. So, I'm pretty much in the organization for as long as I choose to stick around.

What is your hope for the community?

My hope is to bring a more positive light to the transgender community. It's something that is not very understood. Try to make the resources that are out there more known. I've got several people asking me what doctor I go to, what therapist I go see. Those are things that need to be more out there.

Is there anything you wish your family understood better?

I wish they understood that it was hard for me to learn to live without them. The struggles I'm going through could be lessened by the fact that they were just around. It's hard to go from having someone in your life that you call every day when something arises, to not having them at all. It's one thing to lose a loved one through death, but it's a whole other thing to watch them walk out.

I want to be at a certain point in my life where they look at the work I have done for the community, and they feel proud of what I'm doing. We just haven't reached that point yet where they're fully proud of everything that I'm doing. They are more focused on the transition and how it's hurtful to them that I transitioned instead of focusing on what I'm actually doing for others.

What other activities are you involved in?

I currently hold the title of Mr. Gay Evansville. It's a Pageant title through the drag community. I work on things, mostly through our local animal shelters, such as doing fundraisers to help cover their vet costs and the living expenses for animals at the shelter, as well doing Dog Adoption Day to help the adoption rates. That's where my main focus is right now: making sure I follow the platform for that title, doing my work with River City Pride and integrating it into the community, working two jobs, and trying to maintain a social life outside of all that.

Is there anything you wanted to talk about that I didn't ask you?

When it comes to LGBTQ, it more or less comes down to there's not enough outreach, and I don't think there's enough education. That is something I'm working on myself within the local community in which I live, and I've also been in contact with different people throughout the city and other cities as well so we can do community outreach together.

Matty Slaydon

Queering Indy Executive Director
They/Them
27 years old

"We have something to contribute too, and we're just people."

I was born in Alexandria, Louisiana. I came to Indiana about five years ago. I am the Executive Director of a nonprofit organization called Queering Indy. Queering Indy was founded three years ago. I've been a member for a little over a year, and I took over as Executive Director a few months ago. I also do some part-time work, and I'm a full-time student. I have a Maine Coon, which is a very large cat!

My major is Health and Human Services for nonprofit management. I want to run nonprofits. My plan is to pursue a master's program immediately after my bachelor's degree. I'd like to attend Carnegie Mellon University, but wouldn't we all. (Laughs).

What are your hobbies and interests?

I don't have a lot of spare time for hobbies because I am running the nonprofit and taking 20 credits in school and working part-time, and I have a boyfriend. We like to go out to eat, try new restaurants, that sort of thing. I would call myself an armchair television critic. I like to watch drama, and I like to read speculative fiction, fantasy, and science fiction.

My favorite author is Terry Pratchett. He is unfortunately deceased, but he wrote satirical fantasy, and he used fantasy as a lens to critique problems in the real world: politics, military, police.

Can you share a little about your journey?

From around age 12 to 15, I went back and forth. I said I was bi (bisexual), and then said I was straight, and then said I was gay. When I was 18, I had some experiences with cisgender women, and I called myself gay. Then when I was 20, I met a trans nonbinary person and said, "That's what I am." I didn't come out as trans nonbinary until I was 23. Then, there are offshoots of that.

A trans binary person is someone, for example, who is male to female. And there are nonbinary transgender and gender-fluid people who move back and forth between those identities. For me, I just don't identify as either gender. I subscribe to the idea that gender is a social construct. To say boys like cars and girls like Barbie's,™ well why is that? Why is it a boy thing to like a car and a girl thing to like a doll? I think there are rules we have made up as a society so that we can slot people into easily understandable and identifiable groups, and I just don't subscribe to that notion. I also don't feel much like a man, and I don't really feel much like a woman either. If I had to pick, I feel more feminine. But I don't care to choose between the two. So, transgender is just an umbrella term. If you were to draw a diagram, it would be trans at the top and then underneath that would be binary, nonbinary. All gender diverse people are trans.

What do you think is important for allies to know to be more supportive of the transgender community?

More people need to know plenty of things! One thing that comes to mind immediately is something that we in my nonprofit work take very seriously, which is: "Nothing about us without us."

The mission statement of my nonprofit is: We are an LGBTQIA grassroots nonprofit out of Indianapolis, Indiana, working to service the LGBTQIA community of the greater Indianapolis area. We specifically focus on raising up the voices of marginalized groups within our population, specifically trans people and queer people of color. I thought a long time about how I could service queer people of color and what programming I can build and what services I could offer.

Recently, an organization by and for queer people of color, BU Wellness, was throwing a ball in honor of the 50th Anniversary of Stonewall. A friend of mine was talking about what we were going to do for Stonewall, and said, "Hey, I'm going to go clean your toilets. This is y'alls day. Stonewall was a movement created by trans women of color. This is your day. What can I do?" That really got me thinking about how we should help. I have a lot of privilege as a white person who looks like a man. It is not my job to provide services to other populations who might not be as well serviced as I am. It's my job to go find out what they're already doing for themselves and say, "How can I help?"

I think that translates very well to the relationship between allies and the queer community. We already know what we need. We know the services that our community could benefit from. We don't need allies to come out and say, "We just founded this nonprofit that's going to give chest binders to trans men." We need you to say, "Hey, here's some money for chest binders for the organization you've already had going for 30 years." To some people that is counterintuitive because they want to help. Generally, when we understand help, particularly as white people, it's: "What can we do because these downtrodden groups are so underserved. They couldn't possibly figure it out for themselves right now." Well, they have, and they are figuring it out! They just need support. So, that's an important thing to remember.

Just listen to us. When we say we need a thing, that's what we need.

I think that politically, as far as elections and legislation and those sorts of things, allies need to understand the intersectionality (oppression resulting from an overlap of various social identities) as part of the problem, such as voting for a Republican because of their fiscal policies. People will say they are not a "single-issue" voter, and they won't vote against someone just because of their anti-LGBTQ policies. But what you're saying when you do that is, "Your rights and your life are not an important enough issue to vote against somebody." Your life is not important to me is the logical conclusion of that argument. You're free to vote how you choose, but at least acknowledge that you are not an ally.

One of the biggest problems that we face, politically in America as queer people, is the motion of the Overton Window being so far to the right. So, the Overton Window is the idea of what the center of politics is. Globally, the Overton Window tends to stay slightly to the left. America is so far to the right and has moved so far to the right—even in the last ten years—that we look at Democrats and call them "leftists." But when you compare them to other leftists in the world, they're fairly conservative and fairly far right.

That motion to the right is something that dramatically affects our community because the center is not inherently moral. It's just a point between two points: the middle between two points. What happens when that middle point is between: It's okay to be trans and be alive, and it's not okay to be trans and be alive? What's the middle point that we settle for there? Do we continue to vote for Democrats and throw our weight as a community behind particularly centrist Democrats and those policies? I think there's a huge danger when we say the middle point is between my right to live and not to live.

What are your future hopes and dreams for the community?

I would like to see a world where binary gender isn't something that is forced in our day-to-day lives. We need to understand that the body you have does not dictate the way that you feel or the way that you present yourself, and for kids to grow up knowing that they can literally be anything they want. Not just, "You can be a doctor or you can be a fireman." But truly, if you want to be the one wearing a dress and you want to shave your head, pierce your face, and tattoo your name across your forehead, you can. Knowing that things like modesty, by choosing to wear long skirts or choosing to show cleavage, all of those choices are fine based on the way you feel and what you want to do with your body.

I'd also like to see more queer people living publicly, such as trans people being your doctor. Having the barriers that trans people face, particularly black trans women, removed so they have the same opportunities that cisgender people have, particularly white cisgender people. Cisgender means not trans. It means you were born feeling like you connect with your body, and you identify with the sex that you were assigned at birth.

I was raised in a conservative Christian household by southern parents who didn't have the first idea of what trans meant. They knew what gay meant, and they knew they didn't like it. All the hurtful things they did to fix me or change my mind or make me feel bad about who I am, did not work and will not work on anybody. What they should've been concerned about and what I think conservative Christians everywhere should be concerned about is: loving their child as hard as they can because that's the Christ-like thing to do.

If you look at the suicide statistics for kids who are queer and have unsupportive parents, you are increasing the chances of your child dying when you don't accept them. That's not a bleeding heart liberal opinion. That's a fact, a hard number fact, and you can disagree with it, but you can also disagree with the sky being blue. It's not going to change it. So, if you want your child to live, you need to accept them for who they are.

I have been through everything that white conservative Christian people are afraid of. I have been through lots of things and fought through all of those things. Now, I am enrolled in school. I have my own place and my own car. I'm in a successful, happy relationship. I'm literally paying money to go to school so I can help people.

I think if you look past those things that people are afraid of—that a subset of people are afraid of—you see that we are just normal people who want to do the best we can in the world. Sure, not all of us want to work in nonprofits. Some of us just want to do the same things everyone else does. You know, go to work, come home, have a glass of wine, and watch a bunch of HBO, and go to bed. And that's okay. We're really not that different.

A lot of us have had different experiences because of who we are. But, at the end of the day, we have something to contribute too, and we're just people.

Destinee Salinas

Medical Case Manager
She/Her/Hers
38 years old

> *"My hope is that the killings of us stop, everywhere.
> Not just here but around the world."*

I moved to Minneapolis, MN, around age 30. I have three cats. I work at JustUs Health. Prior to that, I worked as the Medical Case Manager at a hospital called Hennepin Healthcare where I worked with individuals living with HIV and AIDS. I helped them find resources for housing and resources for whatever their needs, and I helped them with their paperwork, such as paperwork for insurance, Social Security Disability, Food Shelves, rental assistance, and so on.

What are your hobbies or interests?

I like to do makeup for myself and other people. I used to perform drag for a little while, but I stopped because this job takes up so much of my time. Drag shows are female impersonation, entertaining. I also like to play video games.

My favorite TV show is called "Pose." One of my favorite books is *Becoming* by Michelle Obama. I find that book very interesting.

Can you share a bit about your journey?

I realized I was female when I was 19 years old. Even before that, I knew there was something different about me and that I wasn't the same as everybody else. I enjoyed the feminine side of my life growing up. As a child, I would play with girl stuff. I did things in school that girls normally do, like cheerleading and being in the Color Guard in high school. That was fun. When I turned 19, I moved away from home and saw drag shows for the first time. In doing drag performances, I found myself because being female and wearing female clothes and doing shows, I realized this is who I am, even outside of doing drag. I am a trans woman. My father is Mexican/Indian and so I am Hispanic and also Two-Spirit.

Some of the hard parts about transitioning were the criticism I got from other people, being criticized and discriminated against and being threatened, both verbally and physically. Those are the hardest parts of going through my transition.

What do you think is important for people to know to be better allies?

It's important for allies to approach us as who we are. Also, make sure to get the pronouns right. If someone has questions to ask, ask the appropriate kinds of questions. That way they're not being offensive to anyone who is nonbinary or transgender.

Most of the time, trans men and trans women are happy to answer questions. We are happy to educate people as to who we are and what we go through every day. Do your research and try not to come off sounding judgmental or harsh. An offensive question would be asking somebody about female or male private body parts. Another offensive question would be asking someone their birth name or asking somebody why they want to get surgery. So, private information is something a trans man or trans woman would not typically be comfortable answering.

One thing allies could do better is meeting us where we're at. Do you know what I mean by that? So, not being judgmental. For example, in my role on my job when I am working with people, I'm being myself. I'm not acting like I'm more superior than they are just because I'm at work. I joke. I kid around with people. I know when to be serious, but I don't take that seriousness to a level where I'm intimidating somebody. Just being respectful of our gender: what we identify as.

Also, don't misrepresent us, in books, in movies, and in conversations. Especially on the news channels, trans men and trans women are often misrepresented. For example, when someone is murdered, instead of saying a female trans woman they say male. Also, even religious groups like to misrepresent us because of what the Bible "says." It's all across the board. People misrepresent us all the time, especially trans women. Whether it's in office spaces or the President of the United States, just don't misrepresent us. Even people on the streets, some guy will call out something like, "Hey, you're a dude in a dress!" Or "You're a man, you shouldn't be wearing those clothes." It happens all the time, everywhere. The harassment of trans people needs to stop.

What are your future goals and dreams for your life?

My future goals and dreams for my life are to complete and graduate from the college I am attending and to be an advocate for other trans women and trans men. I already met one goal that I've been trying to achieve for years. Ever since I moved to Minnesota and started working in the field of HIV and AIDS at the hospital, my goal was to be a Medical Case Manager. I felt like I would be great at it. That's something I wanted to do. I enjoy helping people, and I am so proud of myself for completing that goal. I became a Case Manager this year. Also, eventually, I would like to meet someone and get married.

Does your family support you?

I am blessed to have the family I have. They have been very supportive, very accepting. They don't ever call me by my other name. I have one older sister and three brothers, and even my brothers refer to me as their sister.

What is your hope for the community?

My hope for the community, for anywhere, is that people will be more accepting toward us. Also, we don't want to have to worry about being discriminated against in applying for jobs. We are very much discriminated against when applying for jobs. It's hard to find an actual job for a trans person depending on where you're living.

There have been a lot of killings and a lot of discrimination against trans men and trans women. Most of what we hear about is the killings of trans women and all of that needs to be stopped.

My hope is that the killings of us stop, everywhere. Not just here but around the world.

Addison J. Smith

Library Music Collection Coordinator & Community Volunteer
They/Them/Their/Themself
48 years old

> *"People who are attacked for hate crimes live in our community. That's why I do this work.*
> *I want people in the community to feel there is someplace safe they can go."*

I was born in Hinesville, Georgia, Fort Stewart Army Base, but I was raised in West Virginia. I lived in Hurricane, West Virginia, until I was 28 years old. It's spelled like hurricane but the pronunciation actually maintains the old English: Herakin.

I came to Indiana for graduate school and did my master's degree at Ball State University. I got a Master in Music Composition. I was going to do a doctorate in Music Theory and Composition. But as I was exposed more and more to how new professors were treated, I decided I didn't want to be an academic. Then, I got a second master's degree in Digital Storytelling, which is basically new media journalism. I have one daughter who is 14 years old.

What is your current occupation?

I am the Music Collection Coordinator at Ball State University Library. I hire, train, and discipline the student assistants. I am in charge of both circulation activities and reserves and the music collection front office. I do payroll, budgeting, and so on.

What got you interested in music?

My mom tells me that I started humming at 2 weeks old. I would hum myself to sleep, for years. I was in band and played various types of instruments in high school. I was in marching band, concert band, and jazz band. I played a double bass guitar in jazz band. I played the guitar, tuba, and everything else. I used to play the piano, but I can't anymore because of an injury I got while learning to play the violin. My wrist doesn't move well anymore.

I went to Marshall University for my undergrad and was in the band there. I started off as a Tuba Performance major and then switched over to Composition. I got a BFA in Music and then went on to get my graduate degrees.

What are your hobbies or interests?

I write. I had been writing an advice column online called, "Ask Addi," and people would occasionally write in to ask questions about gender and sexuality. Some people would write in to tell me I am mentally ill, and I would get to tell them they are wrong. (Laughs). Most of my hobbies have become volunteering. I teach gender theory as a diversity sensitivity training. I like computer games and bicycling. I ride my bike, and I need to do it more. I'm putting on weight. But it's been too hot most of the summer. That's the problem with HRT (Hormone Replacement Therapy). You sweat a lot, and I got really dehydrated trying to bike ride. So, I don't do as much of that right now.

I am really into Jim Butcher's *The Dresden Files* book series. I grew up on the sci-fi classics. It's a modern fantasy series about a wizard who lives in Chicago and no one knows he's a wizard. Well, he lives out in the open as a wizard but no one will believe him. As the series goes on, it gets more and more into the fantastical realms. It's like Sam Spade with magic, and it's really interesting. I also like watching TV police procedurals, like "NCIS" or "Law and Order," maybe because none of the cops are bigoted or anti-queer, so it's nice to see.

My favorite singer is Christine and the Queens. She's a French artist who uses a lot of '80s and '90s sounds, but very modern. She uses the she pronoun but is also genderqueer. We don't all use "they." Here, every fifteenth person I talk to knows who she is. In France, she's headlining stadium tours. She's actually amazing: amazing voice, amazing dancer, amazing performer. She writes all of her own music. She produced her last album. She wrote all her music and created her choreography as she was writing the music!

As for sports, I love watching women's soccer. I used to be a big football fan, but the game just seems to be getting slower and slower. Out of the 60 minutes on the clock, which ends up taking four hours, the ball is in play for 11 minutes. It gets really boring waiting for people to hike the ball. I like soccer, gymnastics. I always watch the winter games. I hate winter, but I love the winter games. I cried several times during the Women's World Cup. That was an amazing run. Megan Rapinoe is younger than me, but she's already my hero.

What would you like to share about your journey?

Most of my life I knew there was something a little different about me. I didn't relate to men very well at all. Actually, I often said that I hate men: the attitudes, the one-upmanship. I always got along better with women. I always identified, not with the super feminine characters, but with the strong female characters like Princess Leia or Wonder Woman. I always thought, you know, I like women. It's okay being male. I never really thought about gender issues. An ex-girlfriend at the time, who I am still a really close friend with, we broke up because she's gay, and I was presenting male at the time. But we remained good friends. She started dating someone who is nonbinary, and they identified as genderqueer. I had never heard this phrase before, and so I looked it up. I started reading this webpage about being genderqueer and their typical responses to things. I just realized, "Oh hell, that's me!" (Laughs)

I was around 43 years old, and it was a revelation. Looking back at a lot of the issues I'd had in my life, the whole hating men thing and identifying with butch women and sexual issues I had being the male in sex, it all made sense suddenly. I basically started a psychological reevaluation, and I started pulling down filters and barriers that I'd put up in order to fit in with most people. I hid parts of myself while I was married, and for society in general, just so I didn't get picked on as much. But once I started this journey, it was like: "I can't do this anymore because I'm missing a large part of myself." I started identifying as genderqueer myself and then I just kept pulling back the onion layers of denial.

Eventually, I figured out that I am still nonbinary, but the reason I identified with and was more attracted to soft butch lesbians was because I was one, deep down. Once I got there, I knew I had to change. I started identifying as Addison.

I'm letting myself be me.

I started transitioning. I lost a lot of weight and started going by Addison full time. I died my hair red for about three years, presenting myself as more fem and experimenting with the look I want to have. After losing a bunch of weight, I started HRT (Hormone Replacement Therapy). The reason I lost the weight is because I knew the hormone therapy was going to make me gain. I gained more than I thought, and it's annoying. (Laughs). I had gotten down to 144 pounds, and I looked good, a size 6.

But yeah, my body started changing. The fat started going into more feminine areas and leaving some areas. Most of my body hair fell off, which was nice because I always hated being hairy anyway. My chest started to develop, and I never want to be big chested. I wanted to be a small B or full B, and I made it. My face has changed remarkably. You don't realize when you see yourself every day. The change is gradual. But if you go back and actually look at old Facebook pictures, you can see the progress. The Facebook comparisons remind me that, yes, I am changing even though it may not feel like it every day. And that's just through the hormones. I haven't had any surgeries. People don't realize that hormones do a lot of the work.

For someone reading this who does not know, what does the term genderqueer mean for you?

Genderqueer is one of the nonbinary identities. There are lots of them actually. For nonbinary people, we just don't really relate to the societal definitions of man or woman. I look at the stereotypical feminine and that's not me. I look at the stereotypical masculine and that sure as hell is not me. I'm way closer to the feminine than the masculine, but I can't call myself a woman and have it resonate. I am Addi. I am somewhere in-between and there are a lot of us—a lot more nonbinary people than people realize. Almost half my friends go by "they" now.

I use they and their and themself, which confuses some people. Yes, themself is a pronoun to describe me. Technically, I am a transfeminine nonbinary person with an androgynous presentation. Colloquially, I am a soft butch trans lesbian. But it's like asking, "Why do you know you're a woman?" And the answer is, you just do. I know I'm nonbinary just because I am. There's no logic to it.

We can get more technical. The brain is not male or female. People talk about the masculine brain and the female brain and that's just bullshit. It's more about systems and some people have in their brain an internal rule that says, "I am a woman." They will identify with being a woman based on what our culture says a woman is.

Another thing people don't understand is that our gender roles and expectations are all culturally defined. We're not set with those at birth. Those are things we pick up on as we grow. If your brain says, "I am a woman," you are going to be looking at the women and picking up their roles, no matter what your body is. And same thing if you have a female body but your brain is wired with an internal rule that says, "I'm a man." You're going to be looking at men, knowing that's how you're supposed to be. Nonbinary people are somewhere in-between, and we pick up both and that's the rule our brain works under. People will say, "No, that's not right. You have *these* genitals. Therefore, you must have this brain." Well, it doesn't work that way. The body and the brain develop differently, and sometimes they don't match. People will say, "But you have an Y chromosome." Well, what about all the men with XXY or XYY chromosomes, along with the range of chromosome complements and variations?

People try to use science, and it drives me crazy because the science actually agrees with me. The science says our brains are not masculine or feminine. Our gender is on a spectrum, and so is your body. People don't realize that the human body is not even as dimorphic (representing two distinct forms) as other species. Our species is way more on a continuum than it is male or female. There is variation. People try to justify bigotry with bad science.

What does genderqueer mean? It means I don't think like you. That's all it means. It is not better or worse. It's just different.

What would be helpful for allies to know to be more supportive of the transgender community?

Listen to us. If someone says, "I am a nonbinary person, and I prefer to use they pronouns," then just try your best. We're not going to jump on your head if you misgender us, as long as you're not doing it maliciously. So, try to use our pronouns.

Also, try to understand that a trans woman is a woman and their brain is wired to be a woman, no matter what their body looks like. Same goes for a trans man and for nonbinary people also. That's the number one thing. Even people who consider themselves allies will try to tell me what my identity means, like genderqueer means this. No, you're not genderqueer or any form of nonbinary, and you're reading something off a bad website. Shut up and listen to the person who identifies that way. It's called "cisplaining" which is kind of like "mansplaining." And that's another thing: Cisgender is not a slur! Oh my God! That is one of the stupidest things people have come up with recently. It's an academic term, and people need to deal with it.

Another thing allies need to do is actually hang out with people in the community. Some people call themselves allies because they have their one queer friend. That's not an ally. That's somebody with one queer friend. Allies are going to be there for the community, not just that one friend. They are going to be there to protect people against bigots. Sometimes we need protection. Sometimes we need someone to write their senator or their representative. We need allies to act on their belief that we are just like everybody else. We don't need performative allyship. We don't need someone to say, "Look, I'm an ally" waving their hand in the air and then not actually doing anything to help.

In terms of protection, for example, there is a Facebook post going around right now. Apparently, there was a guy at Target™ who was misgendering a trans woman. And this other large man came up and said, "You need to leave her alone." And the other guy says, "Him!" And so this large man turns to the trans woman and says, "What pronoun do you prefer?" And she says, "She." And so he turns back to the other guy and says, "No, you will apologize to *her*." So, he knew to ask for the pronouns. He didn't speak for us. Instead, he amplified what we were saying.

He was there because this person was being verbally attacked. Most trans women on HRT (Hormone Replacement Therapy) don't have the musculature to get into a fight because we lose a lot of muscle mass, and we don't want to fight anyway. We just want to be left alone.

That's what I would say to everybody: *Let us be us.* If you see us, let us go to the bathroom, let us get a sandwich, and let us buy something at Target.™ You don't have to jump on our heads just because we're different. That's what I tell everybody. But for allies, if you see someone attacking us, verbally or physically, lend a hand.

Definitely be involved in the community! We like our allies. There are some jokes you're not going to get and some jokes you can't make. Learn those. And yes, be respectful.

What are your future goals or dreams for yourself?

I want to keep working as an activist. I'd like to get a job someplace where I can be an activist most the time. Something like ACLU (American Civil Liberties Union) or a Pride organization where I can spend my time working on these issues, educating people, and doing events. I am really good at event planning. I am on the Board of Directors of GenderNexus where I am the treasurer and also head of the messaging and marketing committee.

GenderNexus is a psychological services and social services provider for people in the trans and nonbinary community. We do individual therapy sessions. We do group therapy sessions. We do a clothing drive. We do a lot of social networking for people within the trans and nonbinary community. Like today, instead of going to yoga, I am here talking with you. We also do a Coffee Klatch, which is getting together and having coffee. It's usually Sunday mornings. We provide all the caseworkers for the gender diverse kids who are at IU Riley Hospital. Riley Hospital didn't have anybody who worked with gender diverse people.

So, they came to us. Whenever they have a younger trans person or non-binary person that needs a caseworker, it ends up on our docket. It is very important work, and that's why I'm really into it.

I am also on the Board of Directors of Indy Pride. At Indy Pride, we do more than put on the Pride Festival and the parade. We have an education series. We will be doing panel discussions on intersectionality within the queer community: nonbinary identities, gay trans people like myself. A lot of people think that your gender identity and your sexual identity are matched, like trans women must be into men. There are a lot of trans lesbians and a lot of trans gay men. We will do a panel on that discussion, and we're hoping for queer and racial minorities. We might do more lecture series as well.

We also do fundraisers. We have fundraisers for other organizations as well because Indy Pride serves as a clearinghouse. We have a lot of people under our 501(c)(3) umbrella, and we can raise funds for them so they become part of Pride. We work with employee resource groups and business resource groups, which are basically groups that have a common interest within large corporations. They have LGBTQ groups, and we network with them. We help other Prides around the state.

At Pride, we do way more than the festival. The festival is our fundraiser. People come to Pride and listen to music and end up funding scholarships, education and career fairs, and everything else. That's what I want to do with my life: find a paid position within one of these activist groups. Right now my work is as a volunteer, which is mandatory for board members.

Moving to Indy is a main goal for my life. I have fallen in love with Indy. I do a lot of things in Indianapolis, and I really like this town.

What are your hopes and dreams for the community?

I would like to see the community support each other. Sometimes there is a lot of infighting within the LGBTQ community, such as nonbinary people versus drag queens or lesbians versus bisexual women. Infighting doesn't make any sense as far as I'm concerned. As soon as you start discriminating against one group within our alliance, everybody is brought down. We're just shooting ourselves in the foot with that kind of nonsense, and I would really like people to cut it out.

I would also like to see us move into more positions of power. We have one state gay representative. There are other people in our community who would do well as a legislator or city councilperson or something similar. I would like to have some representation.

In terms of Indianapolis being a bit more accepting than other parts of the state, Indy is like this bubble of queerness. It's like the rest of the state is really negative. If you come to Indy, there are Pride flags, and there are businesses, such as restaurants, that don't care if you are LGBTQ. Don't get me wrong. There are some places where you just don't go. But there are plenty of places to go, which is something you can't say for most of the state. Muncie only has three or four places where I actually feel comfortable. Outside of Indianapolis, discrimination is hard-baked into a lot of places.

I would love if people could start making connections outside of our community. A lot of the things that national religious leaders and political leaders say about us are bunk. It doesn't make a bit of sense. When you live in a town of 1,000 people, that means there's probably going to be maybe 30, 40, maybe up to 100 people who are actually in the LGBTQ community. Most of them are going to be closeted because it's safer. Meanwhile, everybody else in town is listening to some person speaking on a program like Fox News or some radio personality talking about the so-called LGBTQ agenda and saying these horrible, ridiculous, and stupid things about queer people. And people believe it! They are taught to believe that our community is the enemy. So LGBTQ people can't step out and say, "Hey, you know, I'm gay or queer. You know me, this is fine." Because then it's, "Oh, you're gay? You're fired." If you come out in some parts of this state, you're basically done in that community. So, I don't know how we can remedy that. I know we are having more Pride festivals. I just wish we could get past the propaganda, and let people see us for who we are.

I've been called a gay supremacist or a trans supremacist. What the hell does that even mean? Treating me like you would treat anybody else does not mean I think I'm superior to you. That means I think I'm like you. But people have been taught by a lot of radio, television, and Internet that we are evil and have some kind of agenda against "normal" people. I would love to be able to break down the barriers so that people can see *we are* normal people. We are just not like everybody else. Our brains are wired slightly differently. That doesn't make us evil! Different is good. Most communities, and our country, benefit when we have a wider array of citizens. We need some way for people to see that our differences don't make us evil. They just make us different.

I've been told so many times that I'm evil or mentally ill and should be confined. It's ridiculous. I had one person tell me, from Ask Addi, that HRT (hormone replacement therapy) was a disrupter like DDT, which is a poison! There is this radio personality guy with a gay frog conspiracy who claimed that stuff was put in the water to make people gay, and people believed that crap! There are a lot of people who are damaged by this stuff. I have friends whose family kicked them out because they believe this bizarre crap about trans people. The queer community makes up 4 percent to 10 percent of the population, depending on which survey you're looking at. Yet, we make up 40 percent of the homeless population because of parents kicking their kids out and landlords finding out that their tenant is gay or trans and then kicking them out because that's legal in a lot of states.

Lies and disinformation are harming people. There are people who literally die, sometimes at their own hand and sometimes in the street. We lost hundreds of transgender people around the world, killed just because they are trans. Mostly black transgender women and also Latinx and indigenous transgender people across the United States were murdered. And not all cases are reported! The LGBTQ community as a whole has become one of the top targets for hate crimes.

People who are attacked for hate crimes live in our community. That's why I do this work. I want people in the community to feel there is someplace safe they can go. I want them to feel proud of who they are. People ask, "Why are you proud to be gay? I'm not proud to be straight?" And I say, "You're not getting it. Pride is the opposite of shame and most people want us to feel shame for being who we are." A Pride celebration is saying, "No, I will not be ashamed of myself because I'm different than the majority."

I am the director of education at Indy Pride so I can teach people within our community. Occasionally, when I am brought in someplace like a medical clinic, some people can barely look at me. A lot of people are fine, but I noticed that there were a couple of older men who could barely look at me, and I got to teach them about being trans, and I'm hoping they actually learned something. Also, it's not just to talk to other queer people. It's hopefully to open up some eyes and teach other people.

I did one talk at the public library, and there were a lot of queer people and queer allies, but there were a few cishet (cisgender heterosexual) people who brought their kids. I got to teach them and their kids. I also got waylaid into a conversation about what is the difference between a transgender person and a transvestite. It took me almost fifteen minutes to get them to understand that I'm not a cross-dresser. I am a feminine person dressed in feminine clothing. It's not the same thing. Educating people, helping people in the community, that's why I do this volunteer work.

Cambria York

Stage Technician, Opera Singer, Political & Labor Organizer
They/Them/Theirs and *Ze/Hir/Hirs*
29 years old

> *"Reinforcement of the gender binary and so-called*
> *"normal" is just one aspect of existence:*
> *one small aspect in a wide variety of different ways*
> *to live and to thrive."*

I was born and raised in Florida. I lived in the Panhandle and also in southern Alabama. I came to Indiana about four years ago to move in with my partner and to pursue better opportunities for work and education. Also, I felt personally that I needed to take the plunge to just move a very far distance away from my hometown so I could more accurately live as myself.

I wish to add an asterisk to that explanation. A lot of people tend to make assumptions about moving from the Deep South to the Midwest. Here's the thing: Some of the most stalwartly, active, intensely loving, and truly militantly devoted towards liberation communities of queer and trans people that I've ever seen have been in the Deep South, and we have always been there. I didn't move because of any false perception of the Midwest being more progressive. Frankly, the state of Indiana is only a little different from Florida in that respect.

Also, the concept that queer people are obligated to move from the rural place we grew up in, or otherwise live in, to various metropolitan areas like San Francisco, New York, Los Angeles, Seattle, Chicago, or Miami in order to live to our fullest, is so shortsighted and not true at all. If you feel like you have to leave your home for a place with more resources, that's one thing. But to assume that we are only in the cities and that we are only able to have a fully rewarding life in cities is just plain erasure of the rural queer life, of which there is a wealth.

What is your current educational or job situation?

I studied as an undergrad at the University of West Florida, and I also took some classes at Butler University after I moved to Indiana. I am a voice major and also pursuing a professional career in opera. I still sing. I still do work as a singer. However, my career has since shifted to technical work since I found that autonomy over my own body is a lot more applicable when you are behind the scenes as a stage manager.

The opera industry is a very toxic industry. There is a lot of pressure put upon singers to fit a certain body type. I had teachers who are tenors or very light baritones go to the gym six days a week and are on specialized diets every six months because they're prepping for a role that needs to look a certain way. That's just not healthy and not practical for me. With my voice type, I'm okay having a robust body because I am a dramatic baritone. However, there's also pressure put upon transgender vocalists to go back in the closet. That is changing and some trans women and trans male vocalists are finding a niche. But in many cases it is still experimental, and you will find conservative-minded directors and conductors who rail against that without failing.

I am a career stagehand. I work with IATSE (International Association of Theatrical Stage Employees). I've done lighting, video, sound design, carpentry, and many other things. There are a lot of skill sets that are expected of us. A whole crew of technicians set up places such as the Convention Center, the Murat Theatre, and Clowes Memorial Hall. Basically, we set up the majority of major performance centers in town.

What are your hobbies or favorite books?

I am an avid writer. I am a political and labor organizer. I enjoy playing Dungeons & Dragons with my friends, who all happen to be queer and transgender. My partner and I also are closing on a house and that is a priority for us, to hunker down and get a base of operations. Two books I like come to mind: *Smoke Gets In Your Eyes* by Caitlin Doughty. That was her memoir. She is a major leader in the death positive movement, which is about reclaiming the rituals surrounding death and end-of-life care from corporately owned funeral homes.

Another favorite book I recommend everyone read is Leslie Feinberg's *Rainbow Solidarity in Defense of Cuba*. Leslie was the first person I knew who told me you could be a nonbinary trans person, and you could also be a butch lesbian at the same time. You can also be a lot of things. Leslie used several pronoun sets: ze, hir, hirs. She also used she/her, which was part of her life. One major thing people in America forget, because it's very easy not to know, is that Cuba enacted the most progressive AIDS treatment program ever during a time when the State Department here wouldn't even acknowledge gay people, let alone admit there was an AIDS crisis.

How do you self-identify?

For me, it is not "identifying as." It is, *I am*. I am Two-Spirit. I am also agender. Encompassing those, I am also transgender and nonbinary. I am also pansexual. So, it might be better to ask someone: "What gender are you?" or "What is your sexuality?" How do you self-identify is a good softball version of that question. It's not bad, inherently. It's just that it's less comprehensive.

What do the terms Two-Spirit, agender, transgender, nonbinary, and pansexual, mean to you?

First of all, I belong to the Mvskoke (Creek) Nation and to be Two-Spirit varies nation to nation. I can tell you what Two-Spirit means for me though. It means to encompass a place of spiritual importance in your community. It is a responsibility as well as a burden, but it is also a celebration. For me, the context is that I'm a midwife to the dying. I am a counselor. I grow herbs in my garden for the express purpose of remedies. I occupy a space that is inherently liminal, which means I can do things and go places cisgender men and cisgender women cannot. There are special circles for Two-Spirit people reserved just for our needs.

I should add that Two-Spirit is not an interchangeable term with being a LGBTQ indigenous person or gay native. Despite being an English language term, Two-Spirit was intended as a Pan-Indigenous term to carry on traditional meanings in various languages. There are ceremonial roles that are conferred onto us by our respective elders. There's also a lot that goes under the umbrella term that is outside of the ceremonial and cultural context. There's also being gender nonconforming, being transgender, being third or even fourth gender. No one indigenous culture's gender or sexual categories apply to everyone. Even within those contexts, there is diversity. Many nations have a lot of genders, and I mean *a lot* of genders. The gender binary was a fairly recent insertion by colonial conquest.

Agender is, ironically enough, that my gender is having no gender. All of this is my own personal definition. Agender is the state of not identifying with any particular gender. If you ask me what being agender is you're going to get a different definition than asking twelve other people.

To be transgender is to be a gender other than the one you were assigned at birth. That's a very basic answer.

To be nonbinary is to have a gender that is not a binary gender: male or female, man or woman. It's also a good umbrella term for folks who might be gender nonconforming. Gender nonconforming sometimes goes with being nonbinary. They're not mutually exclusive. There is sort of a Venn diagram that happens where some people who are gender nonconforming might not be nonbinary and people who are nonbinary might not be gender nonconforming. But it happens a lot at the same time.

For me, pansexuality is my attraction to a myriad of genders, presentations, and people. There is a corny quote: "I'm attracted to people, not body parts." That in itself is not entirely accurate. For example, it's like bisexual women who are attracted to mostly women, but maybe there's this one guy out there. For me, being pansexual is: Yes, I still have preferences, but the potential for an attraction is still there, and I don't hold myself to any particular set values of I am only attracted to this or that. It's constantly changing for me too.

What would you like to share of your personal journey?

I was a gender nonconforming kid from an early age. I'm not going to ignore that being called the pronouns expected of my assigned sex didn't affect me. I deeply resented that for a very long time and especially after I hit puberty and into high school. There was a lot of self-loathing, and I went to really dark place. It wasn't until my late teens and early 20s that I actually realized: *Hey, misery isn't the norm. You might actually have gender dysphoria and also a lot of internalized homophobia. Maybe you should work through that.*

More than that is rediscovering that my people have *always* had this. (Motions to hirself). Reinforcement of the gender binary and so-called "normal" is just one aspect of existence: one small aspect in a wide variety of different ways to live and to thrive. As soon as I was able to own that, I was able to fully breathe and to become something bigger than the struggles I have inside myself.

There is absolutely a level of violence against nonbinary and trans people. I have been harassed. I have been physically attacked. I was arrested at an anti-Trump rally, and they put me in the wrong holding cell. I didn't tell them anything regarding my gender because I knew the police would probably abuse me more for not being cisgender and also probably put me in isolation. I didn't want to risk that because I didn't remember any important phone numbers, and the people who were locked up with me did. I didn't want to be alone. So, that was a difficult situation to be in. I have had to physically defend myself for simply being who I am.

When I was first trying to come out, I faced a lot of oppression from my friends and family, honestly, because they saw it as deviant. They saw it as embarrassing because what the neighbors would think and what their church friends would think. That put a lot of pressure on me because my schedule during high school was highly regulated. If I wasn't going to school, I was most likely doing marching band, and if I wasn't in marching band, I was doing something else. I eventually found a greater degree of freedom, but it was through much struggle.

I haven't sustained any serious injuries because I learned to defend myself from a young age. But it's tiresome being on your guard all the time, I'll tell you that.

What are your life goals and dreams?

A pipe dream goal would be to see the complete decolonization of North America in my lifetime. But that's a very lofty goal. A lesser goal would be to host a community space available to members of the various communities I occupy. For example, no questions asked for emergency housing and to help with the ever-present problem of food precarity, in this city in particular. There are great programs out there, but they are sometimes a bit out of reach for many people.

There's a lot I want out of life. Another really big thing I want to do within the next ten years is become a certified death doula.

What can people do to be better allies to the transgender and nonbinary community?

When looking to help someone, center on them first and less so on yourself. Also, if you see something, say something. Don't be a bystander. Don't be afraid to act if you can. A lot of us make excuses: "That's not my business. That would be rude of me to step in. They're just having a lively discussion or whatever." No, they are yelling at each other and close to blows. If you're physically capable of stepping in, do it. Learn how to de-escalate conflicts. That is extremely important. There are books and resources that teach how to do that. It's something I learned how to do for others as well as myself. It is something we have the power to do.

Secondly, understand that you are working towards something that is much greater than yourself. Don't get me wrong. Individuals are highly valued. But it is not about building clout for your own personal brand or anything like that. It is about service to improve conditions for everyone because all these struggles are interconnected. That is something a lot of people forget.

Another thing I highly, highly recommend is pay more attention to defending youths. Often, folks who are minors feel very alone and when they're not alone, they feel talked down to, as if they are not, you know, just people but younger.

The last thing is work towards an understanding of gender and sexuality that is freed from the confines of American Protestantism and the scars of colonialism because that is something that we are still contending with 400 years later. One of the unions I'm a member of is the IWW (Industrial Workers of the World). Their slogan is: "An injury to one is an injury to all."

At the end of the day, every struggle is in fact interconnected. The struggle for housing is a worker's struggle. It is a disabilities rights issue. It is an anti-racist issue. The struggle for protections in the workplace is a transgender issue. It is a women's issue. It is all kinds of things and more. The struggle for LGBTQ liberation is also the struggle for workers' liberation is also the struggle for the liberation of colonized people. So again, linking all the struggles together. The reason I specify this is because many times people get so caught up in one single issue they literally forget that all these things are connected and share common problem sources.

Ultimately, the people and entities that continually push intergenerational poverty and mass incarceration in black, undocumented, and indigenous communities are the same ones that constantly push for the erosion of queer and transgender rights. They say they are defending religion when, in fact, they are pushing a specific political motive. They are the same people and same entities that own more wealth than 99 percent of the population.

Is there anything else you wanted to talk about that I didn't ask?

I am a firm believer that people should not be complacent politically or ethically. You may not be interested in politics, but politics are extremely interested in you. The mainstream political spectrum in the United States is so far to the right. They are more interested in subduing political interests than they are stirring it up.

I just want to encourage everyone to meet their neighbors and look into the struggles that are happening in their areas. I feel like everyone deserves better. More than that, I feel like we not only deserve a better world, we have to make it better because climate change is going to get worse if we can't stop the people and entities that are aggravating it. The major corporations that are agitating climate change to an untenable breaking point, more often than not, are men who just want to watch the world burn. We are at that point: Either we work to make a better world, or we lose the one we've always had—and you can absolutely quote me on that.

Kimberly Acoff

IYG Director of Programing, Freedom Fighter
She/Her/Hers
53 years old

> *"My hope for the community is that we all can live as a community ...*
> *that we can be an American community, a great melting pot,*
> *free to dream and live our best lives."*

I was born in Selma, Alabama. I lived in Fort Wayne, Indiana, since sixth grade. I lived with my adoptive parents, who are really my aunt and uncle. My uncle moved to Fort Wayne to get work.

I have a Master in Business Administration from Indiana Wesleyan University.

I have a nephew I helped raise like a child. I also have a daughter who is transgender in my family of choice. I have a cat that I got from my best friend who was transgender who had a heart attack and died. I got the cat from her parents when she passed.

What are your hobbies or favorite books?

I love walking, reading, and taking short trips. My favorite books are anything written by Toni Morrison and Maya Angelo. There's a theme there. (Laughs). I also like Julia Cameron (author of *The Artist's Way*).

Can you tell me a little about your personal journey?

I knew from age 6 that I was in the wrong body. I didn't necessarily have the words and truly didn't have the wherewithal to know the identification of it all, but I knew I was a girl trapped in a boy's body. Of course, I had no agency to do anything about that at age 6. I did ask my grandmother about it. My grandparents were taking care of us at that time because both of my parents were alcoholics, and my dad was very violent. I said to my grandmother one day, "How can I be a girl?" And she said, "Kiss your elbow." (Laughs). So I spent my early years trying to kiss my elbow. (Chuckling). She thought that was an impossible thing!

I have five siblings. I grew up with the two youngest. I am the third oldest. My two older sisters grew up with my paternal grandparents. They split the kids up. When my grandparents died, my mother tried to resume custody and found it to be impossible with her drinking and mental illness. So, the three of us were put into foster care. I had always been the one who made things work for us in our family so that we didn't get taken away. Of course, that became too much for a child to do at the age of 10. Social services stepped in. My aunt and uncle lived in New York, and they had to move to Indiana to get us. At that time, you could not transfer children to different states. Today that is allowed. So, that's really good.

I presented as male up until about age 27 and then I realized that I no longer wanted to live that falsehood. I was thought of as gay of course. I was very effeminate. My best friend was Marlena Bridgewater. We started the journey of trying to become our authentic selves. She was Caucasian, and I am black. But what we found out is that much of our lives were very similar. She grew up in the area and knew Fort Wayne more than I did. I didn't have a car when I was growing up. But she had a car in high school, and we would go on these road trips and just dream. We would be driving around for hours, just around town and around the different counties, dreaming about when we could be our authentic selves.

Then, Marlena started making real moves to make that happen. She got on hormones, and I soon followed about six months later. She started to get injections through the black market. I was afraid. So, I didn't do that. This is in the mid-'90s. Hormones were not as readily available because doctors in the area were not willing to prescribe them to trans people who presented as female. As for transitioning, Fort Wayne had very few doctors who would do that.

The feminization process is a long process. Marlena was kind of in a hurry to get more feminized and started doing black-market hormones. I watched and went to every session and helped her through that process. She started to get the counseling because you needed so much counseling in order for a doctor to see you for surgery. Neither one of us had the money anyway. (Laughs). We were dreaming and at least taking these steps that we believed were right. Two years later, Marlena had completed her consultation, and she had got this big packet and letter that said she was ready for surgery. But she had no money. I had been working two jobs as a nurse aide, saving money, but I had not had the consultation because I had been busy working two jobs. I said to Marlena, "Can I see that counseling packet of yours?" I borrowed it over the weekend, and I retyped everything in it. Only instead of her name, I put my name on it. (Laughs).

We found a doctor to do surgery. He was in Brussels, Belgium, and is one of the first doctors to be doing SRS (sexual reassignment surgery), and he was a pioneer in that surgery. Marlena had been in correspondence with him, and he said once she had the money to send in her packet. I wrote him as well, and he said once I had the money, I could send my packet. So, I sent him a Travelers Check, and I sent the packet that I had typed up, and then I received the date of the surgery. Marlena and I were over the moon!

Only, we still did not know if it was going to happen. The hospital stay was covered in the money that I sent, but there was a two-week stay over in a hotel room so that the doctor could take some of the sutures out and see if you were healing okay. I didn't know how naïve I was because if anything had gone wrong, I would have needed to stay longer, and I didn't even count on that. So, I worked overtime at my jobs to get money for the hotel stay and for food and for the flight itself. I don't remember my birthday (transition day), but it is also my Godchild's birthday. My female cis friend was giving birth at the same time I was having surgery. So, that was memorable.

I had surgery in Brussels. I stayed my two weeks. Things went well. The doctors were able to remove the sutures that he was supposed to remove, and I got on my way. I was very weak. I couldn't eat the food there because it's just not the same for me, and plus I was just sick from the surgery. I lost a lot of weight and when I was coming back to the United States, I was in a wheelchair being pulled to my flight at the airport.

When I got back to the United States, I had to find a doctor that would take out the rest of the sutures and also for my aftercare. I'll never forget him. He was wonderful. This was in New Haven (Ind.). He was very caring, and he was also the one prescribing my hormones and Marlena's hormones, and he readily took that on. He had brought in a lot of doctors and nurses to see this. I know it is because they are interested to know if they had never seen this sort of surgery before. But, it made me feel like a specimen. And so that's one of the things that we can do better in the medical practice is to remember that we are still dealing with humans. No matter where we're meeting the patient at, you have to ensure their dignity and their humanity.

For that healing process, I stayed with my friend Marlena for three months, on her couch. I had my own apartment, but I could not help myself. She was very helpful with the care. Like most transgender people, female to male or male to female, we take care of each other as best we can. We are each of other's families and caretakers. We are whatever we need to be to each other to help get through it.

That surgery more than allowed me to be free to be my authentic self. It allowed me to be free to accomplish every other dream I had, including education, and jobs that were fulfilling, and to be able to follow passions of mine, like being an advocate for social justice and all those sort of things. After that, I thought to myself, "I didn't ever believe this to be possible." I've learned that with determination and grit anything is possible—not easy, but possible.

I had a learning disability in school. Well, I still have it because it doesn't go away. I had failed three grades and graduated at the ripe age of 21 from high school. I always thought of myself as being dumb. If you are smart enough to be able to articulate and you seem normal, then they assumed that you were normal and didn't look into your inability to learn in the way that average students learn. I went undiagnosed and was labeled as lazy by my family and the school system.

I remember my sixth-grade teacher and ninth-grade teachers really took an interest in me and in my learning. They tailored the learning for me, and I got good grades. The sixth-grade teacher was teaching everything: English, math, and so on. The way he tailored it was so that I could get it, and I got good grades, and I understood. There was learning. After his class, the teachers didn't tailor anything, and they didn't care that I couldn't learn the way other students were learning. Then, I got to the ninth grade and this teacher, a science teacher, tailored it in that same type of way. I didn't think about it at that time. I just thought those two teachers were amazing, and I learned something and it stuck with me.

By the time I got surgery, I knew that I could learn if things were tailored for me to learn. After I got the surgery, I was able to think about school, and I wanted to try. I had tried college right after high school and failed miserably. And so I thought, "I want to go to college, and I want to get a degree." I thought about what those two teachers had done and thought, "Okay, I'm going to have to do this for myself. No professor is going to tailor it for me. I'm going to tailor it myself."

I would go to classes and take notes as best as I could, which was difficult because when things were said I could not process them as fast as they were being spoken. I had to get the major words down, because I would miss the others, and then put down those thoughts as best I could. I told myself that for every one hour of class, I needed to spend two hours studying. That became my second job: studying.

I had turned a closet into an office, and I would go into this closet and study. Imagine going into this closet willingly when I had prayed and worked to get out! (Laughs). So, I would go into this closet and study, sometimes for six to eight hours. I knew enough to know that I needed to break it up. I would allocate six or eight hours to studying, but I would do it in thirty-minute increments and allow myself fifteen-minute breaks. My first semester, I only took two classes. I wanted to see if that really would work. Well, I came out with A's in those classes. I said, "Oh, let me take two more classes." I had four classes the next semester, and I came out with A's. Then I said, "Okay, this is a winning formula." So, I took a full load and came out with all A's. That just snowballed into one semester following the next.

The next thing I knew I was walking across the stage, magna cum laude. That surpassed my wildest dreams. It was one thing to think I could get some good grades, but it was another thing to think that I could carry a 4.0.

My learning disability was never diagnosed. I knew after I had been in social services awhile that I was environmentally delayed by things that had been happening to me in my early childhood life which made me have a learning disability: the violence, the drinking, the abuse to us, trying to protect my younger siblings, and the emotional trauma of it all. Even though I was never diagnosed, there was PTSD (Post-Traumatic Stress Disorder) there because I would wake up to violence and go to sleep to violence.

I went on to get my master's degree because after I graduated with my bachelor's degree I said, "Okay, I have the winning formula. I know what I need to do." I went on to duplicate the same thing.

What is important for allies to know to be more supportive of the transgender community?

Speak up. Get out and vote on the issues that matter. Call your representatives and make them aware that you are allies, and you are out here.

It's more than just being an ally. It's about recognizing humanity and ensuring that every person is given what the constitution guarantees each person: the right to freedom and the right to liberty and justice for all. That doesn't have to be an ally just for LGBTQ individuals. That's a Freedom Fighter for the rights of mankind.

What are your future goals and dreams for your life?

I am working on a book, but I am not quite sure how to put that together. That's on my Bucket List: to get that book done. Right now, it's all in journals. And then, advocating for freedom for LGBTQ individuals and individuals who are facing injustice at any juncture, whether LGBTQ or not.

Also, to be a model in the hopes and dreams of the young people who are identifying as LGBTQ. I want them to know that no matter what obstacles and barriers they face, they can fulfill their dreams—with determination and grit and hope and, yes, help from people like you and me who are wanting to do the right thing and wanting to ensure that the system does the right thing for individuals. We can ensure that they have a better life.

No one should have to be oppressed or depressed and discriminated against in this day and time. I think we can change what is currently happening, what we see today. Where we see things that appear to be going in reverse, we can set it right. That's what allies have to do. That's what I have to do.

What is your hope for the community?

My hope for the community is that we all can live as a community, as a whole, as Americans. And that we can be an American community, a great melting pot, free to dream and live our best lives.

❧

AFTERWORD

As the individuals in this book emphasized, there are *a lot* of things everyone can do to make the world safer for people who are transgender and to provide more support for them and their families. With valuable input from Kit Malone, American Civil Liberties Union (ACLU) and Board Member of Trinity Haven, the following are significant action steps that will make a difference in the lives of transgender individuals in our communities.

PRACTICAL ACTION STEPS FOR ALLIES

- **Show up!**
  Attend LGBTQ+ events in your area. Don't wait for an invitation. Proximity—choosing to be in relationship with transgender individuals—makes a positive difference. Organizations post community events on their websites all the time featuring workshops, spoken word artists, art shows, educational programs, speakers, parent groups, youth groups, and Pride events. Take your friends, your family, and your children. Find a Transgender Day of Remembrance happening in your area in November. Fellowship helps everyone gain a better understanding of transgender lives.

- **Speak up!**
  Don't let cruel language and hate speech go unchecked. Verbal violence is violence. Engage in uncomfortable conversations

with family members, work colleagues, civic leaders, healthcare providers, school educators and administrators, politicians, and friends. Report incidents of bullying, harassment, or violence that occur in the workplace, in schools, on social media, and in your community.

- **Contact Local Lawmakers!**
  Remind representatives not to use their power to attack people. Don't wait until something is on the docket or in the media. Contact them *anytime.* Let lawmakers know you care about the lives of transgender individuals and their families.

- **Donate to Organizations Supporting Transgender Individuals!**
  Organizations need financial support and volunteers to continue the work of advocating and educating on behalf of transgender people and their families. Consider making a financial contribution to sustain these crucial, ongoing efforts. Learn more about the organizations listed in the Community Resource section.

- **Lift Up!**
  Be fully present for people. Encourage transgender individuals and their families to take up space: at restaurants, organizational gatherings, business meetings, and public events. Offer transgender people the use of community spaces for events. Hire and promote transgender people! Form friendships. Appreciate the talents and gifts of each beautiful human you encounter. Open your heart, wider.

COMMUNITY RESOURCES

This list is a small sampling of LGBTQ organizations that provide resources for transgender individuals, family members, and allies. Check websites for additional resources, community events, and specific information pertaining to educators, families, medical providers, legal services, legislative updates, faith groups, suicide prevention, homelessness, and more. Universities often have LGBTQ+ website information as well. Get involved and stay informed.

RESOURCES REFERENCED IN BOOK
Indy Pride, Inc. has an extensive list of resources: https://indypride.org/community-resources/

Additional Resources:

ACLU of Indiana: www.aclu-in-org.
BU Wellness Network: www.brothersunited.org
Damien Center (AIDS service organization): http://www.damien.org
Free Mom Hugs: www.freemomhugs.org
GEKCO (Gender Expansive Kids and Company) www.INgekco.com
(Facebook group). http://indianatransgendernetwork.com/resources/
advocacy/gekco-gender-expansive-kids-central-indiana
GenderNexus: www.gendernexus.org

Indiana Pride of Color https://www.facebook.com/IndianaPOC
(Facebook group)
Indiana Transgender Network: www.indianatransgendernetwork.com
Indiana Youth Group: www.indianayouthgroup.org
Muncie Outreach: www.muncieoutreach.org
Queering Indy (Facebook group) www.facebook.com
Queerly Indy: www.queerlyindy.com
River City Pride, Evansville https://inrivercitypride.org
Trinity Haven (housing and service provider for LGBTQ+ youth at risk
for homelessness) www.trinityhaven.org

National Resources
Indy Pride, Inc. has a list of Transgender National Organizations:
https://indypride.org/community-resources

Additional Resources:

Gender Spectrum: www.genderspectrum.org
GLAAD (media resources): www.GLAAD.org
Human Rights Campaign (HRC): www.hrc.org
PFLAG (family resources): www.PFLAG.org
The Trevor Project (suicide prevention): www.thetrevorproject.org
TransParent (connecting families): www.transparentusa.org
Trans People of Color Coalition (TPOCC): www.transpoc.org

GLOSSARY OF TERMS

The Human Rights Campaign (HRC) website offers excellent guidance for anyone who is unfamiliar with basic LGBTQ+ terminology. Language rapidly changes as knowledge evolves. In addition, people define for themselves what labels (if any) apply to their lives and may or may not agree with terms used by others. Nevertheless, understanding how current language is used helps in our efforts to communicate respectfully.

For additional information, please visit the HRC website: https://www. hrc.org/resources/glossary-of-terms

Ally | A person who is not LGBTQ but shows support for LGBTQ people and promotes equality in a variety of ways.

Androgynous | Identifying and/or presenting as neither distinguishably masculine nor feminine.

Asexual | The lack of a sexual attraction or desire for other people.

Biphobia | Prejudice, fear or hatred directed toward bisexual people.

Bisexual | A person emotionally, romantically or sexually attracted to more than one sex, gender or gender identity though not necessarily simultaneously, in the same way, or to the same degree.

Cisgender | A term used to describe a person whose gender identity aligns with those typically associated with the sex assigned to them at birth.

Closeted | Describes an LGBTQ person who has not disclosed their sexual orientation or gender identity.

Coming out | The process in which a person first acknowledges, accepts and appreciates their sexual orientation or gender identity and begins to share that with others.

Gay | A person who is emotionally, romantically or sexually attracted to members of the same gender.

Gender dysphoria | Clinically significant distress caused when a person's assigned birth gender is not the same as the one with which they identify. According to the American Psychiatric Association's Diagnostic and Statistical Manual of Mental Disorders (DSM), the term – which replaces Gender Identity Disorder – "is intended to better characterize the experiences of affected children, adolescents, and adults."

Gender-expansive | Conveys a wider, more flexible range of gender identity and/or expression than typically associated with the binary gender system.

Gender expression | External appearance of one's gender identity, usually expressed through behavior, clothing, haircut or voice, and which may or may not conform to socially defined behaviors and characteristics typically associated with being either masculine or feminine.

Gender-fluid | According to the Oxford English Dictionary, a person who does not identify with a single fixed gender; of or relating to a person having or expressing a fluid or unfixed gender identity.

Gender identity | One's innermost concept of self as male, female, a blend of both or neither – how individuals perceive themselves and what they call themselves. One's gender identity can be the same or different from their sex assigned at birth.

Gender non-conforming | A broad term referring to people who do not behave in a way that conforms to the traditional expectations of their gender, or whose gender expression does not fit neatly into a category.

Genderqueer | Genderqueer people typically reject notions of static categories of gender and embrace a fluidity of gender identity and often, though not always, sexual orientation. People who identify as "genderqueer" may see themselves as being both male and female, neither male nor female, or as falling completely outside these categories.

Gender transition | The process by which some people strive to more closely align their internal knowledge of gender with its outward appearance. Some people socially transition, whereby they might begin dressing, using names and pronouns and/or be socially recognized as another gender. Others undergo physical transitions in which they modify their bodies through medical interventions.

Homophobia | The fear and hatred of or discomfort with people who are attracted to members of the same sex.

Intersex | An umbrella term used to describe a wide range of natural bodily variations. In some cases, these traits are visible at birth, and in others, they are not apparent until puberty. Some chromosomal variations of this type may not be physically apparent at all.

Lesbian | A woman who is emotionally, romantically or sexually attracted to other women.

LGBTQ | An acronym for "lesbian, gay, bisexual, transgender and queer."

Non-binary | An adjective describing a person who does not identify exclusively as a man or a woman. Non-binary people may identify as being both a man and a woman, somewhere in between, or as falling completely outside these categories. While many also identify as transgender, not all non-binary people do.

Outing | Exposing someone's lesbian, gay, bisexual or transgender identity to others without their permission. Outing someone can have serious repercussions on employment, economic stability, personal safety or religious or family situations.

Pansexual | Describes someone who has the potential for emotional, romantic or sexual attraction to people of any gender though not necessarily simultaneously, in the same way or to the same degree.

Queer | A term people often use to express fluid identities and orientations. Often used interchangeably with "LGBTQ."

Questioning | A term used to describe people who are in the process of exploring their sexual orientation or gender identity.

Same-gender loving | A term some prefer to use instead of lesbian, gay or bisexual to express attraction to and love of people of the same gender.

Sex assigned at birth | The sex (male or female) given to a child at birth, most often based on the child's external anatomy. This is also referred to as "assigned sex at birth."

Sexual orientation | An inherent or immutable enduring emotional, romantic or sexual attraction to other people.

Transgender | An umbrella term for people whose gender identity and/ or expression is different from cultural expectations based on the sex they were assigned at birth. Being transgender does not imply any specific sexual orientation. Therefore, transgender people may identify as straight, gay, lesbian, bisexual, etc.

Transphobia | The fear and hatred of, or discomfort with, transgender people.

Source: HRC website: https://www.hrc.org/resources/glossary-of-terms

ACKNOWLEDGMENTS

I wish to express my heartfelt gratitude to everyone who shared their stories with such intelligence, grace, and fortitude. It takes courage to live an authentic life, and it takes bravery to speak honestly from the heart. *Thank you!*

As always, I am eternally grateful for life's universal wellspring of creativity and love.

I am also grateful to friends and family members who sustain my spirit during challenges. My daughter's prior work at a LGBTQ+ nonprofit in Thailand, which focuses on HIV education and prevention, served as a model for me of the countless ways we can contribute our time, energy, and talents toward helping each other. A friend who frequents Bali, Suzi Wagman, heightened my awareness of transgender issues across the globe and then brought that awareness home to me with the idea of advocating for transgender equality in my local community.

Love and gratitude for friends (old and new) and other close relations who happen to be transgender, nonbinary, and/or gender nonconforming. I will not sit silently by while anyone criticizes your right to be who you are on this planet. My personal prayer is that this book moves everyone to do something to help in the collective determination to get rid of prejudice, hate, bigotry, and violence and while doing so, elicits a tremendous *outpouring of love.*

Special thanks to Jenni White, Trinity Haven founding Executive

Director. This book would not have been possible without her encouragement and belief in the project. Trinity Haven provides services and housing for LGBTQ+ youth at risk of homelessness.

Thanks to Kit Malone, American Civil Liberties Union (ACLU) and Trinity Haven Board Member, for enlightening conversation that formed the Action Steps for Allies. Kit is an amazing Freedom Fighter who goes above and beyond on behalf of the transgender community. I greatly admire her tenacity and unstinting courage.

Thanks to the following people for their professional expertise, talents, and friendship:

Proofreading: Addison J. Smith, Transgender Educator, Board Member of GenderNexus and Indy Pride.

Cover Photo Image: Mark A. Lee (30 years of work in the LGBTQ community) Great Exposures. www.greatexposures.net

Author Photo: Emily Schwank (parent of nonbinary child and LGBTQ+ ally). www.raincliffsphotography.com

Author Website: Le Weaver, CircleWebWorks (longtime friend whose professional work is always exemplary). www.circlewebworks.com To order additional book copies (discounts available for nonprofits and bulk orders) or to request a speaking appearance, contact the author via her website: www.dianaensign.com

I also want to thank the Indiana Arts Commission. This project is made possible by support of the Indiana Arts Commission, a state agency. The individual artist development grant helped circulate funds back into the community for services provided.

INDIANA ARTS COMMISSION
MAKING THE ARTS HAPPEN

A *Freedom to Be* **GoFundMe**™ campaign will raise funds to provide book copies *free of charge* for rural libraries, schools, small nonprofit organizations, and/or low-income individuals. Books are one way we can educate others and ourselves about significant LGBTQ+ issues in our communities. All funds will be used *solely* to produce book copies for distribution to other organizations. (No funds will be paid to the author). Please consider making a contribution.

ABOUT THE AUTHOR

Diana J. Ensign, JD, is an award-winning author who writes about the human spirit. Ensign has two prior books. *Heart Guide: True Stories of Grief and Healing* shares intimate and poignant guidance for people who are grieving the death of a loved one. *Heart Guide* is an Independent Publisher Book Awards (IPPY) Gold Medal Winner. *Traveling Spirit: Daily Tools for Your Life's Journey* provides spiritual practices for dealing with life's challenges. A percentage of the profits from *Traveling Spirit* go to support the Lambi Fund of Haiti (working on reforestation in Haiti, along with women's and girl's health, nutrition, and education). She is a frequent speaker and workshop facilitator.

For close to 30 years, Ensign has actively supported social justice endeavors. Working first as a lawyer in employment discrimination, she focused on age, race, national origin, disability, gender, and pregnancy discrimination under federal law. Later, she wrote articles, essays, and blogs about the environment, LGBTQ equality, homelessness, and nonviolence. While serving as chair of a social justice committee, she organized various community outreach efforts. The death of her father after his military service served as a stimulus to understand the disease of addictions, leading to a public program with veterans. More recently, she became involved with a nonprofit social service organization that works in Belle-Riviere, Haiti, to meet the community's basic human needs for food, clean water, health, education, and sustainable commerce.

Always, her writing focuses on building heart connections among diverse people so that our sense of compassion is strengthened and our shared humanity is respected, honored, and valued. It is her desire to use writing as a powerful tool to break down the barriers, both within ourselves and within our communities, that separate us. In all her writing, the deeper message is the same: love, compassion, and service of humanity.

Her books and her blog, *Spirituality for Daily Living,* are available on her website: www.dianaensign.com

www.ingramcontent.com/pod-product-compliance
Lightning Source LLC
Chambersburg PA
CBHW031203270326
41931CB00006B/379

THE NATIONAL BEING

THE
NATIONAL BEING

SOME THOUGHTS ON
AN IRISH POLITY

BY

A. E.

Facsimile edition,
Coracle Press, 2007
First edition, Macmillan and Co., 1917

For information, address:
Coracle Press, P.O. Box 151011
San Rafael, California 94915, USA

ISBN-13: 978-1-59731-304-9
(pbk.: alk. paper)
ISBN-13: 978-1-59731-305-6
(hardcover: alk. paper)

THE NATIONAL BEING

I

In the year nineteen hundred and fourteen Anno Domini, amid a world conflict, the birth of the infant State of Ireland was announced. Almost unnoticed this birth, which in other times had been cried over the earth with rejoicings or anger. Mars, the red planet of war, was in the ascendant when it was born. Like other births famous in history, the child had to be hidden away for a time, and could not with pride be shown to the people as royal children were wont to be shown. Its enemies were unforgiving, and its friends were distracted with mighty happenings in the world. Hardly did they know whether it would not be deformed if it survived : whether this was the Promised, or another child yet to be conceived in the womb of the Mother of Parliaments. Battles were threatened between two hosts, secular champions of two spiritual traditions, to decide its fate. That such a conflict threatened showed indeed that there was something of iron fibre in

the infant, without which in their make-up individuals or nations do nothing worthy of remembrance. Hercules wrestled with twin serpents
in his cradle, and there were twin serpents of
sectarianism ready to strangle this infant State
of ours if its guardians were not watchful, or if
the infant was not itself strong enough to destroy
them.

It is about the State of Ireland, its character
and future, I have here written some kind of
imaginative meditation. The State is a physical
body prepared for the incarnation of the soul of
a race. The body of the national soul may be
spiritual or secular, aristocratic or democratic,
civil or militarist predominantly. One or other
will be most powerful, and the body of the race
will by reflex action affect its soul, even as through
heredity the inherited tendencies and passions of
the flesh affect the indwelling spirit. Our brooding over the infant State must be dual, concerned
not only with the body but the soul. When we
essay self-government in Ireland our first ideas
will, in all probability, be borrowed from the
Mother of Parliaments, just as children before
they grow to have a character of their own repeat
the sentiments of their parents. After a time, if
there is anything in the theory of Irish nationality,
we will apply original principles as they are from
time to time discovered to be fundamental in
Irish character. A child in the same way makes
discoveries about itself. The mood evoked by
picture or poem reveals a love of beauty ; the

harsh treatment of an animal provokes an out-
burst of pity; some curiosity of nature draws
forth the spirit of scientific inquiry, and so, as
the incidents of life reveal the innate affinities
of a child to itself, do the adventures of a nation
gradually reveal to it its own character and the
will which is in it.

For all our passionate discussions over self-
government we have had little speculation over
our own character or the nature of the civilization
we wished to create for ourselves. Nations
rarely, if ever, start with a complete ideal. Certainly we have no national ideals, no principles
of progress peculiar to ourselves in Ireland,
which are a common possession of our people.
National ideals are the possession of a few people
only. Yet we must spread them in wide commonalty over Ireland if we are to create a civilization worthy of our hopes and our ages of struggle
and sacrifice to attain the power to build. We
must spread them in wide commonalty because
it is certain that democracy will prevail in Ireland.
The aristocratic classes with traditions of government, the manufacturing classes with economic
experience, will alike be secondary in Ireland to
the small farmers and the wage-earners in the
towns. We must rely on the ideas common
among our people, and on their power to discern
among their countrymen the aristocracy of character and intellect.

Civilizations are externalizations of the soul
and character of races. They are majestic or

mean according to the treasure of beauty, imagination, will, and thought laid up in the soul of the
people.   That great mid-European State, which
while I write is at bay surrounded by enemies,
did not arrive at that pitch of power which made
it dominant in Europe simply by militarism.
That military power depended on and was fed by
a vigorous intellectual life, and the most generally
diffused education and science existing perhaps
in the world.   The national being had been
enriched by a long succession of mighty thinkers.
A great subjective life and centuries of dream
preceded a great objective manifestation of power
and wealth.   The stir in the German Empire
which has agitated Europe was, at its root, the
necessity laid on a powerful soul to surround
itself with equal external circumstance.   That
necessity is laid on all nations, on all individuals,
to make their external life correspond in some
measure to their internal dream.   A lover of
beauty will never contentedly live in a house
where all things are devoid of taste.   An intellectual man will loathe a disordered society.
We may say with certainty that the external
circumstances of people are a measure of their
inner life.   Our mean and disordered little
country towns in Ireland, with their drink-shops,
their disregard of cleanliness or beauty, accord
with the character of the civilians who inhabit
them.   Whenever we develop an intellectual
life these things will be altered, but not in priority
to the spiritual mood.   House by house, village

by village, the character of a civilization changes
as the character of the individuals change.   When
we begin to build up a lofty world within the
national soul, soon the country becomes beautiful
and worthy of respect in its externals.   That
building up of the inner world we have neglected.
Our excited political controversies, our playing
at militarism, have tended to bring men's thoughts
from central depths to surfaces.   Life is drawn
to its frontiers away from its spiritual base, and
behind the surfaces we have little to fall back on.
Few of our notorieties could be trusted to think
out any economic or social problem thoroughly
and efficiently.   They have been engaged in
passionate attempts at the readjustment of the
superficies of things.   What we require more
than men of action at present are scholars, economists, scientists, thinkers, educationalists, and
littérateurs, who will populate the desert depths
of national consciousness with real thought and
turn the void into a fullness.   We have few
reserves of intellectual life to draw upon when
we come to the mighty labour of nation-building.
It will be indignantly denied, but I think it is
true to say that the vast majority of people in
Ireland do not know the difference between good
and bad thinking, between the essential depths
and the shallows in humanity.   How could
people, who never read anything but the newspapers, have any genuine knowledge of any
subject on earth or much imagination of anything
beautiful in the heavens ?

What too many people in Ireland mistake for thoughts are feelings. It is enough to them to vent like or dislike, inherited prejudices or passions, and they think when they have expressed feeling they have given utterance to thought. The nature of our political controversies provoked passion, and passion has become dominant in our politics. Passion truly is a power in humanity, but it should never enter into national policy. It is a dangerous element in human life, though it is an essential part of our strangely compounded nature. But in national life it is the most danger-ous of all guides. There are springs of power in ourselves which in passion we draw on and are amazed at their depth and intensity, yet we do not make these the master light of our being, but rather those divine laws which we have appre-hended and brooded upon, and which shine with clear and steady light in our souls. As creatures rise in the scale of being the dominant factor in life changes. In vegetation it may be appetite ; instinct in bird and beast ; for man a life at once passionate and intellectual ; but the greater beings, the stars and planets, must wheel in the heavens under the guidance of inexorable and inflexible law. Now the State is higher in the scale of being than the individual, and it should be dominated solely by moral and intellectual prin-ciples. These are not the outcome of passion or prejudice, but of arduous thought. National ideals must be built up with the same conscious deliberation of purpose as the architect of the

Parthenon conceived its lofty harmony of shining marble lines, or as the architect of Rheims Cathedral designed its intricate magnificence and mystery. Nations which form their ideals and marry them in the hurry of passion are likely to repent without leisure, and they will not be able to divorce those ideals without prolonged domestic squabbles and public cleansing of dirty linen. If we are to build a body for the soul of Ireland it ought not to be a matter of reckless estimates or jerry-building. We have been told, during my lifetime at least, not to criticize leaders, to trust leaders, and so intellectual discussion ceased and the high principles on which national action should be based became less and less understood, less and less common possessions. The nation was not conceived of as a democracy freely discussing its laws, but as a secret society with political chiefs meeting in the dark and issuing orders. No doubt our political chieftains loved their country, but love has many degrees of expression from the basest to the highest. The basest love will wreck everything, even the life of the beloved, to gratify ignoble desires. The highest love conspires with the imaginative reason to bring about every beautiful circumstance around the beloved which will permit of the highest development of its life. There is no real love apart from this intellectual brooding. Men who love Ireland ignobly brawl about her in their cups, quarrel about her with their neighbour, allow no freedom of thought of her or service of her other than their

own, take to the cudgel and the rifle, and join
sectarian orders or lodges to ensure that Ireland
will be made in their own ignoble image.   Those
who love Ireland nobly desire for her the highest
of human destinies.   They would ransack the
ages and accumulate wisdom to make Irish life
seem as noble in men's eyes as any the world
has known.   The better minds in every race,
eliminating passion and prejudice, by the exercise
of the imaginative reason have revealed to their
countrymen ideals which they recognized were
implicit in national character.   It is such discoveries we have yet to make about ourselves to
unite us to fulfil our destiny.   We have to discover what is fundamental in Irish character,
the affections, leanings, tendencies towards one
or more of the eternal principles which have
governed and inspired all great human effort,
all great civilizations from the dawn of history.
A nation is but a host of men united by some
God - begotten mood, some hope of liberty or
dream of power or beauty or justice or brotherhood, and until that master idea is manifested to
us there is no shining star to guide the ship of our
destinies.

Our civilization must depend on the quality
of thought engendered in the national being.
We have to do for Ireland—though we hope
with less arrogance—what the long and illustrious
line of German thinkers, scientists, poets, philoso-
phers, and historians did for Germany, or what
the poets and artists of Greece did for the

Athenians : and that is, to create national ideals
which will dominate the policy of statesmen, the
actions of citizens, the universities, the social
organizations, the administration of State departments, and unite in one spirit urban and rural
life. Unless this is done Ireland will be like
Portugal, or any of the corrupt little penny-
dreadful nationalities which so continually disturb
the peace of the world with internal revolutions
and external brawlings, and we shall only have
achieved the mechanism of nationality, but the
spirit will have eluded us.

What I have written hereafter on the national
being, my thoughts on an Irish polity, are not to
be taken as an attempt to deal with more than
a few essentials. I offer it to my countrymen,
to start thought and discussion upon the principles which should prevail in an Irish civilization.
If to readers in other countries the thought appears
primitive or elementary, I would like them to
remember that we are at the beginning of our
activity as a nation, and we have yet to settle
fundamentals. Races hoary with political wisdom
may look with disdain on the attempts at political
thinking by a new self-governing nationality, or
the theories of civilization discussed about the
cradle of an infant State. To childhood may be
forgiven the elemental character of its thought
and its idealistic imaginations. They may not
persist in developed manhood ; but if youth has
never drawn heaven and earth together in its
imaginations, manhood will ever be undistin-

guished. This book only begins a meditation in which, I hope, nobler imaginations and finer intellects than mine will join hereafter, and help to raise the soul of Ireland nigher to the ideal and its body nigher to its soul.

II

THE building up of a civilization is at once the noblest and the most practical of all enterprises, in which human faculties are exalted to their highest, and beauties and majestics are manifested in multitude as they are never by solitary man or by disunited peoples. In the highest civilizations the individual citizen is raised above himself and made part of a greater life, which we may call the National Being. He enters into it, and it becomes an oversoul to him, and gives to all his works a character and grandeur and a relation to the works of his fellow-citizens, so that all he does conspires with the labours of others for unity and magnificence of effect. So ancient Egypt, with its temples, sphinxes, pyramids, and symbolic decorations, seems to us as if it had been created by one grandiose imagination; for even the lesser craftsmen, working on the mummy case for the tomb, had much of the mystery and solemnity in their work which is manifest in temple and pyramid. So the city States in ancient Greece in their day were united by ideals to a harmony of art and architecture and literature. Among the Athenians at their highest the ideal of the State

so wrought upon the individual that its service
became the overmastering passion of life, and in
that great oration of Pericles, where he told how
the Athenian ideal inspired the citizens so that
they gave their bodies for the commonwealth, it
seems to have been conceived of as a kind of
oversoul, a being made up of immortal deeds and
heroic spirits, influencing the living, a life within
their life, moulding their spirits to its likeness.
It appears almost as if in some of these ancient
famous communities the nation ideal became a
kind of tribal deity, that began first with some
great hero who died and was immortalized by
the poets, and whose character, continually
glorified by them, grew at last so great in song
that he could not be regarded as less than a demi-
god.   We can see in ancient Ireland that Cuchulain, the dark sad man of the earlier tales, was
rapidly becoming a divinity, a being who summed
up in himself all that the bards thought noblest
in the spirit of their race ; and if Ireland had a
happier history no doubt one generation of bardic
chroniclers after another would have moulded
that half-mythical figure into the Irish ideal of
all that was chivalrous, tender, heroic, and
magnanimous, and it would have been a star to
youth, and the thought of it a staff to the very
noblest.   Even as Cuchulain alone at the ford
held it against a host, so the ideal would have
upheld the national soul in its darkest hours, and
stood in many a lonely place in the heart.   The
national soul in a theocratic State is a god ; in an

aristocratic age it assumes the character of a hero;
and in a democracy it becomes a multitudinous
being, definite in character if the democracy is a
real social organism.   But where the democracy
is only loosely held together by the social order,
the national being is vague in character, is a mood
too feeble to inspire large masses of men to high
policies in times of peace, and in times of war it
communicates frenzy, panic, and delirium.

None of our modern States create in us such
an impression of being spiritually oversouled by
an ideal as the great States of the ancient world.
The leaders of nations too have lost that divine
air that many leaders of men wore in the past,
and which made the populace rumour them as
divine incarnations. It is difficult to know to
what to attribute this degeneration. Perhaps
the artists who create ideals are to blame. In
ancient Ireland, in Greece, and in India, the
poets wrote about great kings and heroes, enlarging on their fortitude of spirit, their chivalry
and generosity, creating in the popular mind an
ideal of what a great man was like; and men
were influenced by the ideal created, and strove
to win the praise of the bards and to be recrowned
by them a second time in great poetry. So we
had Cuchulain and Oscar in Ireland; Hector
of Troy, Theseus in Greece; Yudisthira, Rama,
and Arjuna in India, all bard-created heroes
moulding the minds of men to their image. It
is the great defect of our modern literature that
it creates few such types. How hardly could

one of our modern public men be made the hero of an epic. It would be difficult to find one who could be the subject of a genuine lyric. Whitman, himself the most democratic poet of the modern world, felt this deficiency in the literature of the later democracies, and lamented the absence of great heroic figures. The poets have dropped out of the divine procession, and sing a solitary song. They inspire nobody to be great, and failing any finger-post in literature pointing to true greatness our democracies too often take the huckster from his stall, the drunkard from his pot, the lawyer from his court, and the company promoter from the director's chair, and elect them as representative men. We certainly do this in Ireland. It is—how many hundred years since greatness guided us? In Ireland our history begins with the most ancient of any in a mythical era when earth mingled with heaven. The gods departed, the half-gods also, hero and saint after that, and we have dwindled down to a petty peasant nationality, rural and urban life alike mean in their externals. Yet the cavalcade, for all its tattered habiliments, has not lost spiritual dignity. There is still some incorruptible spiritual atom in our people. We are still in some relation to the divine order ; and while that incorrupted spiritual atom still remains all things are possible if by some inspiration there could be revealed to us a way back or forward to greatness, an Irish polity in accord with national character.

III

In formulating an Irish polity we have to take into account the change in world conditions. A theocratic State we shall have no more. Every nation, and our own along with them, is now made up of varied sects, and the practical dominance of one religious idea would let loose illimitable passions, the most intense the human spirit can feel. The way out of the theocratic State was by the drawn sword and was lit by the martyr's fires. The way back is unthinkable for all Protestant fears or Catholic aspirations. Aristocracies, too, become impossible as rulers. The aristocracy of character and intellect we may hope shall finally lead us, but no aristocracy so by birth will renew its authority over us. The character of great historic personages is gradually reflected in the mass. The divine right of kings is followed by the idea of the divine right of the people, and democracies finally become ungovernable save by themselves. They have seen and heard too much of pride and greatness not to have become, in some measure, proud and defiant of all authority except their own. It may be said the history of democracies is not one to fill us with confidence, but the truth is the world has yet to see the democratic State, and of the yet untried we may think with hope. Beneath the Athenian and other ancient democratic States lay a substratum of humanity in slavery, and the culture, beauty, and bravery of these extraordinary peoples were made possible by the workers in an underworld who had no part in the bright civic life.

We have no more a real democracy in the world to-day. Democracy in politics has in no country led to democracy in its economic life. We still have autocracy in industry as firmly seated on its throne as theocratic king ruling in the name of a god, or aristocracy ruling by military power ; and the forces represented by these twain, superseded by the autocrats of industry, have become the allies of the power which took their place of pride. Religion and rank, whether content or not with the subsidiary place they now occupy, are most often courtiers of Mammon and support him on his throne. For all the talk about democracy our social order is truly little more democratic than Rome was under the Caesars, and our new rulers have not, with all their wealth, created a beauty which we could imagine after-generations brooding over with uplifted heart.

The people in theocratic States like Egypt or Chaldea, ruled in the name of gods, saw rising out of the plains in which they lived an architecture so mysterious and awe-inspiring that they might well believe the master-minds who designed the temples were inspired from the Oversoul. The aristocratic States reflected the love of beauty which is associated with aristocracies. The oligarchies of wealth in our time, who have no divine sanction to give dignity to their rule nor traditions of lordly life like the aristocracies, have not in our day created beauty in the world. But whatever of worth the ancient systems produced was not good enough to make permanent their social order. Their civilizations, like ours, were built on the unstable basis of a vast working-class with no real share in the wealth and grandeur it helped to create. The character of his kingdom was revealed in dream to Nebuchadnezzar by an image with a golden head and feet of clay, and that image might stand as symbol of the empires the world has known. There is in all a vast population living in an underworld of labour whose freedom to vote confers on them no real power, and who are most often scorned and neglected by those who profit by their labours. Indifference turns to fear and hatred if labour organizes and gathers power, or makes one motion of its myriad hands towards the sceptre held by the autocrats of industry. When this class is maddened and revolts, civilization shakes and totters like cities when the earthquake stirs beneath their foundations. Can we master these arcane human forces? Can we, by any device, draw this

c

submerged humanity into the light and make
them real partners in the social order, not partners
merely in the political life of the nation, but,
what is of more importance, in its economic
life ?   If we build our civilization without integrating labour into its economic structure, it
will wreck that civilization, and it will do that
more swiftly to-day than two thousand years
ago, because there is no longer the disparity of
culture between high and low which existed in
past centuries.   The son of the artisan, if he
cares to read, may become almost as fully master
of the wisdom of Plato or Aristotle as if he had
been at a university.   Emerson will speak to
him of his divinity ; Whitman, drunken with
the sun, will chant to him of his inheritance of
the earth.   He is elevated by the poets and
instructed by the economists.   But there are
not thrones enough for all who are made wise
in our social order, and failing even to serve in
the social heaven these men will spread revolt
and reign in the social hell.   They are becoming
too many for higher places to be found for them
in the national economy.   They are increasing
to a multitude which must be considered, and
the framers of a national polity must devise a
life for them where their new-found dignity of
spirit will not be abased.   Men no more will be
content under rulers of industry they do not
elect themselves than they were under political
rulers claiming their obedience in the name of
God.   They will not for long labour in industries

where they have no power to fix the conditions of their employment, as they were not content with a political system which allowed them no power to control legislation.   Ireland must begin its imaginative reconstruction of a civilization by first considering that type which, in the earlier civilizations of the world, has been slave, serf, or servile, working either on land or at industry, and must construct with reference to it.   These workers must be the central figures, and how their material, intellectual, and spiritual needs are met must be the test of value of the social order we evolve.

IV

In Ireland we begin naturally our consideration
of this problem with the folk of the country,
pondering all the time upon our ideal—the
linking up of individuals with each other and
with the nation. Since the destruction of the
ancient clans in Ireland almost every economic
factor in rural life has tended to separate the
farmers from each other and from the nation,
and to bring about an isolation of action ; and
that was so until the movement for the organization of agriculture was initiated by Sir Horace
Plunkett and his colleagues in that patriotic
association, the Irish Agricultural Organization
Society. Though its actual achievement is great ;
though it may be said to be the pivot round which
Ireland has begun to swing back to its traditional
and natural communism in work, we still have
over the larger part of Ireland conditions prevailing which tend to isolate the individual from
the community.

When we examine rural Ireland, outside this
new movement, we find everywhere isolated and
individualistic agricultural production, served

with regard to purchase and sale by private
traders and dealers, who are independent of
economic control from the consumers or producers, or the State. The tendency in the
modern world to conduct industry in the grand
manner is not observable here. The first thing
which strikes one who travels through rural
Ireland is the immense number of little shops.
They are scattered along the highways and at
the cross-roads ; and where there are a few
families together in what is called a village, the
number of little shops crowded round these
consumers is almost incredible. What are all
these little shops doing ? They are supplying
the farmers with domestic requirements : with
tea, sugar, flour, oil, implements, vessels, clothing,
and generally with drink. Every one of them
almost is a little universal provider. Every one
of them has its own business organization, its
relations with wholesale houses in the greater
towns. All of them procure separately from
others their bags of flour, their barrels of porter,
their stocks of tea, sugar, raisins, pots, pans,
nails, twine, fertilizers, and what not, and all
these things come to them paying high rates
to the carriers for little loads. The trader's
cart meets them at the station, and at great
expense the necessaries of life are brought together. In the world-wide amalgamation of
shoe-makers into boot factories, and smithies
into ironworks, which is going on in Europe and
America, these little shops have been overlooked.

Nobody has tried to amalgamate them, or to
economize human effort or cheapen the distribution of the necessaries of life. This work of
distribution is carried on by all kinds of little
traders competing with each other, pulling the
devil by the tail ; doing the work economically,
so far as they themselves are concerned, because
they must, but doing it expensively for the
district because they cannot help it. They do
not serve Ireland well. The genius of amalgamation and organization cannot afford to pass by
these shops, which spring up in haphazard
fashion, not because the country needs them,
but because farmers or traders have children to
be provided for. To the ignorant this is the
easiest form of trade, and so many are started in
life in one of these little shops after an apprentice-
ship in another like it. These numerous com-
petitors of each other do not keep down prices.
They increase them rather by the unavoidable
multiplication of expenses ; and many of them,
taking advantage of the countryman's irregularity
of income and his need for credit, allow credit
to a point where the small farmer becomes a
tied customer, who cannot pay all he owes, and
who therefore dares not deal elsewhere. These
agencies for distribution do not by their nature
enlarge the farmer's economic knowledge. His
vision beyond them to their sources of supply is
blocked, and in this respect he is debarred from
any unity with national producers other than
his own class.

Let us now for a little consider the small
farmer around whom have gathered these multitudinous little agencies of distribution. What
kind of a being is he ? We must deal with
averages, and the small farmer is the typical
Irish countryman. The average area of an
Irish farm is twenty-five acres or thereabouts.
There are hundreds of thousands who have more
or less. But we can imagine to ourselves an
Irish farmer with twenty-five acres to till, lord of
a herd of four or five cows, a drift of sheep, a
litter of pigs, perhaps a mare and foal : call him
Patrick Maloney and accept him as symbol of
his class. We will view him outside the operation
of the new co-operative policy, trying to obey
the command to be fruitful and replenish the
earth. He is fruitful enough. There is no race
suicide in Ireland. His agriculture is largely
traditional. It varied little in the nineteenth
century from the eighteenth, and the beginnings
of the twentieth century show little change in
spite of a huge department of agriculture. His
butter, his eggs, his cattle, horses, pigs, and sheep
are sold to local dealers. He rarely knows
where his produce goes to—whether it is devoured
in the next county or is sent across the Channel.
It might be pitched into the void for all he knows
about its destiny. He might be described almost
as the primitive economic cave-man, the darkness
of his cave unillumined by any ray of general
principles. As he is obstructed by the traders in
a general vision of production other than his

own, so he is obstructed by these dealers in a general vision of the final markets for his produce. His reading is limited to the local papers, and these, following the example of the modern press, carefully eliminate serious thought as likely to deprive them of readers. But Patrick, for all his economic backwardness, has a soul. The culture of the Gaelic poets and story-tellers, while not often actually remembered, still lingers like a fragrance about his mind. He lives and moves and has his being in the loveliest nature, the skies over him ever cloudy like an opal ; and the mountains flow across his horizon in wave on wave of amethyst and pearl. He has the unconscious depth of character of all who live and labour much in the open air, in constant fellowship with the great companions—with the earth and the sky and the fire in the sky. We ponder over Patrick, his race and his country, brooding whether there is the seed of a Pericles in Patrick's loins. Could we carve an Attica out of Ireland ?

Before Patrick can become the father of a Pericles, before Ireland can become an Attica, Patrick must be led out of his economic cave : his low cunning in barter must be expanded into a knowledge of economic law ; his fanatical concentration on his family—begotten by the isolation and individualism of his life—be sublimed into national affections ; his unconscious depths be sounded, his feeling for beauty be awakened by contact with some of the great literature of the world. His mind is virgin soil, and we may hope that, like all virgin soil, it will be immensely fruitful when it is cultivated. How does the policy of co-working make Patrick pass away from his old self? We can imagine him as a member of a committee getting hints of a strange doctrine called science from his creamery manager. He hears about bacteria, and these dark invisibles replace, as the cause of bad butter-making, the wicked fairies of his childhood. Watching this manager of his society he learns a new respect for the man of special or expert knowledge. Discussing the business of his association with other members he becomes something of a practical economist. He knows now where his produce goes. He learns that he has to compete with Americans, Europeans, and Colonials—indeed with the farmers of the world, hitherto concealed from his view by a mountainous mass of middlemen. He begins to be interested in these countries and reads about them. He becomes a citizen of the world. His horizon is no longer bounded by the wave of blue hills beyond his village. The roar of the planet begins to sound in his ears. What is more important is that he is becoming a better citizen of his own country. He meets on his committee his religious and political opponents, not now discussing differences but identities of interest. He also meets the delegates from other societies in district conferences or general congresses, and those who meet thus find their interests are common, and a new friendliness springs up between North and South, and local co-operation leads on to national co-operation. The best intellects, the best business men in the societies, meet in the big centres as directors of federations and wholesales, and they get an all-Ireland view of their industry. They see the parish from the point of view of the nation, and this vision does not desert them when they go back to the parish. They realize that their interests are bound up with national interests, and they discuss legislation and administration with practical knowledge. Eyes getting keener every year, minds getting more instructed, begin to concentrate on Irish public men. Presently Patrick will begin to seek for men of special knowledge and administrative ability to manage Irish affairs. Ireland has hitherto been to Patrick a legend, a being mentioned in romantic poetry, a little dark Rose, a mystic maiden, a vague but very simple creature of tears and aspirations and revolts. He now knows what a multitudinous being a nation is, and in contact with its complexities Patrick's politics take on a new gravity, thoughtfulness, and intellectual character.

Under the influence of these associations and the ideas pervading them our typical Irish farmer gets drawn out of his agricultural sleep of the ages, developing rapidly as mummy-wheat brought out of the tomb and exposed to the eternal forces which stimulate and bring to life. I have taken an individual as a type, and described the original circumstance and illustrated the playing of the

new forces on his mind.   It is the only way we
can create a social order which will fit our character
as the glove fits the hand.   Reasoning solely
from abstract principles about justice, democracy,
the rights of man and the like, often leads us into
futilities, if not into dangerous political experi-
ments.   We have to see our typical citizen in
clear light, realize his deficiencies, ignorance, and
incapacity, and his possibilities of development,
before we can wisely enlarge his boundaries.   The
centre of the citizen is the home.   His circumference ought to be the nation.   The vast majority
of Irish citizens rarely depart from their centre,
or establish those vital relations with their circumference which alone entitle them to the privileges of citizenship, and enable them to act with
political wisdom.   An emotional relationship is
not enough.   Our poets sang of a united Ireland,
but the unity they sang of was only a metaphor.
It mainly meant separation from another country.
In that imaginary unity men were really separate
from   each   other.   Individualism,   fanatically
centring itself on its family and family interests,
interfered on public boards to do jobs in the
interests of its kith and kin.   The co-operative
movement connects with living links the home,
the centre of Patrick's being, to the nation, the
circumference of his being.   It connects him with
the nation through membership of a national
movement, not for the political purposes which
call on him for a vote once every few years, but
for economic purposes which affect him in the

course of his daily occupations. This organization of the most numerous section of the Irish democracy into co-operative associations, as it develops and embraces the majority, will tend to make the nation one and indivisible and conscious of its unity. The individual, however meagre his natural endowment of altruism, will be led to think of his community as himself; because his income, his social pleasures even, depend on the success of the local and national organizations with which he is connected. The small farmers of former times pursued a petty business of barter and haggle, fighting for their own hand against half the world about them. The farmers of the new generation will grow up in a social order, where all the transactions which narrowed their fathers' hearts will be communal and national enterprises. How much that will mean in a change of national character we can hardly realize, we who were born in an Ireland where petty individualism was rampant, and where every child had it borne in upon him that it had to fight its own corner in the world, where the whole atmosphere about it tended to the hardening of the personality.

We may hope and believe that this transformation of the social order will make men truly citizens, thinking in terms of the nation, identifying national with personal interests. For those who believe there is a divine seed in humanity, this atmosphere, if any, they may hope will promote the swift blossoming of the divine seed which

in the past, in favourable airs, has made beauty
or grandeur or spirituality the characteristics
of ancient civilizations in Greece, in Egypt, and
in India.   No one can work for his race without
the hope that the highest, or more than the
highest, humanity has reached will be within
reach of his race also.   We are all laying foundations in dark places, putting the rough-hewn
stones together in our civilizations, hoping for
the lofty edifice which will arise later and make
all the work glorious.   And in Ireland, for all
its melancholy history, we may, knowing that we
are human, dream that there is the seed of a
Pericles in Patrick's loins, and that we might
carve an Attica out of Ireland.

V

In Ireland we must of necessity give special thought to the needs of the countryman, because our main industry is agriculture. We have few big cities. Our great cities are almost all outside our own borders. They are across the Atlantic. The surplus population of the countryside do not go to our own towns but emigrate. The exodus does not enrich Limerick or Galway, but New York. The absorption of life in great cities is really the danger which most threatens the modern State with a decadence of its humanity. In the United States, even in Canada, hardly has the pioneer made a home in the wilderness when his sons and his daughters are allured by the distant gleam of cities beyond the plains. In England the countryside has almost ceased to be the mother of men—at least a fruitful mother. We are face to face in Ireland with this problem, with no crowded and towering cities to disguise the emptiness of the fields. It is not a problem which lends itself to legislative solution. Whether there be fair rents or no rents at all, the child of the peasant, yearning for a fuller life, goes where

life is at its fullest. We all desire life, and that
we might have it more abundantly,—the peasant
as much as the mystic thirsting for infinite being,
—and in rural Ireland the needs of life have
been neglected.

The chief problem of Ireland—the problem
which every nation in greater or lesser measure
will have to solve—is how to enable the countryman, without journeying, to satisfy to the full his
economic, social, intellectual, and spiritual needs.
We have made some tentative efforts. The long
war over the land, which resulted in the trans-
ference of the land from landlord to cultivator,
has advanced us part of the way, but the Land
Acts offered no complete solution. We were
assured by hot enthusiasts of the magic of pro-
prietorship, but Ireland has not tilled a single
acre more since the Land Acts were passed. Our
rural exodus continued without any Moses to
lead us to Jerusalems of our own. At every
station boys and girls bade farewell to their
friends ; and hardly had the train steamed out
when the natural exultation of adventure made
the faces of the emigrants glow because the world
lay before them, and human appetites the country
could not satisfy were to be appeased at the end
of the journey.

How can we make the countryside in Ireland
a place which nobody would willingly emigrate
from ? When we begin to discuss this problem
we soon make the discovery that neither in the
new world nor the old has there been much first-

class thinking on the life of the countryman. This will be apparent if we compare the quality of thought which has been devoted to the problems of the city State, or the constitution of widespread dominions, from the days of Solon and Aristotle down to the time of Alexander Hamilton, and compare it with the quality of thought which has been brought to bear on the problems of the rural community.

On the labours of the countryman depend the whole strength and health, nay, the very existence of society, yet, in almost every country, politics, economics, and social reform are urban products, and the countryman gets only the crumbs which fall from the political table. It seems to be so in Canada and the States even, countries which we in Europe for long regarded as mainly agricultural. It seems only yesterday to the imagination that they were colonized, and yet we find the Minister of Agriculture in Canada announcing a decline in the rural population in Eastern Canada. As children sprung from the loins of diseased parents manifest at an early age the same defects in their constitution, so Canada and the States, though in their national childhood, seem already threatened by the same disease from which classic Italy perished, and whose ravages to-day make Great Britain seem to the acute diagnoser of political health to be like a fruit—ruddy without, but eaten away within and rotten at the core. One expects disease in old age, but not in youth. We expect young countries to sow their wild oats, to have a few revolutions before they settle down to national housekeeping ; but we are not moved by these troubles—the result of excessive energy—as we are by symptoms of premature decay. No nation can be regarded as unhealthy when a virile peasantry, contented with rural employments, however discontented with other things, exists on its soil. The disease which has attacked our great populations here and in America is a discontent with rural life. Nothing which has been done hitherto seems able to promote content. It is true, indeed, that science has gone out into the fields, but the labours of the chemist, the bacteriologist, and the mechanical engineer are not enough to ensure health. What is required is the art of the political thinker, the imagination which creates a social order and adjusts it to human needs. The physician who understands the general laws of human health is of more importance to us here than the specialist. The genius of rural life has not yet appeared. We have no fundamental philosophy concerning it, but we have treasures of political wisdom dealing with humanity as a social organism in the city States or as great nationalities. It might be worth while inquiring to what extent the wisdom of a Solon, an Aristotle, a Rousseau, or an Alexander Hamilton might be applied to the problem of the rural community. After all, men are not so completely changed in character by their rural environment that their social needs do not, to a large extent, coincide with the needs

D

of the townsman. They cannot be considered
as creatures of a different species. Yet statesmen
who have devoted so much thought to the constitution of empires and the organization of great
cities, who have studied their psychology, have
almost always treated the rural problem purely
as an economic problem, as if agriculture was a
business only and not a life.

Our great nations and widespread empires
arose in a haphazard fashion out of city States
and scattered tribal communities. The fusion
of these into larger entities, which could act
jointly for offence or defence, so much occupied
the thoughts of their rulers that everything else
was subordinated to it. As a result, the details
of our modern civilizations are all wrong. There
is an intensive life at a few great political or industrial centres, and wide areas where there is
stagnation and decay. Stagnation is most obvious
in rural districts. It is so general that it has
been often assumed that there was something
inherent in rural life which made the countryman
slow in mind as his own cattle. But this is not
so, as I think can be shown. There is no reason
why as intense, intellectual, and progressive a
life should not be possible in the country as in
the towns. The real reason for the stagnation
is that the country population is not organized.
We often hear the expression, " the rural community," but where do we find rural communities ?
There are rural populations, but that is altogether
a different thing. The word " community "

implies an association of people having common
interests and common possessions, bound together by laws and regulations which express
these common interests and ideals, and define the
relation of the individual to the community.   Our
rural populations are no more closely connected,
for the most part, than the shifting sands on the
seashore.   Their life is almost entirely individualistic.   There are personal friendships, of course,
but few economic or social partnerships.   Everybody pursues his own occupation without regard
to the occupation of his neighbours.   If a man
emigrates it does not affect the occupation of
those who farm the land all about him.   They
go on ploughing and digging, buying and selling,
just as before.   They suffer no perceptible
economic loss by the departure of half-a-dozen
men from the district.   A true community would,
of course, be affected by the loss of its members.
A co-operative society, if it loses a dozen members,
the milk of their cows, their orders for fertilizers,
seeds, and feeding-stuffs, receives serious injury
to its prosperity.   There is a minimum of trade
below which its business cannot fall without
bringing about a complete stoppage of its work
and an inability to pay its employees.   That is
the difference between a community and an
unorganized population.   In the first the interests
of the community make a conscious and direct
appeal to the individual, and the community,
in its turn, rapidly develops an interest in the
welfare of the member.   In the second, the

interest of the individual in the community is only sentimental, and as there is no organization, the community lets its units slip away or disappear without comment or action. We had true rural communities in ancient Ireland, though the organization was rather military than economic. But the members of a clan had common interests. They owned the land in common. It was a common interest to preserve it intact. It was to their interest to have a numerous membership of the clan, because it made it less liable to attack. Men were drawn by the social order out of merely personal interests into a larger life. In their organizations they were unconsciously groping, as all human organizations are, towards the final solidarity of humanity—the federation of the world.

Well, these old rural communities disappeared. The greater organizations of nation or empire regarded the smaller communities jealously in the past, and broke them up and gathered all the strings of power into capital cities. The result was a growth of the State, with a local decay of civic, patriotic, or public feeling, ending in bureaucracies and State departments, where paid officials, devoid of intimacy with local needs, replaced the services naturally and voluntarily rendered in an earlier period. The rural population, no longer existing as a rural community, sank into stagnation. There was no longer a common interest, a social order turning their minds to larger than individual ends. Where

feudalism was preserved, the feudal chief, if the
feeling of *noblesse oblige* was strong, might act
as a centre of progress, but where this was lacking
social decay set in.   The difficulty of moving
the countryman, which has become traditional,
is not due to the fact that he lives in the country,
but to the fact that he lives in an unorganized
society.   If in a city people want an art gallery
or public baths or recreation grounds, there is
a machinery which can be set in motion ; there
are corporations and urban councils which can
be approached.   If public opinion is evident—
and it is easy to organize public opinion in a
town—the city representatives will consider the
scheme, and if they approve and it is within their
power as a council, they are able to levy rates to
finance the art gallery, recreation grounds, public
gardens, or whatever else.   Now let us go to a
country district where there is no organization.
It may be obvious to one or two people that the
place is perishing and the intelligence of its
humanity is decaying, lacking some centre of
life.   They want a village hall, but how is it to
be obtained ?   They begin talking about it to
this person or that.   They ask these people to
talk to their friends, and the ripples go out
weakening and widening for months, perhaps
for years.   I know of districts where this has
happened.   There are hundreds of parishes in
Ireland where one or two men want co-operative
societies or village halls or rural libraries.   They
discuss the matter with their neighbours, but

find a complete ignorance on the subject, and
consequent lethargy. There is no social organism with a central life to stir. Before enthusiasm
can be kindled there must be some knowledge.
The countryman reads little, and it is a long and
tedious business before enough people are excited
to bring them to the point of appealing to some
expert to come in and advise.

More changes often take place within a dozen
years after a co-operative society is first started
than have taken place for a century previous. I
am familiar with a district—in the north-west of
Ireland. It was a most wretchedly poor district.
The farmers were at the mercy of the gombeen
traders and the agricultural middlemen. Then
a dozen years ago a co-operative society was
formed. I am sure that the oldest inhabitant
would agree with me that more changes for the
better for farmers have taken place since the
co-operative society was started than he could
remember in all his previous life. The reign of
the gombeen man is over. The farmers control
their own buying and selling. Their organization markets for them the eggs and poultry. It
procures seeds, fertilizers, and domestic requirements. It turns the members' pigs into bacon.
They have a village hall and a woman's organization. They sell the products of the women's
industry. They have a co-operative band, social
gatherings, and concerts. They have spread out
into half-a-dozen parishes, going southward and
westward with their propaganda, and in half-a-

dozen years, in all that district, previously without organization, there will be well-organized farmers' guilds, concentrating in themselves the trade of their district, having meeting-places where the opinion of the members can be taken, having a machinery, committees, and executive officers to carry out whatever may be decided on : and having funds, or profits, the joint property of the community, which can be drawn upon to finance their undertakings. It ought to be evident what a tremendous advantage it is to farmers in a district to have such organizations, what a lever they can pull and control. I have tried to indicate the difference between a rural population and a rural community, between a people loosely knit together by the vague ties of a common latitude and longitude, and people who are closely knit together in an association and who form a true social organism, a true rural community, where the general will can find expression and society is malleable to the general will. I assert that there never can be any progress in rural districts or any real prosperity without such farmers' organizations or guilds. Wherever rural prosperity is reported of any country inquire into it, and it will be found that it depends on rural organization. Wherever there is rural decay, if it is inquired into, it will be found that there was a rural population but no rural community, no organization, no guild to promote common interests and unite the countrymen in defence of them.

VI

I⊤ is the business of the rural reformer to create
the rural community. It is the antecedent to
the creation of a rural civilization. We have to
organize the community so that it can act as one
body. It is not enough to organize farmers in
a district for one purpose only—in a credit
society, a dairy society, a fruit society, a bacon
factory, or in a co-operative store. All these may
be and must be beginnings ; but if they do not
develop and absorb all rural business into their
organization they will have little effect on character. No true social organism will have been
created. If people unite as consumers to buy
together they only come into contact on this
one point ; there is no general identity of interest.
If co-operative societies are specialized for this
purpose or that—as in Great Britain or on the
Continent—to a large extent the limitation of
objects prevents a true social organism from being
formed. The latter has a tremendous effect on
human character. The specialized society only
develops economic efficiency. The evolution of
humanity beyond its present level depends ab-

solutely on its power to unite and create true social organisms. Life in its higher forms is only possible because of the union of myriads of tiny lives to form a larger being, which manifests will, intelligence, affection, and the spiritual powers. The life of the amœba or any other uni-cellular organism is low compared with the life in more complex organisms, like the ant or bee. Man is the most highly developed living organism on the globe ; yet his body is built up of in-numerable cells, each of which might be described as a tiny life in itself. But they are built up in man into such a close association that what affects one part of the body affects all. The pain which the whole being feels if a part is wounded, if one cell in the human body is hurt, should prove that to the least intelligent. The nervous system binds all the tiny cells together, and they form in this totality a being infinitely higher, more powerful, than the cells which compose it. They are able to act together and achieve things im-possible to the separated cells. Now humanity to-day is, to some extent, like the individual cells. It is trying to unite together to form a real organism, which will manifest higher qualities of life than the individual can manifest. But very few of the organisms created by society enable the individual to do this. The joint-stock companies or capitalist concerns which bring men together at this work or that do not yet make them feel their unity. Existence under a common government effects this still less. Our

modern states have not yet succeeded in building
up that true national life where all feel the identity
of interest ; where the true civic or social feeling
is engendered and the individual bends all his
efforts to the success of the community on which
his own depends ; where, in fact, the ancient
Greek conception of citizenship is realized, and
individuals are created who are ever conscious
of the identity of interest between themselves
and their race. In the old Greek civilizations
this was possible because their States were small,
indeed their ideal State contained no more
citizens than could be affected by the voice of a
single orator. Such small States, though they
produced the highest quality of life within themselves, are no longer possible as political entities.
We have to see whether we could not, within our
widespread nationalities, create communities by
economic means, where something of the same
sense of solidarity of interest might be engendered
and the same quality of life maintained. I am
greatly ambitious for the rural community. But
it is no use having mean ambitions. Unless
people believe the result of their labours will
result in their equalling or surpassing the best
that has been done elsewhere, they will never
get very far. We in Ireland are in quest of a
civilization. It is a great adventure, the building
up of a civilization—the noblest which could be
undertaken by any persons. It is at once the
noblest and the most practical of all enterprises,
and I can conceive of no greater exaltation for

the spirit of man than the feeling that his race
is acting nobly; and that all together are performing a service, not only to each other, but to
humanity and those who come after them, and
that their deeds will be remembered. It may
seem a grotesque juxtaposition of things essentially
different in character, to talk of national idealism
and then of farming, but it is not so. They are
inseparable. The national idealism which will
not go out into the fields and deal with the
fortunes of the working farmers is false idealism.
Our conception of a civilization must include,
nay, must begin with the life of the humblest,
the life of the average man or manual worker,
for if we neglect them we will build in sand. The
neglected classes will wreck our civilization.
The pioneers of a new social order must think
first of the average man in field or factory, and so
unite these and so inspire them that the noblest
life will be possible through their companionship.
If you will not offer people the noblest and best
they will go in search of it. Unless the countryside can offer to young men and women some
satisfactory food for soul as well as body, it will
fail to attract or hold its population, and they will
go to the already overcrowded towns; and the
lessening of rural production will affect production
in the cities and factories, and the problem of
the unemployed will get still keener. The
problem is not only an economic problem. It
is a human one. Man does not live by cash alone,
but by every gift of fellowship and brotherly

feeling society offers him. The final urgings
of men and women are towards humanity. Their
desires are for the perfecting of their own life,
and as Whitman says, where the best men and
women are there the great city stands, though it
is only a village. It is one of the illusions of
modern materialistic thought to suppose that as
high a quality of life is not possible in a village as
in a great city, and it ought to be one of the aims
of rural reformers to dissipate this fallacy, and
to show that it is possible—not indeed to concentrate wealth in country communities as in the
cities—but that it is possible to bring comfort
enough to satisfy any reasonable person, and to
create a society where there will be intellectual
life and human interests. We will hear little
then of the rural exodus. The country will
retain and increase its population and productive-
ness. Like attracts like. Life draws life to
itself. Intellect awakens intellect, and the
country will hold its own tug for tug with the
towns.

Now it may be said I have talked a long while
round and round the rural community, but I
have not suggested how it is to be created. I am
coming to that. It really cannot be created. It
is a natural growth when the right seed is planted.
Co-operation is the seed. Let us consider Ireland.
Twenty-five years ago there was not a single
co-operative society in the country. Individualism was the mode of life. Every farmer manu-
factured and sold as seemed best in his eyes. It

was generally the worst possible way he could have
chosen.   Then came Sir Horace Plunkett and
his   colleagues,   preaching   co-operation.   A
creamery was established here, an agricultural
society there, and having planted the ideas it was
some time before the economic expert could
decide whether they were planted in fertile soil.
But that question was decided many years ago.
The co-operative society, started for whatever
purpose originally, is an omnivorous feeder, and
it exercises a magnetic influence on all agricultural
activities ;   so that we now have societies which
buy milk, manufacture and sell butter, deal in
poultry and eggs, cure bacon, provide fertilizers,
feeding-stuffs, seeds, and machinery for their
members, and even cater for every requirement
of the farmer's household.   This magnetic power
of attracting and absorbing to themselves the
various rural activities which the properly constituted co-operative societies have, makes them
develop rapidly, until in the course of a decade
or a generation there is created a real social
organism, where the members buy together,
manufacture together, market together, where
finally their entire interests are bound up with
the interests of the community.   I believe in
half a century the whole business of rural Ireland
will be done co-operatively.   This is not a wild
surmise, for we see exactly the same process going
on in Denmark, Germany, Italy, and every
country where the co-operative seed was planted.
Let us suppose that in a generation all the rural

industries are organized on co-operative lines, what kind of a community should we expect to find as the result ? How would its members live ? what would be their relations to one another and their community ? The agricultural scientist is making great discoveries. The mechanical engineer goes from one triumph to another. The chemist already could work wonders in our fields if there was a machinery for him to work through. We cannot foretell the developments in each branch, but we can see clearly that the organized community can lay hold of discoveries and inventions which the individual farmer cannot. It is little for the co-operative society to buy expensive threshing sets and let its members have the use of them, but the individual farmer would have to save a long time before he could raise several hundred pounds. The society is a better buyer than the individual. It can buy things the individual cannot buy. It is a better producer also. The plant for a creamery is beyond the individual farmer ; but our organized farmers in Ireland, small though they are, find it no trouble to erect and equip a creamery with plant costing two thousand pounds. The organized rural community of the future will generate its own electricity at its central buildings, and run not only its factories and other enterprises by this power, but will supply light to the houses of its members and also mechanical power to run machinery on the farm. One of our Irish societies already supplies electric light for the town it works in.   In the organized rural community the eggs, milk, poultry, pigs, cattle, grain, and wheat produced on the farm and not consumed, or required for further agricultural production, will automatically be delivered to the co-operative business centre of the district, where the manager of the dairy will turn the milk into butter or cheese, and the skim milk will be returned to feed the community's pigs.   The poultry and egg department will pack and dispatch the fowl and eggs to market. The mill will grind the corn and return it ground to the member, or there may be a co-operative bakery to which some of it may go.   The pigs will be dealt with in the abattoir, sent as fresh pork to the market or be turned into bacon to feed the members.   We may be certain that any intelligent rural community will try to feed itself first, and will only sell the surplus.   It will realize that it will be unable to buy any food half as good as the food it produces.   The community will hold in common all the best machinery too expensive for the members to buy individually.   The agricultural labourers will gradually become skilled mechanics, able to direct threshers, binders, diggers, cultivators, and new implements we have no conception of now.   They will be members of the society, sharing in its profits in proportion to their wages, even as the farmer will in proportion to his trade. The co-operative community will have its own carpenters, smiths, mechanics, employed in its workshop at repairs or in making those things which can profitably be made locally.   There may be a laundry where the washing—a heavy burden for the women—will be done : for we may be sure that every scrap of power generated will be utilized.   One happy invention after another will come to lighten the labour of life. There will be, of course, a village hall with a library and gymnasium, where the boys and girls will be made straight, athletic, and graceful.   In the evenings, when the work of the day is done, if we went into the village hall we would find a dance going on or perhaps a concert.   There might be a village choir or band.   There would be a committee-room where the council of the community would meet once a week ;   for their enterprises would have grown, and the business of such a parish community might easily be over one hundred thousand pounds, and would require constant thought.   There would be no slackness on the part of the council in attending, because their fortunes would depend on their communal enterprises, and they would have to consider reports from the managers and officials of the various departments.   The co-operative community would be a busy place.   In years when the society was exceptionally prosperous, and earned larger profits than usual on its trade, we should expect to find discussions in which all the members would join as to the use to be made of these profits : whether they should be altogether divided or what portion of them should be devoted to some public purpose. We may be certain that there would be animated discussions, because a real solidarity of feeling would have arisen and a pride in the work of the community engendered, and they would like to be able to outdo the good work done by the neighbouring communities.

One might like to endow the village school with a chemical laboratory, another might want to decorate the village hall with reproductions of famous pictures, another might suggest removing all the hedges and planting the roadsides and lanes with gooseberry bushes, currant bushes, and fruit trees, as they do in some German communes to-day. There would be eloquent pleadings for this or that, for an intellectual heat would be engendered in this human hive, and there would be no more illiterates or ignoramuses. The teaching in the village school would be altered to suit the new social order, and the children of the community would, we may be certain, be instructed in everything necessary for the intelligent conduct of the communal business. The spirit of rivalry between one community and another, which exists to-day between neighbouring creameries, would excite the imagination of the members, and the organized community would be as swift to act as the unorganized community is slow to act. Intelligence would be organized as well as business. The women would have their own associations, to promote domestic economy, care of the sick and the children. The girls would have their own

E

industries of embroidery, crochet, lace, dress-making, weaving, spinning, or whatever new industries the awakened intelligence of women may devise and lay hold of as the peculiar labour of their sex. The business of distribution of the produce and industries of the community would be carried on by great federations, which would attend to export and sale of the products of thousands of societies. Such communities would be real social organisms. The individual would be free to do as he willed, but he would find that communal activity would be infinitely more profitable than individual activity. We would then have a real democracy carrying on its own business, and bringing about reforms without pleading to, or begging of, the State, or intriguing with or imploring the aid of political middlemen to get this, that, or the other done for them. They would be self-respecting, because they would be self-helping above all things. The national councils and meetings of national federations would finally become the real Parliament of the nation ; for wherever all the economic power is centred, there also is centred all the political power. And no politician would dare to interfere with the organized industry of a nation.

There is nothing to prevent such communities being formed. They would be a natural growth once the seed was planted. We see such communities naturally growing up in Ireland, with perhaps a little stimulus from outside from rural

reformers and social enthusiasts. If this ideal
of the organized rural community is accepted
there will be difficulties, of course, and enemies
to be encountered. The agricultural middleman
is a powerful person. He will rage furiously.
He will organize all his forces to keep the farmers
in subjection, and to retain his peculiar functions
of fleecing the farmer as producer and the general
public as consumer. But unless we are determined to eliminate the middleman in agriculture
we will fail to effect anything worth while attempt-
ing. I would lay down certain fundamental
propositions which, I think, should be accepted
without reserve as a basis of reform. First,
that the farmers must be organized to have
complete control over all the business connected
with their industry. Dual control is intolerable.
Agriculture will never be in a satisfactory condition if the farmer is relegated to the position of a
manual worker on his land ; if he is denied the
right of a manufacturer to buy the raw materials
of his industry on trade terms ; if other people
are to deal with his raw materials, his milk,
cream, fruit, vegetables, live stock, grain, and
other produce ; and if these capitalist middle
agencies are to manufacture the farmers' raw
material into butter, bacon, or whatever else :
are to do all the marketing and export, paying
farmers what they please on the one hand, and
charging the public as much as they can on the
other hand. The existence of these middle
agencies is responsible for a large proportion of

the increased cost of living, which is the most acute domestic problem of modern industrial communities. They have too much power over the farmer, and are too expensive a luxury for the consumer. It would be very unbusinesslike for any country to contemplate the permanenc. in national life of a class whose personal interests are always leading them to fleece both producer and consumer alike. So the first fundamental idea for reformers to get into their minds is that farmers, through their own co-operative organizations, must control the entire business connected with agriculture. There will not be so much objection to co-operative sale as to co-operative purchase by the farmers. But one is as necessary as the other. We must bear in mind, what is too often forgotten, that farmers are manufacturers, and as such are entitled to buy the raw materials for their industry at wholesale prices. Every other kind of manufacturer in the world gets trade terms when he buys. Those who buy—not to consume, but to manufacture and sell again—get their requirements at wholesale terms in every country in the world. If a publisher of books is approached by a bookseller he gives that bookseller trade terms, because he buys to sell again. If I, as a private individual, want one of those books I must pay the full retail price. Even the cobbler, the carpenter, the solitary artist, get trade terms. The farmer, who is as much a manufacturer as the shipbuilder, or the factory proprietor, is as much entitled to trade terms when he buys the raw materials for his industry. His seeds, fertilizers, ploughs, implements, cake, feeding-stuffs are the raw materials of his industry, which he uses to produce wheat, beef, mutton, pork, or whatever else ; and, in my opinion, there should be no differentiation between the farmer when he buys and any other kind of manufacturer. Is it any wonder that agriculture decays in countries where the farmers are expected to buy at retail prices and sell at wholesale prices ? We must not, to save any friction, sell the rights of farmers. The second proposition I lay down is that this necessary organization work among the farmers must be carried on by an organizing body which is entirely controlled by those interested in agriculture—farmers and their friends. To ask the State or a State Department to undertake this work is to ask a body influenced and often controlled by powerful capitalists, and middle agencies which it should be the aim of the organization to eliminate. The State can, without obstruction from any quarter, give farmers a technical education in the science of farming ; but let it once interfere with business, and a horde of angry interests set to work to hamper and limit by every possible means ; and compromises on matters of principle, where no compromise ought to be permitted, are almost inevitable.

A voluntary organizing body like the Irish Agricultural Organization Society, which was the first to attempt the co-operative organization of farmers in these islands, is the only kind of body which can pursue its work fearlessly, unhampered by alien interests. The moment such a body declares its aims, its declaration automatically separates the sheep from the goats, and its enemies are outside and not inside. The organizing body should be the heart and centre of the farmers' movement, and if the heart has its allegiance divided, its work will be poor and ineffectual, and very soon the farmers will fall away from it to follow more single-hearted leaders. No trades union would admit representatives of capitalist employers on its committee, and no organization of farmers should allow alien or opposing interest on their councils to clog the machine or betray the cause. This is the best advice I can give reformers. It is the result of many years' experience in this work. An industry must have the same freedom of movement as an individual in possession of all his powers. An industry divided against itself can no more prosper than a household divided against itself. By the means I have indicated the farmers can become the masters of their own destinies, just as the urban workers can, I think, by steadfastly applying the same principles, emancipate themselves. It is a battle in which, as in all other battles, numbers and moral superiority united are irresistible ; and in the Irish struggle to create a true democracy numbers and the power of moral ideas are with the insurgents.

VII

It would be a bitter reproach on the household
of our nation if there were any unconsidered,
who were left in poverty and without hope and
outside our brotherhood. We have not yet
considered the agricultural labourer—the proletarian of the countryside. His is, in a sense,
the most difficult problem of any. The basis of
economic independence in his industry is the
possession of land, and that is not readily to be
obtained in Ireland. The earth does not upheave
itself from beneath the sea and add new land to
that already above water in response to our need
for it. Yet I would not pass away from the rural
labourer without, however inadequately, indicat-
ing some curves in his future evolution. These
labourers are not in Ireland half so numerous as
farmers, for it is a country of small holdings,
where the farmer and his family are themselves
labourers. Labour is badly paid, and, owing
to the lack of continuous cropping of the land,
it is often left without employment at seasons
when employment is most needed. No class
which is taken up to-day and dropped to-morrow

will in modern times remain long in a country.
Employers often act as if they thought labour
could be taken up and laid down again like a pipe
and tobacco.   None have contributed so to
thicken the horde of Irish exiles as the rural
labourers.   Three hundred thousand of them
in less than my lifetime have left the fields of
Ireland for the factories of the new world.   Yet
I can only rejoice if Irishmen, who are badly
dealt with in their motherland, find an ampler
life and a more prosperous career in another land.
A wage of ten or eleven shillings a week will
bind none but the unaspiring lout to his country.
But I would like to make Ireland a land which,
because of the human kindness in it, few would
willingly leave.   The agricultural proletarian,
like all other labour, should be organized in a
national union.   That is bound to come.   But
the agricultural labourer should, I think, no more
than labour in the cities, make the raising of
wages his main or only object.   He should rather
strive to make himself economically independent ;
or, in the alternative, seek for status by integration
into the co-operative communities of farmers by
becoming a member, and by pressing for permanent employment by the community rather
than casual employment by the individual.   Agricultural labour undoubtedly will have to struggle
for better remuneration.   Yet it has to be remembered that agriculture is a protean industry.
It is not like mining, where the colliery produces
coal and nothing but coal, and where the miners

have a practical monopoly of supply. If miners
are dissatisfied with wages and are well organized
they can enforce their terms, and the colliery
owners may almost be indifferent, because they
can charge the increased cost of working to the
public. But agriculture, as I said, is protean
and changes its forms perpetually. If tillage
does not pay this year, next year the farmer may
have his land in grass. He reverts to the cheapest
methods of farming when prices are low, or labour
asks a wage which the farmer believes it would be
unprofitable to pay. In this way pressure on
the farmer for extra wages might result in two
men being employed to herd cows where a dozen
men were previously employed at tillage. The
farmer cannot easily—as the mine-owner—unload
his burden on the general public by the increase
of prices. There are many difficulties, which
seem almost insoluble, if we propose to ourselves
to integrate the rural labourer into the general
economic life of the country by making him a
partner in the industry he works on. But what
I hope for most is first that the natural evolution
of the rural community, and the concentration of
individual manufacture, purchase and sale, into
communal enterprises, will lead to a very large
co-operative ownership of expensive machinery,
which will necessitate the communal employment
of labour. If this takes place, as I hope it will,
the rural labourer, instead of being a manual
worker using primitive implements, will have
the status of a skilled mechanic employed per-

manently by a co-operative community. He should be a member of the society which employs him, and in the division of profits receive in proportion to his wage, as the farmers in proportion to their trade.

A second policy open to agricultural labour when it becomes organized is the policy of collective farming. This I believe will and ought to receive attention in the future. Co-operative societies of agricultural labourers in Italy, Roumania, and elsewhere have rented land from landowners. They then reallotted the land among themselves for individual cultivation, or else worked it as a true co-operative enterprise with labour, purchase and sale all communal enterprises, with considerable benefit to the members. We can well understand a landowner not liking to divide his land into small holdings, with all the attendant troubles which in Ireland beset a landlord with small farmers on his estate. But I think landowners in Ireland could be found who would rent land to a co-operative society of skilled labourers who approached the owner with a well-thought-out scheme. The success of one colony would lead to others being started, as happened in Italy.

This solution of the problem of agricultural labour will be forced on us for many reasons. The economic effects of the great European War, the burden of debt piled on the participating nations, will make Ministers shun schemes of reform involving a large use of national credit, or which would increase the sum of national obligations. Land purchase on the old terms I believe cannot be continued. Yet we will demand the intensive cultivation of the national estate, and increased production of wealth, especially of food-stuffs. The large area of agricultural land laid down for pasture is not so productive as tilled land, does not sustain so large a population, and there will be more reasons in the future than in the past for changing the character of farming in these areas. The policy of collective farming offers a solution, and whatever Government is in power should facilitate the settlement of men in co-operative colonies and provide expert instructors as managers for the first year or two if necessary. Such a policy would not be so expensive as land purchase, and with fair rent fixed, hundreds of thousands of people could be planted comfortably on the land in Ireland and produce more wealth from it than could ever be produced from grazing lands, and agricultural workers and the sons of farmers who now emigrate could become economically independent.

I hope, also, that farmers, becoming more brotherly as their own enterprises flourish, will welcome labourers into their co-operative stores, credit banks, poultry and bee-keeping societies, and allow them the benefits of cheap purchase, cheap credit, and of efficient marketing of whatever the labourer may produce on his allotment. The growth of national conscience and the spirit of human brotherhood, and a feeling of shame that any should be poor and neglected in the national household, will be needed to bring the rural labourer into the circle of national life, and make him a willing worker in the general scheme. If farmers will not, on their part, advance towards their labourers and bring them into the co-operative community, then labour will be organized outside their community and will be hostile, and will be always brooding and scheming to strike a blow when the farmer can least bear it,— when the ground must be tilled or the harvest gathered. And this, if peace cannot be made, will result in a still greater decline of tillage and the continued flight of the rural labourers, and the increase of the area in grass, and the impoverishing of human life and national well-being.

Some policy to bring contentment to small holders and rural workers must be formulated and acted upon. Agriculture is of more importance to the nation than industry. Our task is to truly democratize civilization and its agencies; to spread in widest commonalty culture, comfort, intelligence, and happiness, and to give to the average man those things which in an earlier age were the privileges of a few. The country is the fountain of the life and health of a race. And this organization of the country people into co-operative communities will educate them and make them citizens in the true sense of the word, that is, people continually conscious of their identity of interest with those about them.

It is by this conscious sense of solidarity of interest, which only the organized co-operative community can engender in modern times, that the higher achievements of humanity become possible. Religion has created this spirit at times—witness the majestic cathedrals the Middle Ages raised to manifest their faith.   Political organization engendered the passion of citizenship in the Greek States, and the Parthenon and a host of lordly buildings crowned the hills and uplifted and filled with pride the heart of the citizen.   Our big countries, our big empires, and republics, for all their military strength and science, and the wealth which science has made it possible for man to win, do not create citizenship because of the loose organization of society ; because individualism is rampant, and men, failing to understand the intricacies of the vast and complex life of their country, fall back on private life and private ambitions, and leave the honour of their country and the making of laws and the application of the national revenues to a class of professional politicians, in their turn in servitude to the interests which supply party funds, and so we find corruption in high places and cynicism in the people.   It is necessary for the creation of citizens, for the building up of a noble national life, that the social order should be so organized that this sense of interdependence will be constantly felt.   It is also necessary for the preservation of the physical health and beauty of our race that our people should live

more in the country and less in the cities. I
believe it would be an excellent thing for humanity
if its civilization could be based on rural industry
mainly and not on urban industry. More and
more men and women in our modern civilization
drift out of Nature, out of sweet air, health,
strength, beauty, into the cities, where in the third
generation there is a rickety population, mean in
stature, vulgar or depraved in character, with
the image of the devil in mind and matter more
than the image of Deity. Those who go like it
at first; but city life is like the roll spoken of by
the prophet, which was sweet in the mouth but
bitter in the belly. The first generation are
intoxicated by the new life, but in the third generation the cord is cut which connected them with
Nature, the Great Mother, and life shrivels up,
sundered from the source of life. Is there any
prophet, any statesman, any leader, who will—
as Moses once led the Israelites out of the
Egyptian bondage—excite the human imagination
and lead humanity back to Nature, to sunlight,
starlight, earth-breath, sweet air, beauty, gaiety,
and health ? Is it impossible now to move
humanity by great ideas, as Mahomet fired his
dark hosts to forgetfulness of life ; or as Peter the
Hermit awakened Europe to a frenzy, so that it
hurried its hot chivalry across a continent to the
Holy Land ? Is not the earth mother of us all ?
Are not our spirits clothed round with the substance of earth ? Is it not from Nature we draw
life ? Do we not perish without sunlight and

fresh air ?   Let us have no breath of air and in
five minutes life is extinct.   Yet in the cities
there is a slow poisoning of life going on day by
day.   The lover of beauty may walk the streets
of London or any big city and may look into ten
thousand faces and see none that is lovely.   Is
not the return of man to a natural life on the earth
a great enough idea to inspire humanity ?   Is
not the idea of a civilization amid the green trees
and fields under the smokeless sky alluring ?
Yes, but men say there is no intellectual life
working on the land.   No intellectual life when
man is surrounded by mystery and miracle !
When the mysterious forces which bring to birth
and life are yet undiscovered ; when the earth is
teeming with life, and the dumb brown lips of the
ridges are breathing mystery !   Is not the growth
of a tree from a tiny cell hidden in the earth as
provocative of thought as the things men learn
at the schools ?   Is not thought on these things
more interesting than the sophistries of the
newspapers ?   It is only in Nature, and by
thought on the problems of Nature, that our
intellect grows to any real truth and draws near
to the Mighty Mind which laid the foundations
of the world.

Our civilizations are a nightmare, a bad dream.
They have no longer the grandeur of Babylon or
Nineveh.   They grow meaner and meaner as they
grow more urbanized.   What could be more
depressing than the miles of poverty-stricken
streets around the heart of our modern cities ?

The memory lies on one " heavy as frost and deep almost as life." It is terrible to think of the children playing on the pavements ; the depletion of vitality, with artificial stimulus supplied from the flaring drink-shops. The spirit grows heavy as if death lay on it while it moves amid such things. And outside these places the clouds are flying overhead snowy and spiritual as of old, the sun is shining, the winds are blowing, the fields are green, the forests are murmuring leaf to leaf, but the magic that God made is unknown to these poor folk. The creation of a rural civilization is the greatest need of our time. It may not come in our days, but we can lay the foundations of it, preparing the way for the true prophet when he will come. The fight now is not to bring people back to the land, but to keep those who are on the land contented, happy, and prosperous. And we must begin by organizing them to defend what is left to them ; to take back, industry by industry, what was stolen from them. We must organize the country people into communities, for without some kind of communal life men hold no more together than the drifting sands by the seashore. There is a natural order in which men have instinctively grouped themselves from the dawn of time. It is as natural to them to do so as it is for bees to build their hexagonal cells. If we read the history of civilization we will find people in every land forming little clans co-operating together. Then the ambition of rulers or warriors breaks them up; the greed of powerful men puts an end to them. But, whether broken or not, the moment the rural dweller is left to himself he begins again, with nature prompting him, to form little clans—or nations rather—with his fellows, and it is there life has been happiest. We did this in ancient Ireland. The baronies whose names are on Irish land to-day and the counties are survivals of these old co-operative colonies, where the men owned the land together and elected their own leaders, and formed their own social order and engendered passionate loyalties and affections. It was so in every land under the sun. It was so in ancient India and in ancient Peru. The European farmers, and we in Ireland along with them, are beginning again the eternal task of building up a civilization in nature—the task so often disturbed, the labour so often destroyed. And it is with the hope that we in Ireland will build truly and nobly that I have put together these thoughts on the rural community.

VIII

WE may now consider the proletarian in our
cities. The worker in our modern world is the
subject of innumerable unapplied doctrines. The
lordliest things are predicated of him, which do
not affect in the least the relationship with him
of those who employ his labour. The ancient
wisdom, as it is recounted to him on God's day,
assures him of his immortality : that the divine
signature is over all his being, that in some way
he is co-related with the Eternal, that he is
fashioned in a likeness to It. He is a symbol
of God Himself. He is the child of Deity. His
life is Its very breath. The Habitations of
Eternity await his coming, and the divine event
to which he moves is the dwelling within him of
the Divine Mind, so that Deity may become his
very self. So proud a tale is told of him, and
when he wakens on the morrow after the day of
God he finds that none will pay him reverence.
He, the destined comrade of Seraphim and
Cherubim, is herded with other Children of the
King in fœtid slum and murky alleys, where the
devil hath his many mansions, where light and

air, the great purifiers, are already dimmed and
corrupted before they do him service. He is
insecure in the labour by which he lives. He
works to-day, and to-morrow he may be told
there is no further need for him, and his fate
and the fate of those dependent on him are not
remembered by those who dismissed him. If he
dies, leaving wife or children, the social order
makes but the most inhuman provision for them.
How ghastly is the brotherhood of the State for
its poor the workhouses declare, and our social
decrees which turn loving-kindness into official
acts and make legal and formal what should be
natural impulse and the overflow of the heart.
So great a disparity exists between spiritual
theory and the realities of the social order that it
might almost be said that spiritual theory has no
effect at all on our civilization, and its inhuman
contours seem softened at no point where we could
say, " Here the Spirit has mastery. Here God
possesses the world."

The imagination, following the worker in
our industrial system, sees him labouring without
security in his work, in despair, locked out, on
strike, living in slums, rarely with enough food
for health, bringing children into the world who
suffer from malnutrition from their earliest years,
a pauper when his days of strength are passed.
He dies in charitable institutions. Though his
labours are necessary he is yet not integrated into
the national economy. He has no share of his
own in the wealth of the nation. He cannot

claim work as a right from the holders of economic power, and this absolute dependence upon the autocrats of industry for a livelihood is the greatest evil of any, for it puts a spiritual curse on him and makes him in effect a slave. Instinctively he adopts a servile attitude to those who can sentence him and his children to poverty and hunger without trial or judgment by his peers. A hasty word, and he may be told to draw his pay and begone. The spiritual wrong done him by the social order is greater than the material ill, and that spiritual wrong is no less a wrong because generation after generation of workers have grown up and are habituated to it, and do not realize the oppression ; because in childhood circumstance and the black art of education alike conspire to make the worker humble in heart and to take the crown and sceptre from his spirit, and his elders are already tamed and obsequious.

Yet the workers in the modern world have great qualities. This class in great masses will continually make sacrifices for the sake of a principle. They have lived so long in the depths : many of them have reached the very end of all—the pain which is the utmost life can bear—and have in their character that fearlessness which comes from long endurance and familiarity with the worst hardships. I am a literary man, a lover of ideas, and I have found few people in my life who would sacrifice anything for a social principle ; but I will never forget the exultation

with which I realized in a great labour trouble,
when the masters of industry issued a document
asking men on peril of dismissal to swear never
to join a trades union, that there were thousands
of men in my own city who refused to obey,
though they had no membership or connection
with the objectionable association. Nearly all
the real manhood of Dublin I found was among
the obscure myriads who are paid from twenty
to thirty shillings a week. The men who will
sacrifice anything for brotherhood get rarer and
rarer above that limit of wealth. These men
would not sign away their freedom, their right
to choose their own heroes and their own ideals.
Most of them had no strike funds to fall back on.
They had wives and children depending on them.
Quietly and grimly they took through hunger
the path to the Heavenly City, yet nobody
praised them, no one put a crown upon their
brows. Beneath their rags and poverty there
was in these obscure men a nobility of spirit.
It is in these men and the men in the cabins in
the country that the hope of Ireland lies. The
poor have always helped each other, and it is
they who listen eagerly to the preachers of a social
order based on brotherhood in industry. It is
these workers, always necessary but never yet
integrated into the social order, who must be
educated, who must be provided for, who must
be accepted fully as comrade in any scheme of
life to be devised and which would call itself
Christian. That word, expressing the noblest

and most spiritual conception of humanity, has been so degraded by misuse in the world that we could almost hate it with the loathing we have for evil, if we did not know that Hell can as disguise put on the outward garments of Heaven. Yet what is eternally true remains pure and uncorrupted, and those who turn to it find it there—as all finally must turn to it to fulfil their destiny of inevitable beauty.

IX

OFTEN with sadness I hear people speak of industrial development in Ireland, for I feel they contemplate no different system than that which fills workers with despair in countries where it is more successfully applied. All these energetic people are conspiring to build factories and mills and to fill them with human labour, and they believe the more they do this the better it will be for Ireland. They talk of Ireland as if it was only admirable as a quantity rather than a quality. They express delight at swelling statistics and increased trade, but where do we hear any reflection on the quality of life engendered by this industrial development ? Our civilization is to differ in no way from any other. No new ideal of life is suggested to differentiate us. We are to go on exploiting human labour. Our working classes are to increase and multiply and earn profits for an employing class, as labour has done from time immemorial in Babylon, in Nineveh, in Rome, and in London to-day. But a choice yet remains to us, because the character of our civilization is not yet fixed. It is mainly germinal. It fills the spirit with weariness to think of another nation following the old path, without thought or imagination of other roads leading to new and more beautiful life. Every now and then, when the world was still vast and full of undiscovered wonders, some adventurers would leave the harbour, and steer their galleys past the known coast and the familiar cities and over untravelled seas, seeking some new land where life might be freer and ampler than that they had known. Is the old daring gone ? Are there not such spirits among us ready to join in the noblest of all adventures—the building up of a civilization—so that the human might reflect the divine order ? In the divine order there is both freedom and solidarity. It is the virtue of the soul to be free and its nature to love ; and when it is free and acts by its own will it is most united with all other life. Those planetary spirits who move in solemn motion about the heavens I do not conceive as the slaves of Deity but as its adorers. But that material nature in which the soul is embodied has the dividing quality of the prism, which resolves pure light into distinct rays ; and so on earth we get the principle of freedom and the virtue of solidarity as separated ideals continually at warfare with each other, and the reconcilement on earth of these principles in man is the conquest of matter by the spirit. This dramatic sundering on earth of virtues in unison in the heavens explains the struggle between Protestantism and Catholicism,

between nationality and imperialism, between
individualist and socialist, between dynamic and
static in philosophy. Indeed in the last analysis
all human conflicts are the balancing on earth
of the manifestation of divine principles which
are one in the unmanifest spirit.

The civilization we create, the social order we
build up, must provide for essential freedom for
the individual and for solidarity of the nation.
Now essential freedom is denied to men if they
are in their condition servile. Can we contemplate the permanent existence of a servile class
in Ireland ? For, disguise it how we will, our
present industrial system is practically a form
of slavery for the workers, differing in externals
only from the ages when the serf had a collar
round his neck. He has now freedom to change
from master to master, and can even seek for a
master in other countries ; but he must, in any
case, accept the relation of servant to master.
The old slave could be whipped. In the new
order the wage slave can be starved, and the fact
that many of the rulers of industry use their
power benevolently does not make the existing
relation between employer and employed right,
or the social order one whose permanence can
be justified. Men will gladly labour if they feel
that their labour conspires with that of all other
workers for the general good ; but there is something loathsome to the spirit in the condition of
the labour market, where labour is regarded as a
commodity to be bought and sold like soap or

candles. For that truly describes how it is with
labour in our industrial system : we can buy
labour, which means we can buy human life and
thought, a portion of God's being, and make a
profit out of it. By so selling himself the worker
is enslaved and limited in a thousand ways.
The power of dismissal of one person by another
at whim acts against independence of character,
or the free expression of opinion in thought,
in politics, and in religion. The soul is stunted
in its growth, and spiritual life made subordinate
to material interests. To deny essential freedom
to the soul is the greatest of all crimes, and such
denial has in all ages evoked the deepest anger
among men. When freedom has been threatened
nations have risen up maddened and exultant,
and the clang of martial arms has been heard
and the stony kings of the past have been encountered in battle. In Ireland we shall have
our greatest fight of all to gain this freedom :
not alone material independence for man, but the
freedom of the soul, its right to choose its own
heroes and its own ideals without let or hindrance
by other men.

We have many of the vices of a slave race,
and we treat others as we have been treated. Our
national aspirations were overborne by material
power, and we in turn use cudgel and curse on
our countrymen when they differ from us in
opinion and policy. Men, when they cannot
match their intellect against another's, suppress
him and howl him down, putting faith in their

own brainlessness. I would make the most
passionate plea for freedom in Ireland : freedom
for all to say the truth they feel or know. What
right have we to ask for ourselves what we deny
to another ? The bludgeon at meetings is a blow
struck against heaven. Those who will not
argue or reason are recreants against humanity,
and are prowling back again on all fours in their
minds to the brute. It matters not in what holy
name men war with violence on freedom of
thought, whether in the name of God or nation
they are enemies of both. We are only right in
controversy when we overcome by a superior
beauty or truth. The first fundamental idea
inspiring an Irish polity should be this idea of
freedom in all spheres of thought, and it is most
necessary to fight for this because the devil and
hell have organized their forces in this unfortunate
land in sectarian and secret societies, of which
it might be written they love darkness rather
than light for the old God-given reasons.

X

WHENEVER in Ireland there has been a revolt
of labour it too often finds arrayed against it the
press, the law, and the police. All the great
powers are in entente. The press, without
inquiry, begins a detestable cant about labour
agitators misleading ignorant men. Every wild
phrase uttered by an exasperated worker is quoted
against the cause of labour, and its grievances are
suppressed. We are told nothing about how the
worker lives : what homes, what food, his wage
will provide. The journalist holds up a moral
umbrella, protecting society from the fiery hail
of conscience. The baser sort of clergyman will
take up the parable and begin advocating a servile
peace, glibly misinterpreting the divine teaching
of love to prove that the lamb should lie down
inside the lion, and only so can it be saved soul
and body, forgetful that the peace which was
Christ's gift to humanity was the peace of God
which passes all understanding, and that it was
a spiritual quietude, and that on earth—the
underworld—the gospel in realization was to
bring not peace but a sword.

The law, assured of public opinion, then deals
sternly with whatever unfortunate life is driven
into its pens. I am putting very mildly the
devilish reality, for society is so constituted that
the public, kept in ignorance of the real facts,
believes that it is acting rightly, and so the devil
has conscience on his side and that divine power
is turned to infernal uses. What can labour
oppose to this federation of State and Church, of
press and law, of capital and physical force to
back capital, when it sets about its own liberation
and to institute a new social order to replace
autocracy in industry ? Its allies are few. A
rare thinker, scientist, literary man, artist or
clergyman, impelled by hatred of what is ugly in
life, will speak on its behalf, and may render some
aid and help to tear holes in that moral shield
held up by the press, and may here and there
give to that blinded public a vision of the Hosts
of the Lord arrayed against it. But the only
real power the workers can truly rely on is their
own. Nothing but a spiritual revolution or an
economic revolution will bring other classes into
comradeship with them. The ideal labour should
set before itself is not a transitory improvement
in its wage, because a wage war never truly or
permanently improves the position of labour.
This section or that may, relatively to its own
past or the position of other workers, improve
itself; but capital is like a ship which, however
the tide rises or falls, floats upon it, and is not
sunken more deeply in the water at high tide

than at low tide. Whenever any burden is placed
upon capital it immediately sets about unloading
that burden on the public. Wages might be
doubled by Act of Parliament, and the net result
would be to double prices, if not to increase them
still more. The more the autocrats of industry
are federated the more easily can they unload
on others any burden placed on them.

The value of money is simply what it will
purchase at any time. If the rulers of industry
can halve the purchasing power of money while
doubling wages at the command of the State,
logic leads us to assume that wages boards,
arbitration boards and the like can only be transitory in their meliorating effect ; and to pursue
the attack on the autocrats of industry by the
road of wages alone is to attack them where they
are impregnable, and where, seeming to give way,
they are all the while really losing nothing, and
are only fixing the wage system more permanently
on those who attack them. There are fiery
spirits among the proletarians who hope that
militant labour will at last bring about the social
revolution, taking the earthly paradise by violence.
They believe that if every worker dropped his
tools and absolutely refused to work under the
old system, it would be impossible to continue it.
That is true, but those who advocate this policy
slur over many difficulties, and the relative power
of endurance of both parties. They do not, I
think, take into account the immense power in
the hands of those who uphold the present system.

Those who might be expected to strike are not—at least in Ireland—a majority of the population. They would have far fewer material resources to fall back on than those others whose interests would lead them to preserve the present social order. It is clear, too, when we analyse the forces at the command of labour and capital, that the latter has attached to itself by the bonds of self-interest the scientific men—engineers, inventors, chemists, bacteriologists, designers, organizers, all the intellect of industry—without which, in alliance with itself, revolting labour would be unable to continue production as before. Labour so revolting might indeed for a time bring the work of the nation to a standstill; but unless it could by some means attract to itself men of the class described, it would not be able to take the helm of the ship of industry and guide it with knowledge as the holders of economic power have done in the past. A policy of emancipation should provide labour with a means of attracting to itself that kind of knowledge which is gained in universities, laboratories, colleges of science, and, above all, in the actual guidance of great industrial enterprises. In any trial of endurance those who start with the greatest intellectual, moral, and material resources will win.

I do not deny that the strike is a powerful weapon in the hand of labour, but it is one with which it is difficult to imagine labour dealing a knock-out blow to the present social order. I believe in an orderly evolution of society, at least in Ireland, and doubt whether by revolution people can be raised to an intelligence, a humanity, or a nobility of nature greater than they formerly possessed. Nobody can remain standing on tiptoe. After a little time disorder subsides and some strong man leads the inevitable reaction. In France people revolted against a decadent monarchy, and in a dozen years they had a new emperor. In England they beheaded a king as a protest against tyranny, and they got a dictator in his place who took little or no account of parliaments ; and finally a second Charles, rather worse than the first, came to the throne. The everlasting battle between light and darkness goes on stubbornly all the time, and the gain of the Hosts of Light is inch by inch. Extraordinary efforts, impetuous charges, which seem to win for a moment, too often leave the attacking force tired and exhausted, and the forces of reaction set in and overwhelm them. I am the friend of revolt if people cannot stand the conditions they live under, and if they can see no other way. It is better to be men than slaves. The French Revolution was a tragic episode in history, but when people suffer intolerably and are insulted in their despair it is inevitable blood will be shed. One can only say with Whitman :

Pale, silent, stern, what could I say to that long-accrued
    retribution ?
Could I wish humanity different ?
Could I wish the people made of wood and stone, or that
    there be no justice in destiny or time ?

There is danger in revolution if the revolutionary spirit is much more advanced than the intellectual and moral qualities which alone can secure the success of a revolt.   These intellectual and moral qualities—the skill to organize, the wisdom to control large undertakings, are not natural gifts but the results of experience.   They are evolutionary products.   The emancipation of labour, I believe, will not be gained by revolution but by prolonged effort, continued month by month and year by year, in which first this thing is adventured, then that : each enterprise brings its own gifts of wisdom and experience, and there is no reaction, because, instead of the violent use of certain powers, the whole being is braced : experience, intellect, desire, all strong and working harmoniously, press forward and support each other, and no enterprise is undertaken where the intellect to carry it out is not present together with the desire.   It requires great intellectual and moral qualities to bring about a revolution. A rage at present conditions is not enough.

XI

OUR farmers are already free. The problem with them is not now concerned with freedom, but how they may be brought into a solidarity with each other and the nation. To make our proletarians free and masters of their own energies, in unison with each other and the national being, is the most pressing labour of the many before us. Unless there be economic freedom there can be no other freedom. The right of no individual to subsistence should be at the good will of any other individual. More than mere comfort depends on it. There are eternal and august rights of the soul to be safeguarded, and the economic position of men should be protected by organization and democratic law. I have already discussed some of the avenues through which workers in our time have looked with hope. I have little belief that these roads lead anywhere but back to the old City of Slavery, however they may seem to curve away at the outset. The strike, on whatever scale, is no way to freedom, though the strike—or the threat of it—may bring wages nearer to subsistence level. The art of warfare is too much in the hands of specialists for trust to be placed in revolution. A machine-gun with a few experts behind it is worth a thousand revolutionary workers, however maddened they may be. Does political action, on which so many rely, promise more ? I do not believe it does. I believe that to appeal to legislatures is to appeal to bodies dominated by those interested in maintaining the present social order, although they may act so as to redress the worst evils created by it. In Ireland, for this generation at least, it would be impossible to secure in a legislative assembly majorities representative of the class we wish to see emancipated. It may seem as if I had closed all the paths out of the social labyrinth ; but the way to emancipation has, I think, already been surveyed by pioneers. A policy of social reconstruction is practical, and needs but steady persistence for its realization. That policy—I refer to co-operative action—has been adopted in various forms by workers in many countries ; and what is needed here is to study and co-ordinate these applications of co-working, and to form a general staff of labour who will, on behalf of the workers, examine the weapons fashioned by their class elsewhere, and who will draw up a plan of campaign as the staff of an army do previous to military operations. It will be found that economic action along co-operative lines has, in one country, barriers placed before its expansion which could be set aside by supplementing this action by methods elaborated by the genius of workers elsewhere.

It is not my purpose here to repeat in detail methods of organization, partly technical, which can be found fully described in many admirable books, but rather to indicate the order of advance, the methods of co-ordination of these, and their final absorption and transformation in the national being.   There is a great deal of ignorance about things essential to safe action.   When men are filled with enthusiasm they are apt to apply their new principles rashly in schemes which are bound to fail, just as over-confident soldiers will in battle sometimes rush a position prematurely which they cannot hold, because the general line of their army has not advanced sufficiently to support them.   Sacrifices are made with no permanent result, and the morale of the army is injured.

In the rural districts the advance must, in the nature of things, be from production to consumption, and with urban workers inversely from a control over distribution to a mastery over production.   I have often wondered over the blindness of workers in towns in Ireland, who have made so little use in the economic struggle of the freedom they have to spend their wage where they choose.   They speak of this struggle as the class war ; but they carry on the conflict most energetically where it is most difficult for them to succeed, and hardly at all where it would be comparatively easy for them to weaken the resources of their antagonists.   In warfare much use is made of flanking movements, which aim at cutting the enemy's communication with his base of supply. Frontal attacks are dangerous. It is equally true in economic warfare. The strike is a frontal attack, and those they fight are entrenched deeply with all the artillery of the State, the press, science, and wealth on their side. What would we think of an army which, at the close of each week's fighting, voluntarily surrendered to the enemy the ground, guns, ammunition, and prisoners captured through the previous six days ? Yet this is what our workers do. The power opposed to them is mainly economic, though there is an intellectual basis for it also. But the wages of the workers, little for the individual, yet a large part of the national income if taken for the mass, goes back to strengthen the system they protest against through purchases of domestic requirements. The creation of co-operative stores ought to be the first constructive policy adopted by Irish labour. It ought to be as much a matter of class honour with them to be members of stores as to be in the trade union of their craft. The store may be regarded as the commissariat department of the army of labour. Many a strike has failed of its object, and the workers have gone back defeated, because their neglect of the commissariat made them unable to hold out for that last week when both sides are desperate and at the end of their resources. But it is not mainly as an aid to the strike that I advocate democratizing the distributive trade, but because control over distribution gives a large

measure of control over production.   The history
of co-operative workshops indicates that these
have rarely been successful unless worked in
conjunction with distributive stores.   The retail
trader is not sympathetic with co-operative production.   As the cat is akin to the tiger, so is the
individual trader—no matter on how small a
scale he operates—a kinsman of the great autocrats of industry, and he will sympathize with his
economic kinsmen and will retail their goods in
preference to those produced in co-operative
workshops.

The control of agencies of distribution by the
workers at a certain stage in their development
enables them to start productive enterprises with
more safety and less expense in regard to advertise-
ment than the capitalist can.   In fact the co-
operative store, properly organized, creates a tied
trade for the output of co-operative workshops.
It is a source of financial aid to these, and will
invest funds in them and assist trades unions
gradually to transform themselves into co-operative guilds of producers which should be their
ultimate ideal.   As I shall show later on, the
store will enable the urban worker to enter into
intimate alliance with the rural producer.   Their
interests are really identical.   In every town in
Ireland efforts should be made to democratize
the distributive agencies, and the workers will
have many allies in this, driven by the increased
cost of living to search out the most economical
agencies of purchase.   If the proletarians are

not in a majority in Ireland—a nation where the farmers are the most numerous single class— they certainly form the majority in the cities ; and the co-operative store, while admitting to membership all who will apply, ought to be and would be sympathetic with the efforts of labour to emancipate itself, and would be a powerful lever in its hands. As the stores increase in number, an analysis of their trade will reveal year by year in what directions co-operative production of particular articles may safely be attempted. More and more by this means the producing power and the capital at the disposal of the worker will be placed at the service of democracy. The first steps are the most difficult. In due time the workers will have educated a number of their members, and will have attached to themselves men of proved capacity to be the leaders in fresh enterprises, manufactures of one kind or another, democratic banking in- stitutions, all supporting each other and leaning on each other and playing into each other's hands.

The extent to which this may be carried, and the opportunities for making Ireland a co- operative democracy, I shall presently explain. I do not regard any of these forms of co-operative organization as ideal or permanent. The co- operative movement must be regarded rather as a great turning movement on the part of humanity towards the ideal. The co-operative organizations now being formed in Ireland and over the world will, I am certain, persist and outlast this generation and the next, and will grow into vaster things than we dream of; but the really important change they will bring about in the minds of men will be psychological. Men will become habituated to the thought of common action for the common good. To get so far in civil life is a great step. To-day our civil life is a tangle of petty personal interests and competitions. The co-operative movement is, as I have said, a vast turning movement of humanity heavenwards, or, at least, to bring them face round to the Delectable City. When this psychological change takes place the democratic associations—which have grown up haphazard as the workers found it easiest to create them—will be changed and remodelled by men who will have the mass of people behind them in their efforts to make a more majestic structure of society for the enlargement of the lives and spirits of men.

XII

WE have descended from the national soul to the
material plane, and we must still continue here
for a time, because the doctrine that a sane mind
can only manifest through a sane body is as true
in reference to the State as to the individual,
and necessitates a study of social fabrics. The
soul creates tendencies and habits in the body,
and the body repeats these vibrations automatically
and infects the soul again with its old desires.
Our religious hatreds created sectarian organizations, and these react again in the national soul,
which would, I believe, willingly pass away from
that mood, but finds itself incarnated in organizations habituated to sectarian action, and its
energies are turned into these hateful channels
unwillingly. So a drunkard who now realizes
that intemperance is rotting his nature is conquered by the appetites he set up in the past,
and with his soul in rebellion he yet satisfies the
craving in the body. The individualism in our
economic life reacts on the national being, and
prevents concerted action for the general good.
We have yet to create harmony of purpose in

our economic life, and to bring together interests long separated and unmindful of each other, and make them realize that their interests are identical. It is one of the commonplaces of economics that urban and rural interests are identical : but in truth the townsman and the countryman have always acted as if their interests were opposed, and they know very little of each other. I never like to let these commonplaces of economics pass my frontiers unless they give the countersign to the challenge for truth. People declare in the same way that the interests of labour and capital are identical, and implore them not to fight with one another. But the truth of that statement seems to me to depend largely on whether capital owns labour or labour owns capital. As an abstract proposition it is one of the economic formulæ I would leave instructions at my frontiers to have detained until further inquiry as to its antecedents. All these statements may be true, but to make them operative, to give them a dynamic rather than a static character, we must convince people they are true by close argument and still more so by realistic illustration.

To bring about a high nobility in the national soul we must make harmony in its economic life, and the two main currents of economic energy—the agricultural and urban—must be made to flow so that their action will not defeat each other. Let us take the farmer first. How ought he to wish to see life in the towns develop ?

Should he wish for the triumph of labour or capital : the success of the co-operative movement, the triumph of the multiple shop or the private trader, of guilds of workers or autocrats of industry ? Economic desires generally depend on the nature of the industry men are engaged in. The jeweller would probably desire the permanence of the social order which created most wealthy people who could afford to buy his wares. The farmer's industry, if we consider it closely, is the most democratic of any in its application to society. The produce of the farm, in its final distribution, is divided into portions more or less equal and conditioned in quantity by the digestive powers of an individual. The wealthiest millionaire cannot eat more bread, butter, meat, vegetables, or fruit than the manual labourer would eat if the latter could afford to get such things. In fact he would eat rather less, because the manual worker has a much better appetite, indeed requires more food. It appears to be the interest of the farmer to support any urban movement whose object it is to see that every worker in the towns is remunerated so that he, his wife, and his children can procure as much food as they require. Any underpaid worker in the towns is a wrong to the farmer—a willing customer who yet cannot buy. If there is, let us say, a sum of fifteen hundred pounds a week to be paid away in a town, it is to the interest of farmers that that sum should be paid to a thousand men at the rate of thirty shillings a week rather than to fifty men at thirty pounds a week. In the case of the workers a greater part of the money will be spent on food. But if fifty men have thirty pounds a week each, it will be spent to satisfy the appetites of a much smaller number of people. A larger proportion will be spent on furniture, pictures, motor-cars and what not. It may be spent so as to give some kind of employment, but it will not be a division of the money so much to the interests of the farmer. However we analyse the problem it appears to be to the farmer's interests to support democratic movements in the cities, certainly up to the point where every worker in the towns has a wage which enables himself and his family to eat all they require for health. It is also to the interests of farmers to support any system of distribution of goods which eliminates the element of profit in the sale. After the farmer gets his price it is to his interests that food should be increased in cost as little as possible when the article is transferred to the consumer, because if farm produce has to bear too many profits it will be expensive for the consumer, and there will be a lessened demand. So associations like the co-operative stores, which aim at the elimination of the element of profit in distribution, should be approved of by the farmers.

Now we come to the townsman again. Is it his interest to support the farmers in his own country or to regard the world as his farm ? The argument on the economic side is not so

clear, but it is, I think, just as sound.   If agriculture is neglected in any country the rural population pour into the towns.   The country becomes
a fountain of blackleg labour.   Rural labour
has no traditions of trade unionism, and takes
any work at any price.   There are fewer people
engaged in producing food, and its cost rises.
Food must be imported from abroad ; and there
is national insecurity, as in times of war their is
always the danger of the trade routes overseas
being blocked by an enemy, and this again has to
be provided against by heavy expenditure for
militarist purposes.   The farther away an army
is from its base the more insecure is its position,
and the same thing is true in the industrial life
of nations.   International trade there must always
be.   It is one of the means by which the larger
solidarity of humanity is to be achieved ;   but
that will never come about until there is a nobler
and more human life within the states, and we
must begin by perfecting national life before we
consider empires and world federations.   So in
this essay only the national being is considered.
      I desire to unite countryman and townsman
in one movement, and to make the co-operative
principle the basis of a national civilization.
How are we to prevent them fighting the old
battle between producer and consumer ?   I think
that this can best be brought about by co-operative
federations, which will act for both in manufacture, purchase, and sale, and with which both
rural and urban associations will find it to their

interest to be affiliated. Now the townsman cannot to any extent supply food for his stores by buying farms. To control agricultural production in that way would necessitate a financial operation which the State would shrink from, and which it would be impossible for urban co-operators to finance. We had better make up our minds to let farmers be syndicalists, controlling entirely the processes of agricultural production themselves. They will do it better than the townsman could, more efficiently and more economically. They will never be able, with the world in competition, to put up prices artificially. How can the two main divisions of national life be brought together in a national solidarity? We can find an answer if we remember that farmers are not only producers but consumers. They do not go about naked in the fields. They require clothes, furniture, tea, coffee, sugar, oil, soap, candles, pots and pans—in fact the farmer's wife needs nearly all the things the townsman's wife needs, except that she purchases a little less food. But even here modern conditions are driving the farmer to buy food in the shops rather than to produce it for himself on the farm. Country bread is made in the bakery more and more. Butter, cheese, and bacon are made in factories, and the farmer's tendency is to buy what bread, bacon, and butter he requires, selling the milk to be made into butter to a creamery, the grain to make the bread to a miller, and the pigs to a factory. Co-operative distribution would be as advantageous to the country as in the town. Already in Ireland a considerable number of farmers' societies are enlarging their objects, and are turning what originally were purely agricultural associations into general purposes societies, where the farmer's wife can purchase her domestic requirements as well as her man his machinery, fertilizers, feeding-stuffs, and seeds. It would be to the interest of rural societies to deal with co-operative wholesales just as much as it is in the interest of urban stores to do so. It would be to their interest to take shares in these wholesales and productive federations, and see that they cater for the farmer's interests as much as for the townsman's.

The urban co-operators, on their side, will see the opportunities for productive co-operation the union of rural and urban movements would create. They naturally will desire to employ as many people as possible in co-operative production. Farmers are surrounded by rings of all kinds : machinery manufacturers who will not sell to their societies, manure manufacturers' alliances who keep up prices. It is a great industry, this of supplying the farmer with his fertilizers, feeding-stuffs, cake, machinery. These rural co-operative societies are increasing in number year by year. Farmers want clothes, hats, and boots : and the necessary machinery for their industry is almost entirely of urban manufacture—ploughs, binders, separators, harrows, and many other implements of tillage. It

is an immense industry and yet to be co-operatively exploited. In the towns some progress
has been made in distribution. But a nation
depends upon its wealth producers and not upon
its consumers. Co-operators might double,
treble, or quadruple the distributive trade, and
still occupy only a very secondary position in
national life unless they enter more largely upon
production. We will never make the co-operative idea the fundamental one in the civilization
of Ireland until we employ a very large part of
the population in production. Now we have at
present, thanks to the energy of the pioneers of
agricultural co-operation, a new market opening
in the country for things which the townsman can
produce. Does not this suggest new productive
urban enterprises ? Does it not favour an evolution of manufacturing industry; so that democratic
control may finally replace the autocratic control
of the capitalist ? The trades unions cannot do
this alone by following up any of their traditional
policies. They cannot go into trade on their
own account with any guarantee of success unless
they are associated with agencies of distribution.
But if co-operators—urban and rural—through
their federations invade more and more the field
of production they will draw to themselves the
hearts and hopes of the workers and idealists in
the nation. People are really more concerned
about the making of an income than about the
spending of it. It is a necessity of our policy if it
is to bring about the co-operative commonwealth,

that co-operators must adventure much more largely into production than they have hitherto done.

Now let us see what we have come to. There is a country movement which is not merely one for agricultural production. It is rapidly taking up the distribution of goods. There is an urban movement not merely concerned with distribution but entering upon production. They can be brought into harmony if the same federations act for both branches of the movement. The meeting-place of the two armies should be there. If this policy is adopted there will gradually grow up that unity of purpose between country and urban workers which is the psychological basis and necessary precedent for national action for the common good. The policy of identity of interest must be real, and it can only be real when the identity of interest is obvious, and it can only be made obvious when the symbols of that unity and identity are visible day by day in buildings and manufactures, things which are handled and seen, and in transactions which daily bring that unity to mind. The old poetic ideal of a united Ireland was and could only be a geographical expression, and not a human reality, so long as men were individualist in economics and were competing and struggling with each other for mastery.

By the co-operative commonwealth more is meant than a series of organizations for economic purposes. We hope to create finally, by the

H

close texture of our organizations, that vivid sense of the identity of interest of the people in this island which is the basis of citizenship, and without which there can be no noble national life. Our great nation-states have grown so large, so myriad are their populations, so complicated are their interests, that most people in them really feel no sense of brotherhood with each other. We have yet to create inside our great nation-states social and economic organizations, which will make this identity of interest real and evident, and not seem merely a metaphor, as it does to most people to-day.   The more the co-operative movement does this for its members, the more points of contact they find in it, the more will we tend to make out of it and its branches real social organisms, which will become as closely knit psychically as physically the cells in a human body are knit together.   Our Irish diversities of interest have made us world-famous ; but such industrial and agricultural organizations would swallow up these antagonisms, as the serpents created by the black art of the Egyptian magicians were swallowed up by the rod Aaron cast on the floor, and which was made animate by the white magic of the Lord.

XIII

It will appear to the idealist who has contemplated
the heavens more closely than the earth that the
policy I advocate is one which only tardily could
be put into operation, and would be paltry and
inadequate as a basis for society. The idealist
with the Golden Age already in his heart believes
he has only to erect the Golden Banner and
display it for multitudes to array themselves
beneath its folds ; therefore he advocates not, as
I do, a way to the life, but the life itself. I am
sympathetic with idealists in a hurry, but I do
not think the world can be changed suddenly by
some heavenly alchemy, as St. Paul was smitten
by a light from the overworld. Such light from
heaven is vouchsafed to individuals, but never to
nations, who progress by an orderly evolution in
society. Though the heart in us cries out continually, " Oh, hurry, hurry to the Golden Age,"
though we think of revolutions, we know that the
patient marshalling of human forces is wisdom.
We have to devise ways and means and light
every step clearly before the nation will leave
its footing in some safe if unattractive locality to

plant itself elsewhere. The individual may be reckless. The race never can be so, for it carries too great a burden and too high destinies, and it is only when the gods wish to destroy or chastise a race that they first make it mad. Not by revolutions can humanity be perfected. I might quote from an old oracle, " The gods are never so turned away from man as when he ascends to them by disorderly methods." Our spirits may live in the Golden Age, but our bodily life moves on slow feet, and needs the lantern on the path and the staff struck carefully into the darkness before us to see that the path beyond is not a morass, and the light not a will o' the wisp.

Other critics may say I would destroy the variety of civilization by the inflexible application of a single idea. Well, I realize that the net which is spread for Leviathan will not capture all the creatures of the deep ; and the complexity of human nature is such that it is impossible to imagine a policy, however fitting in certain spheres of human activity, which could be applied to the whole of life. What I think we should aim at is making the co-operative idea fundamental in Irish life. But to say fundamental is not to say absolute. Always there will be enterprising persons—men of creative minds—who will break away from the mass and who will insist, perhaps rightly, on an autocratic control of the enterprises they found, which were made possible alone by their genius, and which would not succeed unless every worker in the enterprise was malleable by

their will.   It is unlikely that State action will
cease, or that any Government we may have will
not respond to the appeal of the people to do this,
that, or the other for them which they are too
indolent to do for themselves, or which by the
nature of things only governments can undertake.
For a principle to be fundamental in a country
does not mean that it must be absolute.   I hope
society in Ireland will be organized that the idea
of democratic control of its economic life will so
pervade Irish thought that it will be in the body
politic what the spinal column is to the body—
the pillar on which it rests, the strongest single
factor in the body. Another illustration may make
still clearer my meaning.   In a red sunsetting
the glow is so powerful that green hills, white
houses, and blue waters, touched by its light,
assume a ruddy colour, partly a local colour, and
partly a reflected light from the sun.   Now in
the same way, what is most powerful in society
multiplies images and shadows of itself, and
produces harmonies with itself which are yet not
identities.   It is by a predominating idea that
nations achieve the practical unity of their citizens,
and national progress becomes possible.   In the
future structure of society I have no doubt there
will be elements to which the socialist, the syndi-
calist, the capitalist, and the individualist will
have contributed.   By degrees it will be discovered what enterprises are best directed by the
State, by municipalities, by groups, or by individuals.   But if the idea of democratic control

is predominant, those enterprises which are
otherwise directed will yet meet the prevalent
mood by adopting the ideas of the treatment of
the workers enforced in democratically controlled
enterprises, and will in every respect, except
control, make their standards equal. All the
needles of being point to the centres where power
is most manifested. The effects of the French
revolution — a democratic upheaval — invaded
men's minds everywhere. Even the autocratic-
ally ruled States, hitherto careless about the
people in their underworlds, had to make advances
to democracy, and give it some measure of the
justice democracy threatened to deal to itself.
Without demanding absolutism I do desire a
predominant democratic character in our national
enterprises, rather than a confused muddle or
struggle of interests where nothing really emerges
except the egoism of those who struggle.

It will be noticed that in all that has preceded
I have referred little to action by government,
though it is on governments that democracies
over the world are now fixing all their hopes.
They believe the State is the right agency to
bring about reforms and changes in society.
And I must here explain why I do not share their
hopes. My distrust of the State in economic
reform is based on the belief that governments
in great nation-states, even representative governments, are not malleable by the general will.
They are too easily dominated by the holders of
economic power, are, in fact, always dominated

by aristocracies with land or by the aristocracies
of wealth.   It is the hand at the helm guides the
ship.   The larger the State is the more easily
do the holders of economic power gain political
power.   The theory of representative government
held good in practice, I think, so long as parliaments were engaged in formulating general
rights, the right, for example, of the individual
to think or profess any religion he pleased ; his
right not to be deprived of liberty or life without
open trial by his fellow - citizens.   So long as
legislatures were affirming or maintaining these
rights, which rich and poor equally desired, they
were justified.   But when legislatures began to
intervene in economic matters, in the struggles
between rich and poor, between capital and labour,
it became at once apparent the holders of economic
power had also political power ; and that the
institution which operated fairly where universal
rights were considered did not operate fairly
when there was a conflict between particular
interests.

The jury of the nation was found to be packed.
At least nine-tenths of the population in Great
Britain, for example, belong to the wage-earning
class.   At least nine-tenths of the members of
legislatures belong to the classes possessing land
or capital.   Now, why any member of the wage-
earning class should look with hope to such
assemblies I cannot understand.   Their ideal is,
or should be, economic freedom, together with
democratic control of industries, an ideal in every

way opposed to the ideal of the majority of the members of the legislatures. The fiction that representative assemblies will work for the general good is proclaimed with enthusiasm ; but the moment we examine their actions we see it is not so, and we discover the cause. Where the nation is capitalist and capitalism is the dominant economic factor, legislatures invariably act to uphold it, and legislation tends to fix the system more securely. We see in Great Britain that wage-earners are now openly regarded by the legislatures as a class who must not be allowed the same freedom in life as the wealthy. They must be registered, inspected, and controlled in a way which the wealthy would bitterly resent if the legislation referred to themselves. After economic inferiority has been enforced on them by capital, the stigma of human inferiority is attached to the wage-earners by the legislature. But I must not be led away from my theme by the bitter reflections which arise in one who lives in the Iron Age and knows it is Iron, who feels at times like the lost wanderer on trackless fields of ice, which never melt and will not until earth turns from its axis.

I wish to see society organized so that it shall be malleable to the general will. But political and economic progress are obstructed because existing political and economic organizations are almost entirely unmalleable by the general will. Public opinion does not control the press. The press, capitalistically controlled, creates public

opinion. Our legislators have grown so secure
that they confess openly they have passed measures
which they knew would be hateful to the majority
of citizens, and which, if they had been voted on,
would never have been passed. The theory of
representative government has broken down. To
tell the truth, the life of the nation is so complicated
that it is difficult for the private citizen to have
any intelligent opinion about national policies,
and we can hardly blame the politician for despis-
ing the judgment of the private citizen. Government departments are still less malleable by public
opinion than the legislature. For an individual
to attack the policy of a Government department
is almost as hopeless a proceeding as if a labourer
were to take pickaxe and shovel and determine
to level a mountain which obstructed his view.
Yet Government departments are supposed to be
under popular control. The Castle in Ireland,
theoretically, was under popular control, but it
was adamantine in policy. If the cant about
popular control of legislation and Government
departments is obviously untrue, how much
more is it in regard to public services like rail-
ways, gas works, mines, the distribution of goods,
manufacture, purchase and sale, which are almost
entirely under private control and where public
interference is bitterly resented and effectively
opposed. What chance has the individual who
is aggrieved against the great carrying companies ? To come lower down, let us take the
farmer in the fairs. What way has he of in-

fluencing the jobbers and dealers to act honestly by him—they who have formed rings to keep down the prices of cattle ?   Are they malleable to public opinion ?   The farmers who have waited all day through a fair know they are not.

When we consider the agencies through which people buy we find the same thing. The increase of multiple shops, combines, and rings makes the use of the limited power a man had to affect a dealer by transferring his custom to another merchant to dwindle yearly. Everywhere we turn we find this adamantine front presented by the legislature, the State departments, by the agencies of production, distribution, or credit, and it is the undemocratic organization of society which is responsible for nine-tenths of our social troubles. All the vested interests backed up by economic and political power conflict with the public welfare, and the general will, which intends the good of all, can act no more than a paralysed cripple can walk. We would all choose the physique of the athlete, with his swift, unfettered, easy movements, rather than the body of the cripple if we could, and we have this choice before us in Ireland.

If we concentrate our efforts mainly on voluntary action, striving to make the co-operative spirit predominant, the general will would manifest itself through organizations malleable to that will, flexible and readily adjusting themselves to the desires of the community. To effect reforms we have not first to labour at the gigantic task of affecting national opinion and securing the majorities necessary for national action.   In any district a hundred or two hundred men can at any time form co-operative societies for production, purchase, sale, or credit, and can link themselves by federation with other organizations like their own to secure greater strength and economic efficiency.   By following this policy steadily we simplify our economic system, and reduce to fewer factors the forces in conflict in society.   We beget the predominance of one principle, and enable that general will for good, which Rousseau theorized about, to find agencies through which it can manifest freely, so changing society from the static condition begot by conflict and obstruction to a dynamic condition where energies and desires manifest freely.

The general will, as Rousseau demonstrated, always intends the good, and if permitted to act would act in a large and noble way.   The change from static to dynamic, from fixed forms to fluid forms, has been coming swiftly over the world owing to the liberation of thought, and this in spite of the obstruction of a society organized,- I might almost say, with egomania as the predominant psychological factor.   The ancient conception of Nature as a manifestation of spirit is incarnating anew in the minds of modern thinkers, and Nature is not conceived of as material, but as force and continual motion ; and they are trying to identify human will with this arcane energy, and let the forces of Nature have freer play in humanity. We begin to catch glimpses of civilizations as far exceeding ours as ours surpasses society in the Stone Age. In all our democratic movements, in these efforts towards the harmonious fusion of human forces, humanity is obscurely intent on mightier collective exploits than anything conceived of before. The nature of these energies manifesting in humanity I shall try to indicate later on. But to let the general will have free play ought to be the aim of those who wish to build up national organizations for whatever purpose; and to let the general will have free play we require something better than the English invention of representative government, which, as it exists at present, is simply a device to enable all kinds of compromises to be made on matters where there should be no compromise, as if right and wrong could come to an agreement honestly to let things be partly right and partly wrong. We are importing into Ireland some political machinery of this antiquated pattern. I have written the foregoing because I dread Irish people becoming slaves of this machine. I fear the importers of this machinery will desire to make it do things it can only do badly, and will set it to work with the ferocity of the new broom and will make it an obstruction, so that the real genius of the Irish people will be unable freely to manifest itself. The less we rely on this machinery at present, and the more we desire a machinery of progress, at once flexible and efficient, the better will it be for us later on.   What must be embodied in State action is the national will and the national soul, and until that giant being is manifested it is dangerous to let the pygmies set powers in motion which may enchain us for centuries to come.

XIV

IT may seem I have spoken lightly of that infant
whose birth I referred to with more solemnity
in the opening pages of this book, and indeed
I am a little dubious about that infant. The
signature of the Irish mind is nowhere present
in it, and I look upon it with something of the
hesitating loyalty the inhabitant of a new Balkan
State might feel for his imported prince, doubtful
whether that sovereign will reflect the will of
his new subjects or whether his policy will not
constrain national character into an alien mould.
The signature of the Irish mind is not apparent
anywhere in this new machinery for self-government. Our politicians seem to have been unaware
that they had any wisdom to learn from the more
obvious failures of representative government as
they knew it. So far as I have knowledge, no
Irishman during the past century of effort for
political freedom took the trouble to think out a
form of government befitting Irish circumstance
and character. We left it absolutely to those
whom we declared incapable of understanding
us or governing us to devise for us a system

by which we might govern ourselves. I do not
criticize those who devised the new machinery
of self-government, but those who did not devise
it, and who discouraged the exercise of political
imagination in Ireland. It is said of an artist
that it was his fantasy first to paint his ideal of
womanly beauty, and, when this was done, to
approximate it touch by touch to the sitter, and
when the sitter cried, " Ah, now it is growing
like ! " the artist ceased, combining the maximum
of ideal beauty possible with the minimum of
likeness. Now if we had thought out the ideal
structure of Irish government we might have
offered it for criticism by those in whose power
it was to accept or reject, and have gradually
approximated it until a point was reached where
the compromise left at least something of our
making and imagination in it. There is nothing
of us in the Act which is in abeyance as I write.
I am less concerned with it than with the creation
of a social order, for the social order in a country
is the strong and fast fortress where national
character is created and preserved. A legislature
may theoretically allow self-government, but by
its constitution may operate against national
character and its expression in a civilization.
We have accepted the principle of representative
government, and that, I readily concede, is the
ideal principle, but the method by which a
representative character is to be given to State
institutions we have not thought out at all. We
have committed the error our neighbours have

committed of assuming that the representative
assembly which can legislate for general interests
can deal equally with particular interests ; that
the body of men who will act unitedly so as to
secure the liberty of person or liberty of thought,
which all desire for themselves, will also act
wisely where class problems and the development
of particular industries are concerned.   The
whole history of representative assemblies shows
that the machinery adequate for the furtherance
and protection of general interests operates un-
justly or stupidly in practice against particular
interests.   The long neglect of agriculture and
the actual condition of the sweated are instances.
I agree that representative government is the
ideal, but how is it to operate in the legislature
and still more in administration ?   Are government departments to be controlled by Parliament
or by the representatives of the particular class
to promote whose interests special departments
were created.   I hold that the continuous efficiency
of State departments can only be maintained when
they are controlled in respect of policy, not
by the casual politician whom the fluctuations of
popular emotion places at their head, but by
the class or industry the State institution was
created to serve.   A department of State can
conceivably be preserved from stagnation by a
minister of strong will, who has a more profound
knowledge of the problems connected with his
department than even his permanent officials.
He might vitalize them from above.   But does

the party system yield us such Ministers ? In practice is not high position the reward of service to party ? Is special knowledge demanded of the controller of a Board of Trade or a Board of Agriculture ? Do we not all know that the vast majority of Ministers are controlled by the permanent officials of their department. Failing great Ministers, the operations of a department may be vitalized by control over its policy exercised, not by a general assembly like Parliament, but by a board elected from the class or industry the department ostensibly was created to serve. An agricultural department controlled by a council or board composed solely of those making their livelihood out of agriculture and elected solely by their own class, would, we may be certain, be practical in its methods. It would receive perpetual stimulus from those engaged in making their living by the industry. Parliaments or senates should confine themselves to matters of general interest, leaving particular or special interests to those who understand them, to the specialists, and only intervene when national interests are involved by a clashing of particular interests. Our State institutions will never fulfil their functions efficiently until they are subject in respect of policy not to general control, but the control of the class they were created to serve.

That ideal can only be realized fully when all industries are organized. But we should work towards it. Parliament may act as a kind of

I

guardian of the unorganized, but, once an industry is organized, once it has come of age, it must resent domination by bodies without the special knowledge of which it has the monopoly within itself. It should not tolerate domination by the unexpert outsider, whatever may be his repute in other spheres. It is only when industries are organized that the democratic system of election can justify itself by results in administration. When a county, let us say, chooses a member of Parliament to represent every interest, only too often it chooses a man who can represent few interests except his own. The greatest common denominator of the constituents is as a rule some fluent utterer of platitudes. But if the farmers in a county, or the manufacturers in a county, or the workers in a county, had each to choose a man to represent them, we may be certain the farmers would choose one whom they regarded as competent to interpret their needs, the manufacturers a man of real ability, and labour would select its best intelligence. Persons engaged in special work rarely fail to recognize the best men in their own industry. Then they judge somewhat as experts, whereas they are by no means experts when they are asked to select a representative to represent everybody in every industry. To secure good government I conceive we must have two kinds of representative assemblies running concurrently with their spheres of influence well defined. One, the supreme body, should be elected by counties or cities to deal

with general interests, taxation, justice, education,
the duties and rights of individual citizens as
citizens.   The other bodies should be elected
by the people engaged in particular occupations
to control the policy of the State institutions
created to foster particular interests.   The average
man will elect people to his mind whose delibera-
tions will be in a sphere where the ideas of the
average man ought to be heard and must be
respected.   The specialists in their department
of industry will elect experts to work in a sphere
where their knowledge will be invaluable, and
where, if it is not present, there will be muddle.

The machinery of government ought never
to be complicated, and ought to be easily understood by the citizens.   In Ireland, where we have
at present no thought of foreign policy, no question
of army or navy, departments of State should fall
naturally into a few divisions concerned with
agriculture, education, local government, justice,
police, and taxation.   The administration of some
of these are matters of national concern, and they
should and must be under parliamentary control,
and that control should be jealously protected.
Others are sectional, and these should be controlled in respect of policy by persons representative of these sections, and elected solely by them.
I think there should also be a department of
Labour.   I am not sure that the main work of
the Minister in charge ought not to be the
organization of labour in its proper unions or
guilds.   It is a work as important to the State

as the organization of agriculture, and indeed from a humanitarian point of view more urgent. Nothing is more lamentable, nothing fills the heart more with despair, than the multitude of isolated workers, sweated, unable to fix a price for their work, ignorant of its true economic value ; connected with no union, unable to find any body to fall back on for help or advice in trouble, neglected altogether by society, which yet has to pay a heavy price in disease, charity, poor rates, and in social disorder for its neglect. Was not the last Irish rising largely composed of those who were economically neglected and oppressed ? Society bears a heavier burden for its indifference than it would bear if it accepted responsibility for the organization of labour in its own defence. The State in these islands recommends farmers to organize for the protection of their interests and assists in the organization, and leaves the organized farmers free to use their organizations as they will. As good a case could be made for the State aiding in the organization of labour for the protection of its own interests. A ministry of labour should seek out all wage-earners ; where there is no trade union one should be organized, and, where one exists, all workers should be pressed to join it. Such a ministry ought to be the city of refuge for the proletarian, and the Minister be the Father of Labour, fighting its battles for an entry into humanity and its rightful place in civilization.

If we consider the problem of representation,

it should not be impossible to devise a system of which the foundation might be the County Councils, where there would be as sub-divisions, committees for local government, agriculture, and technical instruction or trade to deal with local administration in these matters. These committees should send representatives to general councils of local government, agriculture, and trade. The election should not be by the County Council as a body, but by the committees, so that traders would have no voice in choosing a representative for farmers, nor farmers interfere in the choice of manufacturers or traders selecting a representative on a general Council of Trade, and it should be regarded as ridiculous any such intervention as for a War Office to claim it should have a voice along with the Admiralty in the selection of captains and commanders of vessels of war. At these general councils, which might meet twice a year for whatever number of days may be expedient, general policies would be decided and boards elected to ensure the carrying out by the officials of the policies decided upon. By this process of selection men who had to control Boards of Agriculture, Trade, or Local Government would be three times elected, each time by a gradually decreasing electorate, with a gradually increasing special knowledge of the matters to be dealt with. A really useless person may contrive to be chosen as representative by a thousand electors. It requires an able man to convince a committee of ten persons, themselves more or less specialists, that his is the best brain among them. Where national education, a thorny subject in Ireland, is concerned, I think the educationalists in provinces might be asked to elect representatives from their own profession on a Council of Education to act as an advisory body to the Minister of Education. County Council elections are not exactly means by which miracles of culture are discovered. A man who came to be member of a board of control would at least have proved his ability to others engaged on work like his own who have special knowledge of it and of his capacity to deal with it. If this system was accepted, we would not have traders on our Council of Agriculture protesting against the farmers organizing their industry, because none but persons concerned with agriculture would be allowed to be members of agricultural committees, and this would, of course, involve the concentration of merchants and manufacturers upon the work of a Board of Trade and the control of a policy of technical instruction suitable for industrial workers, where agricultural advisers in their turn would be out of place. Control so exercised over the policy of State institutions would vitalize them, and tend to make them enter more intimately into the department of national effort they were created to foster. The stagnation which falls on most Government departments is due to this, that the responsible heads rarely have a knowledge great enough to enable them to inaugurate new methods, that parliamentary control is never adequate, is rarely exercised with knowledge, and there is always a party in power to defend the policy of their Minister, for if one Minister is successfully attacked a whole party goes out of power. We, in Ireland, should desire above all things efficiency in our public servants. They will stagnate in their offices unless they are continually stimulated by intimate connection with the class they work for and who have a power of control. This system would also, I believe, lead to less jobbery. Men in an assembly, where theoretically every class and interest are represented, often conspire to make bad appointments, because only a minority have knowledge of what qualifications the official ought to have, and they are outvoted by representatives who do their friends such good turns often in sheer ignorance that they are betraying their constituents. Where specialists have power, and where the well-being of their own industry is concerned, they never willingly appoint the inefficient. Such an organization of our County Council system would operate also to break up sectarian cliques. The feeling of organized classes, farmers, or industrialists, concerned about their own well-being, would oppose itself to sectarian sentiment where its application was unfitting.

In the system of representative government I have outlined, we would have one supreme or national assembly concerned with general interests, justice, taxation, education, the apportioning of revenue to its various uses, reserving to itself direct control over the policy of the departments of treasury, police, judiciary, all that affects the citizens equally ; and, beneath it, other councils, representative of classes and special interests, controlling the policy and administration of the State departments concerned with their work. Where everybody was concerned everybody would have that measure of control which a vote confers ; where particular interests were concerned these interests would not be hampered in their development by the intervention of busybodies from outside.   Of course on matters where particular interests clashed with general interests, or were unable to adjust themselves to other interests, the supreme Assembly would have to decide. The more sectional interests are removed from discussion in the National Assembly, and the more it confines itself to general interests the more will it approximate to the ideal senate, be less the haunt of greed, and more the vehicle of the national will and the national being.

By the application of the principle of representative government now in force, one is reminded of nothing so much as the palette of an artist who had squeezed out the primary colours and mixed them into a greasy drab tint, where the purity of every colour was lost, or the most powerful pigment was in dull domination.   If the modification of the representative principle I have outlined was in operation, with each interest or industry organized, and freed from alien interference, the effect might be likened to a disc with the seven primary colours raying from a centre, and made to whirl where the motion produced rather the effect of pure light.   We must not mix the colours of national life until conflicting interests muddle themselves into a grey drab of human futility, but strive, so far as possible, to keep them pure and unmixed, each retaining its own peculiar lustre, so that in their conjunction with others they will harmonize, as do the pure primary colours, and in their motion make a light of true intelligence to prevail in the national being.

XV

No policy can succeed if it be not in accord with national character. If I have misjudged that, what is written here is vain. It may be asked, can any one abstract from the chaos which is Irish history a prevailing mood or tendency recurring again and again, and assert these are fundamental ? It is difficult to define national character, even in long-established States whose history lies open to the world ; but it is most difficult in Ireland, which for centuries has not acted by its own will from its own centre, where national activity was mainly by way of protest against external domination, or a readjustment of itself to external power. We can no more deduce the political character of the Irish from the history of the past seven hundred years than we can estimate the quality of genius in an artist whom we have only seen when grappling with a burglar. The political character of a people emerges only when they are shaping in freedom their own civilization. To get a clue in Ireland we must slip by those seven centuries of struggle and study national origins, as the lexicographer, to get the exact meaning of a word, traces it to its derivation. The greatest value our early history and literature has for us is the value of a clue to character, to be returned to again and again in the maze of our infinitely more complicated life and era.

In every nation which has been allowed free development, while it has the qualities common to all humanity, it will be found that some one idea was predominant, and in its predominance regrouped about itself other ideas. With our neighbours I believe the idea of personal liberty has been the inspiring motive of all that is best in its political development, whatever the reactions and oppressions may have been. In ancient Attica the idea of beauty, proportion, or harmony in life so pervaded the minds of the citizens that the surplus revenues of the State were devoted to the beautifying of the city. We find that love for beauty in its art, its literature, its architecture; and to Plato, the highest mind in the Athenian State, Deity itself appeared as Beauty in its very essence. That mighty mid-European State, whose ambitions have upset the world, seems to conceive of the State as power. Other races have had a passion for justice, and have left codes of law which have profoundly affected the life of nations which grew up long after they were dead. The cry of ancient Israel for righteousness rings out above all other passions, and its laws are essentially the laws of a people who desired that morality should prevail.

We have to discover for ourselves the ideas which lie at the root of national character, and so inculcate these principles that they will pervade the nation and make it a spiritual solidarity, and unite the best minds in their service, and so control those passionate and turbulent elements which are the cause of the downfall and wreckage of nations by internal dissensions. I desire as much as any one to preserve our national identity, and to make it worthy of preservation, and this can only be done by the domination of some inspiring ideal which will draw all hearts to it; which may at first have that element of strangeness in it which Ben Jonson said was in all excellent beauty, and which will later become—as all high things we love do finally become—familiar to us, and nearer and closer to us than the beatings of our own hearts.

When ideals which really lie at the root of our being are first proclaimed, all that is external in life protests. So were many great reformers martyred, but they left their ideals behind them in the air, and men breathed them and they became part of their very being. Nationality is a state of consciousness, a mood of definite character in our intellectual being, and it is not perceived first except in profound meditation; it does not become apparent from superficial activities any more than we could, by looking at the world and the tragic history of mankind, discover that the Kingdom of Heaven is within us. That knowledge comes to those who go

within themselves, and not to those who seek
without for the way, the truth, and the life.   But,
once proclaimed, the incorruptible spiritual element in man intuitively recognizes it as truth,
and it has a profound effect on human action.
There is, I believe, a powerful Irish character
which has begun to reassert itself in modern times,
and this character is in essentials what it was
two thousand years ago.   We discover its first
manifestation in the ancient clans.   The clan was
at once aristocratic and democratic.   It was aristocratic in leadership and democratic in its economic
basis.   The most powerful character was elected
as chief, while the land was the property of the
clan.   That social order indicates the true political
character of the Irish.   Races which last for
thousands of years do not change in essentials.
They change in circumstance.   They may grow
better or worse, but throughout their history the
same fundamentals appear and reassert themselves.
We can see later in Irish literature or politics, as
powerful personalities emerged and expressed
themselves, how the ancient character persisted.
Swift, Goldsmith, Berkeley, O'Grady, Shaw,
Wilde, Parnell, Davitt, Plunkett, and many others,
however they differed from each other, in so far
as they betrayed a political character, were
intensely democratic in economic theory, adding
that to an aristocratic freedom of thought.   That
peculiar character, I believe, still persists among
our people in the mass, and it is by adopting a
policy which will enable it to manifest once more

that we will create an Irish civilization, which
will fit our character as the glove fits the hand.
During the last quarter of a century of comparatively peaceful life the co-operative principle
has once more laid hold on the imagination of
the Irish townsman and the Irish countryman.
The communal character is still preserved. It
still wills to express itself in its external aspects
in a communal civilization, in an economic
brotherhood. That movement alone provides
in Ireland for the aristocratic and democratic
elements in Irish character. It brings into
prominence the aristocracy of character and
intelligence which it is really the Irish nature to
love, and its economic basis is democratic. A
large part of our failure to achieve anything
memorable in Ireland is due to the fact that,
influenced by the example of our great neighbours,
we reversed the natural position of the aristocratic
and democratic elements in the national being.
Instead of being democratic in our economic life,
with the aristocracy of character and intelligence
to lead us, we became meanly individualistic in
our economics and meanly democratic in leadership. That is, we allowed individualism—the
devilish doctrine of every man for himself—to
be the keynote of our economic life; where,
above all things, the general good and not the
enrichment of the individual should be considered.
For our leaders we chose energetic, common-
place types, and made them represent us in the
legislature; though it is in leadership above all

that we need, not the aristocracy of birth, but the aristocracy of character, intellect, and will. We had not that aristocracy to lead us. We chose instead persons whose ideas were in no respect nobler than the average to be our guides, or rather to be guided by us. Yet when the aristocratic character appeared, however imperfect, how it was adored! Ireland gave to Parnell —an aristocratic character—the love which springs from the deeps of its being, a love which it gave to none other in our time.

With our great neighbours what are our national characteristics were reversed. They are an individualistic race. This individualism has expressed itself in history and society in a thousand ways. Being individualistic in economics, they were naturally democratic in politics. They have a genius for choosing forcible average men as leaders. They mistrust genius in high places. Intensely individualistic themselves, they feared the aristocratic character in politics. They desired rather that general principles should be asserted to encircle and keep safe their own national eccentricity. They have gradually infected us with something of their ways, and as they were not truly our ways we never made a success of them. It is best for us to fall back on what is natural with us, what is innate in character, what was visible among us in the earliest times, and what, I still believe, persists among us—a respect for the aristocratic intellect, for freedom of thought, ideals, poetry, and imagination, as the qualities to be looked for in leaders, and a bias for democracy in our economic life. We were more Irish truly in the heroic ages. We would not then have taken, as we do to-day, the huckster or the publican and make them our representative men, and allow them to corrupt the national soul. Did not the whole vulgar mob of our politicians lately unite to declare to the world that Irish nationality was impossible except it was floated on a sea of liquor? The image of Kathleen ni Houlihan anciently was beauty in the hearts of poets and dreamers. We often thought her unwise, but never did we find her ignoble; never was she without a flame of idealism in her eyes, until this ignoble crew declared alcohol to be the only possible basis of Irish nationality.

In the remote past we find the national instincts of our people fully manifested. We find in this early literature a love for the truth-teller and for the hero. Indeed they did not choose as chieftains of their clans men whom the bards could not sing. They reverenced wisdom, whether in king, bard, or ollav, and at the same time there was a communal basis for economic life. This heroic literature is, as our Standish O'Grady declared, rather prophecy than history. It reveals what the highest spirits deemed the highest, and what was said lay so close to the heart of the race that it is still remembered and read. That literature discloses the character of the national being, still to be manifested in a civilization, and it must flame out before the tale which began

among the gods is closed. Whatever brings this
communal character into our social order, and at
the same time desires the independent aristocratic
intellect, is in accord with the national tradition.
The co-operative movement is the modern expression of that mood. It is already making a
conquest of the Irish mind, and in its application
to life predisposing our people to respect for the
man of special attainments, independent character,
and intellect. A social order which has made
its economics democratic in character needs such
men above all things. It needs aristocratic
thinkers to save the social order from stagnation,
the disease which eats into all harmonious life.
We shall succeed or fail in Ireland as we succeed
or fail to make democracy prevail in our economic
life, and aristocratic ideals to prevail in our
political and intellectual life.

In all things it is best for a people to obey
the law of their own being. The lion can never
become the ox, and " one law for the lion and the
ox is oppression." Now that the hammer of
Thor is wrecking our civilizations, is destroying
the body of European nationalities, the spirit is
freer to reshape the world nearer to the heart's
desire. Necessity will drive us along with the
rest to recast our social order and to fix our
ideals. Necessity and our own hearts should
lead us to a brotherhood in industry. It should
be horrible to us the thought of the greedy
profiteer, the pursuit of wealth for oneself rather
than the union of forces for the good of all and

K

the creation of a brotherly society. The efforts of individuals to amass for themselves great personal wealth should be regarded as ignoble by society, and as contrary to the national spirit, as it is indeed contrary to all divine teaching. Our ideal should be economic harmony and intellectual diversity. We should regard as alien to the national spirit all who would make us think in flocks, and discipline us to an unintellectual commonalty of belief. The life of the soul is a personal adventure, a quest for the way and the truth and the life. It may be we shall find the ancient ways to be the true ways, but if we are led to the truth blindfolded and without personal effort, we are like those whom the Scripture condemns for entering into Paradise, not by the straight gate, but over the wall, like thieves and robbers. If we seek it for ourselves and come to it, we shall be true initiates and masters in the guild.

No people seem to have greater natural intelligence than the Irish. No people have been so unfortunately cursed with organizations which led them to abnegate personal thought, and Ireland is an intellectual desert where people read nothing and think nothing ; where not fifty in a hundred thousand could discern the quality of thought in the *Politics* of Aristotle or the *Republic* of Plato as being in any way deeper than a leading article in one of their daily papers. And we, whose external life is so mean, whose ignorance of literature is so great, are yet flattered by the suggestion that we have treasures of spiritual and intellectual life which should not be debased by external influences, and so it comes about that good literature is a thing unpurchasable except in some half-dozen of the larger towns. Any system which would suppress the aristocratic, fearless, independent intellect should be regarded as contrary to the Irish genius and inimical to the national being.

XVI

AMONG the many ways men have sought to create a national consciousness, a fountain of pride to the individual citizen, is to build a strong body for the great soul, and it would be an error to overlook—among other modern uprisings of ancient Irish character—the revival of the military spirit and its possible development in relation to the national being. National solidarity may be brought about by pressure from without, or by the fusion of the diverse elements in a nation by a heat engendered from within. But to create national solidarity by war is to attain but a temporary and unreal unity, a gain like theirs who climb into the Kingdom not by the straight gate, but over the wall like a robber. When one nation is threatened by another, great national sacrifices will be made, and the latent solidarity of its humanity be kindled. But when the war is over, when the circumstances uniting the people for a time are past, that spirit rapidly dies, and people begin their old antagonisms because the social order, in its normal working, does not constantly promote a consciousness of identity of interest.

Almost all the great European states have fortified their national being by militarism. Everything almost in their development has been subordinated to the necessities of national defence, and hence it is only in times of war there is any real manifestation of national spirit. It is only then that the citizens of the Iron Age feel a transitory brotherhood. It is a paradoxical phenomenon, possible only in the Iron Age, that the highest instances of national sacrifice are evoked by warfare—the most barbarous of human enterprises. To make normal that spirit of unity which is now only manifested in abnormal moments in history should be our aim ; and as it is the Iron Age, and material forces are more powerful than spiritual, we must consider how these fierce energies. can be put in relation with the national being with least debasement of that being. If the body of the national soul is too martial in character, it will by reflex action communicate its character to the spirit, and make it harsh and domineering, and unite against it in hatred all other nations. We have seen that in Europe but yesterday. The predominance in the body of militarist practice will finally drive out from the soul those unfathomable spiritual elements which are the body's last source of power in conflict, and it will in the end defeat its own object, which is power. When nations at war call up their reserves of humanity to the last man capable of bearing arms, their leaders begin also to summon up those bodiless moods and national sentiments which are the souls of races, and their last and most profound sources of inspiration and deathless courage. The war then becomes a conflict of civilizations and of spiritual ideals, the aspirations and memories which constitute the fundamental basis of those civilizations. Without the inspiration of great memories or of great hopes, men are incapable of great sacrifices. They are rationalists, and the preservation of the life they know grows to be a desire greater than the immortality of the spiritual life of their race. A famous Japanese general once said it was the power to hold out for the last desperate quarter of an hour which won victories, and it is there spiritual stamina reinforces physical power. It is a mood akin to the ecstasy of the martyr through his burning. Though in these mad moments neither spiritual nor material is consciously differentiated, the spiritual is there in a fiery fusion with all other forces. If it is absent, the body unsupported may take to its heels or will yield. It has played its only card, and has not eternity to fling upon the table in a last gamble for victory.

A military organization may strengthen the national being, but if it dominates it, it will impoverish its life. How little Sparta has given to the world compared with Attica. Yet when national ideals have been created they assume an immeasurably greater dignity when the citizens organize themselves for the defence of their ideals, and are prepared to yield up life itself as a sacrifice if by this the national being may be preserved. A creed always gains respect through its martyrs. We may grant all this, yet be doubtful whether a militarist organization should be the main support of the national being in Ireland. The character of the ideal should, I believe, be otherwise created, and I am not certain that it could not be as well preserved and defended by a civil organization, such as I have indicated, as by armed power. Our geographical position and the slender population of our country also make it evident that the utmost force Ireland could organize would make but a feeble barrier against assault by any of the greater States. We have seen how Belgium, a country with a population larger than that of Ireland, was thrust aside, crushed and bleeding, by one stroke from the paw of its mighty neighbour.[1] The military and political institutions of a small country are comparatively easy to displace, but it would be a task infinitely more difficult to destroy ideals or to extinguish a national being based on a social order, democratic and co-operative in character, the soul of the country being continually fed by institutions which, by their very nature, would be almost impossible to alter unless destruction of the whole humanity of the country was aimed at. National ideals, based on a co-operative social order, would have the same power of resistance almost as a religion, which is, of all things, most

[1] Since this book was written Ireland has had a tragic illustration of the truth of what is urged in these pages.

unconquerable by physical force, and, when it is itself militant, the most powerful ally of military power. The aim of all nations is to preserve their immortality. I do not oppose the creation of a national army for this purpose. There are occasions when the manhood of a nation must be prepared to yield life rather than submit to oppression, when it must perish in self-contempt or resist by force what wrong would be imposed by force. But I would like to point out that for a country in the position of Ireland the surest means of preserving the national being by the sacrifice and devotion of the people are economic and spiritual.

Our political life in the past has been sordid and unstable because we were uncultured as a nation. National ideals have been the possession of the few in Ireland, and have not been diffused. That is the cause of our comparative failure as a nation. If we would create an Irish culture, and spread it widely among our people, we would have the same unfathomable sources of inspiration and sacrifice to draw upon in our acts as a nation as the individual has who believes he is immortal, and that his life here is but a temporary foray into time out of eternity.

Yet we have much to learn from the study of military organization. The great problem of all civilizations is the creation of citizens : that is, of people who are dominated by the ideal of the general welfare, who will sink private desire and work harmoniously with their fellow-citizens for

the highest good of their race.   While we may
all agree that war brings about an eruption of
the arcane and elemental forces which lie normally
in the pit of human life, as the forces which cause
earthquakes lie normally asleep in the womb of
the world, none the less we must admit that
military genius has discovered and applied with
mastery a law of life which is of the highest importance to civilization—far more important to
civil even than to military development—and that
is the means by which the individual will forget
his personal danger and sacrifice life itself for the
general welfare.   In no other organization will
men in great masses so entirely forget themselves
as men will in battle under military discipline.
What is the cause of this ?   Can we discover
how it is done and apply the law to civil life ?

The military discipline works miracles.   The
problem before the captains of armies is to take
the body of man, the most naturally egoistic of
all things, which hates pain and which will
normally take to its legs in danger and try to
save itself, and to dominate it so that the body
and the soul inhabiting it will stand still and face
all it loathes.   And the problem is solved in the
vast majority of cases.   After military training
the civilians who formerly would fly before a
few policemen will manfully and heroically stand,
not the blows of a baton, but a whole hail of
bullets, a cannonade lasting through a day ; nay,
they will for weeks and months, day by day, risk
and lose life for a cause, for an idea, at a word of

command. They may not have half as good a
cause to lose life for as they had as a mob of
angry civilians, but they will face death now, and
the chances of mutilation and agony worse than
death. Can we inspire civilians with the same
passionate self-forgetfulness in the pursuit of
the higher ideals of peace ? Men in a regiment
have to a large extent the personal interests
abolished. The organization they now belong
to supports them and becomes their life. By
their union with it a new being is created. Exercise, drill, manœuvre, accentuate that unity, and
esprit de corps arises, so that they feel their highest
life is the corporate one ; and that feeling is
fostered continually, until at last all the units,
by some law of the soul, are as it were in spite of
themselves, in spite of the legs which want to
run, in spite of the body which trembles with
fear, constrained to move in obedience to the
purpose of the whole organism expressed by its
controlling will ; and so we get these devoted
masses of men who advance again and again under
a hail more terrible than Dante imagined falling
in his vision of the fiery world.

There is nothing like it in civilian life, but yet
the aim of the higher minds in all civilizations is
to create a similar devotion to civic ideals, so that
men will not only, as Pericles said, " give their
bodies for the commonwealth," but will devote
mind, will, and imagination with equal assiduity
and self-surrender to the creation of a civilization
which will be the inheritance of all and a cause

of pride to every one, and which will bring to
the individual a greater beauty and richness of
life than he could finally reach by the utmost
private efforts of which he was capable.

I believe that an organization of society, such
as I have indicated, would evolve gradually a
similar passion for the general zeal, having,
without the stern restraint militarism imposes on
its units, a like power of turning the thoughts to
the general good.

I may say also that to create a militarist organization, before the natural principles to be safeguarded are well understood and a common
possession of all the people in the country, would
be a danger akin to the peril of allowing children
to play with firearms. We may find it a bad
business to create natural ideals as they are
required, just as it is a perilous business to try
to create an army when a country is in a state of
war. If we do not rapidly create a national
culture embodying the fundamental ideas we
wish to see prevailing in society our volunteer
armies will be subject to influences from the baser
sort of politicians who would force party aims
on the country. We shall have a wretched
future unless the soul of the country can dominate
the physical forces in it, unless ideals of national
conduct, liberty of speech and thought, of justice
and brotherhood, exist to inspire and guide it,
and are recognized by all and appealed to by all
parties equally.

We are standing on the threshold of nation-

hood, and it is problems like these we should
be setting ourselves to solve, unless we are to
be an unimportant province of the world, a
mere administrative area inhabited by a quite
undistinguished people.

XVII

But there are other methods of devotion to the
national being possible to us through collective
action, and I was moved to imagine one, having
once received a letter from a bloodthirsty corre-
spondent—one of that rather numerous class
whose minds are always loaded with ball cartridge,
whose fingers are always on the trigger, and who
are always calling on the authorities not to hesitate
to shoot. He wrote to me during a railway
strike, advocating military conscription in order
that railway men who went out on strike could
be called up by the military authorities as the
French railway strikers were, and who were subject
to martial law if they disobeyed. I do not think
with those who believe the venerable remedy of
blood-letting is the best cure for social maladies ;
and I would have thought no more about that
stern disciplinarian, but my mind went playing
about the idea of conscription, and there came to
me some thoughts which I wish to put on record
in the hope that our people in some future, when
the social order will create public spirit and the
passion for the State more plentifully than it

does to-day, may recur to the idea and apply it.
Nearly every State in the world demands from
youth a couple of years' service in the army.
There they are trained to defend their country—
even, if necessary, to slay their own countrymen.
There is much that is abhorrent to the imagination
in the idea of war, and I am altogether with that
noble body of men who are trying, by means of
arbitration treaties, to solve national differences
by reason rather than by force. But we all
recognize something noble in the spirit of the
nation where the community agrees that every
man shall give up some years of his life to the
State for the preservation of the State, and may
be called upon to surrender life absolutely in
that service.   While the manhood of a race does
this on the whole with cheerfulness, there must
be something of high character in the manhood
of that nation. A certain gravity attaches to
national decisions which are made, as it were,
upon the slopes of death, because none are exempt
from service, and there is no delirious mob ready
to yell for a war in which it does not run the risk
of having its own dirty skin perforated by bullets.
In Ireland we have never had military conscription, for reasons which are well known to all,
and upon which I need not enter. I am well
satisfied it should be so, for it leaves open to us
the possibility of a much nobler service, one
which has never yet been attempted by any modern
nation, and that is civil conscription.

I throw out this suggestion, which may hold

the imagination of those who have noble concep-
tions of what national life should be and what a
nation should work for, in the hope that some
time it may fructify.   There is a prohibition laid
on the people in this island against conscription
for military purposes.   Is there any reason why
we should not have conscription for civil purposes ?   Why should not every young man in
Ireland give up two years of his life in a comradeship of labour with other young men, and be
employed under skilled direction in great works
of public utility, in the erection of public buildings, the beautifying of our cities, reclamation of
waste lands, afforestation, and other desirable
objects ?   The principle of service for the State
for military purposes is admitted in every country,
even at last by the English-speaking peoples.   It
is easy to be seen how this principle of conscription
could be applied to infinitely nobler ends—to
the building up of a beautiful civilization—and
might make the country adopting it in less than
half a century as beautiful as ancient Attica or
majestic as ancient Egypt.   While other nations
take part of the life of young men for instruction
in war, why should not the State in Ireland, more
nobly inspired, ask of its young men that they
should give equally of their lives to the State,
not for the destruction of life, but for the con-
servation of life ?   This service might be asked
from all—high and low, well and humbly born—
except from those who can plead the reasons
which exempt people abroad from military service.

As things stand to-day, if the State undertakes any public work, it does it more expensively by far than it would be if undertaken by private enterprise. Every person puts up prices for the State or for municipalities. Labour, land, and materials are all charged at the highest possible rates, whereas if there was any really high conception of citizenship and of the functions of the State, the citizens would agree so that works of public utility, or those which conspired to add to national dignity, should be done at least cost to the community. Where there is no national sacrifice there is no national pride. Because there is no national pride our modern civilizations show meanly compared with the titanic architecture of the cities and majestic civilizations of the past. We know from the ruins of these proud cities that he who walked into ancient Rome, Athens, Thebes, Memphis and Babylon, walked amid grandeurs which must have exalted the spirit. To walk into Manchester, Sheffield, or Liverpool is to feel a weight upon the soul. There is no national feeling for beauty in our industrial civilizations.

Let us suppose Ireland had through industrial conscription about fifty thousand young men every year at its disposal under a national works department. What could be done? First of all it would mean that every young man in the country would have received an industrial training of some kind. The work of technical instruction could be largely carried on in connection with this industrial army. People talk of the benefit of discipline and obedience secured by military service. This and much more could be secured by a labour conscription. Every man in the island would have got into the habit of work at a period of life when it is most necessary, and when too many young men have no serious occupation. Parents should welcome the training and discipline for their children, and certificates of character and intelligence given by the department of national works should open up prospects of rapid employment in the ordinary industrial life of the country when the period of public service was closed. For those engaged there would be a true comradeship in labour, and the phrase, "the dignity of labour," about which so much cant has been written, would have a real significance where young men were working together for the public benefit with the knowledge that any completed work would add to the health, beauty, dignity, and prosperity of the State. In return for this labour the State should feed and clothe its industrial army, educate them, and familiarize them with some branch of employment, and make them more competent after this period of service was over to engage in private enterprise. Two years of such training would dissipate all the slackness, lack of precision, and laziness which are so often apparent in young men who have never had any strict discipline in their homes, and whom parental weakness has rendered unfit for the hard business of life.

L

The benefit to those undergoing such a training would of itself justify civil conscription; but when we come to think of the nation—what might not be done by a State with a national labour army under its control? Public works might be undertaken at a cost greatly below that which would otherwise be incurred, and the estimates which now paralyse the State, when it considers this really needed service or that, would assume a different appearance, as it would be embracing in one enterprise technical education and the accomplishment of beneficial works. With such an army under skilled control the big cities could have playgrounds for the children of the cities; public gardens, baths, gymnasiums, recreation rooms, hospitals, and sanatoriums might be built; waste land reclaimed and afforested, and the roadsides might be planted with fruit trees. National schools, picture-galleries, public halls, libraries, and a thousand enterprises which now hang fire because at present labour for public service is the most expensive labour, all could be undertaken. If the State becomes very poor, as indeed it is certain to be, it may be forced into some such method of fulfilling its functions. Are we, with enormous burdens of debt, to hang up every useful public work because of the expense, and spend our lives in paying State debts while the body for whom we work is unable, on account of the expense, to do anything for us in return? If the State is to continue its functions we shall have to commandeer people for its service in times of peace as is done in times of war. There is hardly an argument which could be used to defend military conscription which could not be equalled with as powerful an argument for civil conscription. I am not at all sure that if the State in Ireland decided to utilise two years of every young man's life for State purposes that we could not disband most of our expensive constabulary and make certain squads of our civil recruits responsible for the keeping of public law and order, leaving only the officers as permanent professionals, for of course there must be expert control of the conscripts. The postal service might also be carried on largely by conscripted civilians.

This may appear a fantastic programme, but I would like to see it argued out. It would create a real brotherhood in work, just as the army creates in its own way a brotherhood between men in the same regiments. The nation adopting civil conscription could clean itself up in a couple of generations, so that in respect of public services it would be incomparable. The alternative to this is to starve all public services, to make the State simply the tax-collector, to pay the interest on a huge debt, and so get it hated because it can do nothing except collect money to pay the interest on a colossal national debt. Obviously the State as an agency to bring about civilization cannot perform both services—pay interest on huge public loans, and continue an expensive service. It must find out some way in which public services can be continued, and if possible

improved, and the open way to that is civil conscription and the assertion of a claim to two or
three years of the work of every citizen for
civil purposes, just as it now asserts a claim on
the services of citizens for the defence of the
State.   As national debts are more and more
piled up, it has seemed to many that here must be
an end to what was called social reform, that we
were entering on a black era, and no dawn would
show over Europe for another century.   There
is always a way out of troubles if people are
imaginative enough and brotherly enough to
conceive of it and bold enough to take action when
they have found the way.   The real danger for
society is that it may become spiritless and hide-
bound and tamed, and have none of those high
qualities necessary in face of peril, and the more
people get accustomed to thinking of bold schemes
the better.   They will get over the first shock,
and may be ready when the time comes to put
them into action.   When a country is poor like
Ireland and yet is ambitious of greatness ; when
the aspect of its civilization is mean and when it
yet aspires to beauty ; when its people are living
under unsanitary conditions and yet the longing
is there to give health to all ; when Ireland is
like this, its public men and its citizens might do
much worse than brood over the possibilities of
industrial conscription, and of revising the character of the purposes for which nations have
hitherto claimed service from their young citizens
on behalf of the State.   Debarred by a fate not

altogether unkind from training every citizen in
the arts of war Ireland might—if the love of
country and the desire for service are really so
strong as we are told—suddenly become eminent
among the nations of the world by adopting a
policy which in half a century would make our
mean cities and our backward countryside the
most beautiful in the modern world.

XVIII

I HAVE not in all this written anything about the
relations of Ireland with other countries, or even
with our neighbours, in whose political household
we have lived for so many centuries in intimate
hostility. I have considered this indeed, but did
not wish, nor do I now wish, in anything I may
write, to say one word which would add to that
old hostility. Race hatred is the cheapest and
basest of all national passions, and it is the nature
of hatred, as it is the nature of love, to change us
into the likeness of that which we contemplate.
We grow nobly like what we adore, and ignobly
like what we hate; and no people in Ireland
became so anglicized in intellect and temperament, and even in the manner of expression, as
those who hated our neighbours most. All
hatreds long persisted in bring us to every base-
ness for which we hated others. The only laws
which we cannot break with impunity are divine
laws, and no law is more eternally sure in its
workings than that which condemns us to be
even as that we condemned. Hate is the high
commander of so many armies that an inquiry

into the origin of this passion is at least as needful
as histories of other contemporary notorieties.
Not emperors or parliaments alone raise armies,
but this passion also.   It will sustain nations in
defeat.   When everything seems lost this wild
captain will appear and the scattered forces are
reunited.   They will be as oblivious of danger
as if they were divinely inspired, but if they win
their battle it is to become like the conquered
foe.   All great wars in history, all conquests, all
national antagonisms, result in an exchange of
characteristics.   It is because I wish Ireland to
be itself, to act from its own will and its own
centre, that I deprecate hatred as a force in national
life.   It is always possible to win a cause without
the aid of this base helper, who betrays us ever
in the hour of victory.

When a man finds the feeling of hate for
another rising vehemently in himself, he should
take it as a warning that conscience is battling
in his own being with that very thing he loathes.
Nations hate other nations for the evil which is in
themselves ; but they are as little given to self-
analysis as individuals, and while they are right
to overcome evil, they should first try to understand the genesis of the passion in their own
nature.   If we understand this, many of the
ironies of history will be intelligible.   We will
understand why it was that our countrymen in
Ulster and our countrymen in the rest of Ireland,
who have denounced each other so vehemently,
should at last appear to have exchanged charac-

teristics : why in the North, having passionately protested against physical force movements,
no-rent manifestos, and contempt for Imperial
Parliament, they should have come themselves at
last to organize a physical force movement, should
threaten to pay no taxes, and should refuse obedience to an Act of Parliament. We will understand
also why it was their opponents came themselves
to address to Ulster all the arguments and de-
nunciations Ulster had addressed to them. I
do not point this out with intent to annoy, but
to illustrate by late history a law in national as
well as human psychology. If this unpopular
psychology I have explained was adopted everywhere as true, we would never hear expressions
of hate. People would realize they were first
revealing and then stabbing their own characters
before the world.

Nations act towards other nations as their own
citizens act towards each other. When slavery
existed in a State, if that nation attacked another
it was with intent to enslave. Where there is a
fierce economic competition between citizen and
citizen then in war with another nation, the
object of the war is to destroy the trade of the
enemy. If the citizens in any country could
develop harmonious life among themselves they
would manifest the friendliest feelings towards
the people of other countries. We find that it
is just among groups of people who aim at
harmonious life, co-operators and socialists, that
the strongest national impulses to international

brotherhood arise; and wars of domination are brought about by the will of those who within a State are dominant over the fortunes of the rest. Ireland, a small country, can only maintain its national identity by moral and economic forces. Physically it must be overmastered by most other European nations. Moral forces are really more powerful than physical forces. One Christ changed the spiritual life of Europe; one Buddha affected more myriads in Asia.

The co-operative ideal of brotherhood in industry has helped to make stronger the ideal of the brotherhood of humanity, and no body of men in any of the countries in the great War of our time regarded it with more genuine sorrow than those who were already beginning to promote schemes for international co-operation. It must be mainly in movements inspired with the ideal of the brotherhood of man, that the spirit will be generated which, in the future, shall make the idea of war so detestable that statesmen will find it is impossible to think of that solution of their disputes as they would think now of resorting to private assassination of political opponents. The great tragedy of Europe was brought about, not by the German Emperor, nor by Sir Edward Grey, nor by the Czar, nor by any of the other chiefs ostensibly controlling foreign policy, but by the nations themselves. These men may have been agents, but their action would have been impossible if they did not realize that there was a vast body of national feeling behind them not

opposed to war.   Their citizens were in conflict
with each other already, generating the moods
which lead on to war.   Emperors, foreign secre-
taries, ambassadors, cabinet ministers are not
really powerful to move nations against their will.
On the whole, they act with the will of the nations,
which they understand.   Let any one ruler try,
for example, to change by edict the religion of
his subjects, and a week would see him bereft
of place and power.   They could not do this,
because the will of the nation would be against
it.   They resort to war and prepare for it because
the will of the nation is with them, and this throws
us back on the private citizens, who finally are
individually and collectively responsible for the
actions of the State.   In the everlasting battle
between good and evil, private soldiers are called
upon to fight as well as the captains, and it is
only through the intensive cultivation by individuals and races of the higher moral and
intellectual qualities, until in intensity they
outweigh the mood and passion of the rest, that
war will finally become obsolete as the court of
appeal.   When there is a panic of fire in a crowded
building men are suddenly tested as to character.
Some will become frenzied madmen, fighting
and trampling their way out.   Others will act
nobly, forgetting themselves.   They have no
time to think.   What they are in their total make
up as human beings, overbalanced either for
good or evil, appears in an instant.   Even so,
some time in the heroic future, some nation in a

crisis will be weighed and will act nobly rather
than passionately, and will be prepared to risk
national extinction rather than continue existence
at the price of killing myriads of other human
beings, and it will oppose moral and spiritual
forces to material forces, and it will overcome
the world by making gentleness its might, as all
great spiritual teachers have done.   It comes to
this, we cannot overcome hatred by hatred or
war by war, but by the opposites of these.   Evil
is not overcome by evil but by good ; and any
race like the Irish, eager for national life, ought
to learn this truth—that humanity will act
towards their race as their race acts towards
humanity.   The noble and the base alike beget
their kin.   Empires, ere they disappear, see
their own mirrored majesty arise in the looking-
glass of time.   Opposed to the pride and pomp
of Egypt were the pride and pomp of Chaldaea.
Echoing the beauty of the Greek city state were
many lovely cities made in their image.   Carthage
evoked Rome.   The British Empire, by the
natural balance and opposition of things, called
into being another empire with a civilization of
coal and steel, and with ambitions for colonies and
for naval power, and with that image of itself it
must wrestle for empire.   The great armadas
that throng the seas, the armed millions upon the
earth betray the fear in the minds of races, nay,
the inner spiritual certitude the soul has, that
pride and lust of power must yet be humbled by
their kind.   They must at last meet their equals

face to face, called to them as steel to magnet by some inner affinity. This is a law of life both for individuals and races, and, when this is realized, we know nothing will put an end to race conflicts except the equally determined and heroic development of the spiritual, moral, and intellectual forces which disdain to use the force and fury of material powers.

We may be assured that the divine law is not mocked, and it cannot be deceived. As men sow so do they reap. The anger we create will rend us ; the love we give will return to us. Biologically, everything breeds true to its type : moods and thoughts just as much as birds and beasts and fishes. When I hear people raging against England or Germany or Russia I know that rage will beget rage, and go on begetting it, and so the whole devilish generation of passions will be continued. There are no nations to whom the entire and loyal allegiance of man's spirit could be given. It can only go out to the ideal empires and nationalities in the womb of time, for whose coming we pray. Those countries of the future we must carve out of the humanity of to-day, and we can begin building them up within our present empires and nationalities just as we are building up the co-operative movement in a social order antagonistic to it. The people who are trying to create these new ideals in the world are outposts, sentinels, and frontiersmen thrown out before the armies of the intellectual and spiritual races yet to come into being.

We can all enlist in these armies and be comrades to the pioneers. I hope many will enlist in Ireland. I would cry to our idealists to come out of this present-day Irish Babylon, so filled with sectarian, political, and race hatreds, and to work for the future. I believe profoundly, with the most extreme of Nationalists, in the future of Ireland, and in the vision of light seen by Bridget which she saw and confessed between hopes and tears to Patrick, and that this is the Isle of Destiny and the destiny will be glorious and not ignoble, and when our hour is come we will have something to give to the world, and we will be proud to give rather than to grasp. Throughout their history Irishmen have always wrought better for others than for themselves, and when they unite in Ireland to work for each other, they will direct into the right channel all that national capacity for devotion to causes for which they are famed. We ought not only to desire to be at peace with each other, but with the whole world, and this can only be brought about by the individual citizen at all times pro- testing against sectarian and national passions, and taking no part in them, coming out of such angry parties altogether, as the people of the Lord were called by the divine voice to come out of Babylon. It may seem a long way to set things right, but it is the swift way and the royal road, and there is no other ; and nobody, no prophet crying before his time, will be listened to until the people are ready for him. The congre-

gation must gather before the preacher can deliver
what is in him to say.   The economic brotherhood which I have put forward as an Irish ideal
would, in its realization, make us at peace with
ourselves, and if we are at peace with ourselves
we will be at peace with our neighbours and all
other nations, and will wish them the good-will
we have among ourselves, and will receive from
them the same good-will.   I do not believe in
legal and formal solutions of national antagonisms.
While we generate animosities among ourselves
we will always display them to other nations,
and I prefer to search out how it is national
hatreds are begotten, and to show how that
cancer can be cut out of the body politic.

XIX

IT seems inevitable that the domination of the individual by the State must become ever greater. It is in the evolutionary process. The amalgamation of individuals into nationalities and empires is as much in the cosmic plan as the development of highly organized beings out of unicellular organisms. I believe this process will continue until humanity itself is so psychically knit together that, as a being, it will manifest some form of cosmic consciousness in which the individual will share. Our spiritual intuitions and the great religions of the world alike indicate some such goal as that to which this turbulent cavalcade of humanity is wending. A knowledge of this must be in our subconscious being, or we would find the sacrifices men make for the State otherwise inexplicable. The State, though now ostensibly secular, makes more imperious claims on man than the ancient gods did. It lays hold of life. It asserts its right to take father, brother, and son, and to send them to meet death in its own defence. It denies them a choice or judgment as to whether its action is right or wrong.

Right or wrong, the individual must be prepared to give his body for the commonwealth, and when one gives the body unresistingly, one gives the soul also. The marvellous thing about the authority of the State is that it is recognized by the vast majority of citizens. During eras of peace the citizen may be always in conflict with the policy of the State. He may call it a tyranny, but yet when it is in peril he will die to preserve for it an immortal life. The hold the State establishes over the spirit of man is the more wonderful when we look rearward on history, and see with what labour and sacrifice the State was established. But we see also how readily, once the union has been brought about, men will die to preserve it, even although it is a tyranny, a bad State. For what do they die unless the spirit in man has some inner certitude that the divine event to which humanity tends is a unity of its multitudinous life, and that a State—even a bad State—must be preserved by its citizens, because it is at least an attempt at organic unity? It is a simulacrum of the ideal; it contains the germ or possibility of that to which the spirit of man is travelling. It disciplines the individual in service to that greater being in which it will find its fulfilment, and a bad State is better than no State at all. To be without a State is to prowl backwards from the divinity before us to the beast behind us.

The power the State exerts is a spiritual power, acting on or through the will of man. The

volunteer armies do not really march to die with
more readiness than the conscript armies. The
sacrifice is not readily explicable by material
causes. There is no material reason why the
proletarian—who has no property to defend, who
is more or less sure as a skilled craftsman of
employment under any ruler—should concern
himself whether his ruler be King, Kaiser, or
President. But not one in a hundred proletarians
really thinks like that. It is not the hope of
personal profit works upon men to risk life. Let
some exploiter of industry desire to employ a
thousand men at dangerous work, with the risks
of death or disablement equal to those of war ;
let it be known that one in six will be killed and
another be disabled, and what sum will purchase
the service of workers ? They will risk life for
the State, though given a bare subsistence or a
pay which they would describe as inhuman if
offered by one of the autocrats of industry. Men
working for the State will make the most extraordinary sacrifices ; but they stand stubbornly
and sullenly as disturbers and blockers of all
industry which is run for private profit. Is it
not clear of the two policies for the State to adopt,
to promote personal interests among its citizens
or to unite men for the general good, that the first
path is full of danger to the State, while through
the other men will march cheerfully, though it be
to death, in defence of the State. Something, a
real life above the individual, acts through the
national being, and would almost suggest to us

that Heaven cannot fully manifest its will to
humanity through the individual, but must utter
itself through multitudes.   There must be an
orchestration of humanity ere it can echo divine
melodies.   In real truth we are all seeking in
the majesties we create for union with a greater
Majesty.

I wrote in an earlier page that the ancient
conception of Nature as a manifestation of spirit
was incarnating anew in the minds of modern
thinkers ; that Nature was no longer conceived
of as material or static in condition, but as force
and continual motion ; that they were trying to
identify human will with this arcane energy, and
let the forces of Nature manifest with more power
in society.   The real nature of these energies
manifesting in humanity I do not know, but they
have been hinted at in the Scriptures, the oracles
of the Oversoul, which speak of the whole creation
labouring upwards and the entry of humanity
into the Divine Mind, and of the re-introcession
of That Itself with all Its myriad unity into Deity,
so that God might be all in all.   I believe profoundly that men do not hold the ideas of liberty
or solidarity, which have moved them so powerfully, merely as phantasies which are pleasant
to the soul or make ease for the body ; but
because, whether they struggle passionately for
liberty or to achieve a solidarity, in working for
these two ideals, which seem in conflict, they are
divinely supported, in unison with the divine
nature, and energies as real as those the scientist

studies—as electricity, as magnetism, heat or light—do descend into the soul and reinforce it with elemental energy. We are here for the purposes of soul, and there can be no purpose in individualizing the soul if essential freedom is denied to it and there is only a destiny. Wherever essential freedom, the right of the spirit to choose its own heroes and its own ideals, is denied, nations rise in rebellion. But the spirit in man is wrought in a likeness to Deity, which is that harmony and unity of Being which upholds the universe ; and by the very nature of the spirit, while it asserts its freedom, its impulses lead it to a harmony with all life, to a solidarity or brotherhood with it.

All these ideals of freedom, of brotherhood, of power, of justice, of beauty, which have been at one time or another the fundamental idea in civilizations, are heaven-born, and descended from the divine world, incarnating first in the highest minds in each race, perceived by them and transmitted to their fellow-citizens ; and it is the emergence or manifestation of one or other of these ideals in a group which is the beginning of a nation ; and the more strongly the ideal is held the more powerful becomes the national being, because the synchronous vibration of many minds in harmony brings about almost unconsciously a psychic unity, a coalescing of the subconscious being of many. It is that inner unity which constitutes the national being.

The idea of the national being emerged at

no recognizable point in our history in Ireland.
It is older than any name we know.   It is not
earth-born, but the synthesis of many heroic and
beautiful moments, and these, it must be remembered, are divine in their origin.   Every heroic
deed is an act of the spirit, and every perception
of beauty is vision with the divine eye, and not
with the mortal sense.   The spirit was subtly
intermingled with the shining of old romance,
and it is no mere phantasy which shows Ireland
at its dawn in a misty light thronged with divine
figures, and beneath and nearer to us demi-gods
and heroes fading into recognizable men.   The
bards took cognisance only of the most notable
personalities who preceded them, and of these
only the acts which had a symbolic or spiritual
significance ;   and these grew thrice refined as
generations of poets in enraptured musings along
by the mountains or in the woods brooded upon
their heritage of story, until, as it passed from
age to age, the accumulated beauty grew greater
than the beauty of the hour.   The dream began
to enter into the children of our race, and turn
their thoughts from earth to that world in which
it had its inception.

It was a common belief among the ancient
peoples that each had a national genius or deity
who presided over them, in whose all-embracing
mind they were contained, and who was the
shepherd of their destinies.   We can conceive of
the national spirit in Ireland as first manifesting itself through individual heroes or kings, and

as the history of famous warriors laid hold of the people, extending its influence until it created therein the germs of a kindred nature.

An aristocracy of lordly and chivalrous heroes is bound in time to create a great democracy by the reflection of their character in the mass, and the idea of the divine right of kings is succeeded by the idea of the divine right of the people. If this sequence cannot be traced in any one respect with historical regularity, it is because of the complexity of national life, its varied needs, the vicissitudes of history, and its infinite changes of sentiment. But the threads are all taken up in the end; and ideals which were forgotten and absent from the voices of men will be found, when recurred to, to have grown to a rarer and more spiritual beauty in their quiet abode in the heart. The seeds which were sown at the beginning of a race bear their flowers and fruits towards its close, and already antique names begin to stir us again with their power, and the antique ideals to reincarnate in us and renew their dominion over us.

They may not be recognized at first as a re-emergence of ancient moods. The democratic economics of the ancient clans have vanished almost out of memory, but the mood in which they were established reappears in those who would create a communal or co-operative life in the nation into which those ancient clans long since have melted. The instinct in the clans to waive aside the weak and to seek for an aristocratic and powerful character in their leaders reappears in the rising generation, who turn from the utterer of platitudes to men of real intellect and strong will.   The object of democratic organization is to bring out the aristocratic character in leadership, the vivid original personalities who act and think from their own will and their own centres, who bring down fire from the heaven of their spirits and quicken and vivify the mass, and make democracies also to be great and fearless and free.   A nation is dead where men acknowledge only conventions.   We must find out truth for ourselves, becoming first initiates and finally masters in the guild of life.   The intellect of Ireland is in chains where it ought to be free, and we have individualism in our economics which ought to be co-ordinated and sternly disciplined out of the iniquity of free profiteering.   To quicken the intellect and imagination of Ireland, to co-ordinate our economic life for the general good, should be the objects of national policy, and will subserve the evolutionary purpose. The free imagination and the aspiring mind alone climb into the higher spheres and deflect for us the ethereal currents.   It is the multitude of aristocratic thinkers who give glory to a people and make them of service to other nations, and it is by the character of the social order and the quality of brotherhood in it our civilization will endure.   Without love we are nothing.

XX

I BESEECH audience from the churches for these
thoughts on our Irish polity, and would recall
to them their early history, how when the fiery
spirit of their Lord first manifested on earth, life,
near to It, reflected It as in a glowing glass, and
impulses of true living arose. Material possessions were held in common. There was no
fierce talk of Thine and Mine. His ancient law
counselled poverty to the spirit, lest the gates of
Paradise should grow narrow before it like the
eye of a needle. I believe the fading hold the
heavens have over the world is due to the neglect
of the economic basis of spiritual life. What
profound spiritual life can there be when the
social order almost forces men to battle with each
other for the means of existence ? I know well
that no political mechanics, nothing which is an
economic device only, will of themselves be able
to affect the transfiguration of society and bring
it under the dominion of the spirit. For that,
a far higher quality of thought and action than
is here indicated is necessary. The economist
can provide the daily bread, but that bread of

the coming day which Christ wished his followers
to aspire to must come otherwise.   That should
be the labour of the poets, artists, musicians, and
of the heroic and aristocratic characters who
provide ʰy their life an image to which life can
be modelled.   Therefore I beseech audience not
only of the churches, but of the poets, writers,
and thinkers of Ireland for their aid in this labour.
They alone can create in wide commonalty the
ideals which can dominate society.   It is the work
of the artist to create for us images of desirable
life, to manifest to us the ideal humanity, and to
prefigure that vaster entity which I have called
the national being.   I said in an earlier page
that part of the failure of Ireland must be laid
to the poets who had dropped out of the divine
procession and sang a solitary song ; to the
writers who had turned from contemplating the
great to the portrayal of the little in human nature.
I know how difficult it is to constrain the spirit,
and how futile it is to ask artists or poets to create
what they are not inspired to create.   But we can ask
all men—artists, poets, litterateurs, and scientists
—to be citizens, and if they realize imagina-
tively the spiritual conception of the State, we may
assume that this imaginative realization of the
State will influence the labours of the mind, and
what is done will, consciously or unconsciously,
have reference to that collective being which
must dominate society more and more, which will
dominate it as a tyranny if we fail in our labours,
or liberate and make more majestical the spirit

of man if we imagine rightly.   All greatness is brought about by a conspiracy of the imagination and the will.   Our literature certainly manifests beauty, but not greatness or majesty, for majesty only arises where there is an orchestration of humanity by some mighty conductor ; and as a people we shall never manifest the highest qualities in literature or life until we are under the dominion of one, at least, of the great fundamental ideas which have been the inspiration of races.   Our feebleness arises from our economic individualism. We continually neutralize each other's efforts. Yet there is no less power in humanity to-day than there ever was.   We see now clearly what untamed elemental fires lay underneath the seeming placidity of the world.   There was a feeling in society that, just as the earth itself had settled down to be a habitable globe, and was forgetting its ancient ferocities of earthquake that opened up gulfs between land and land and rended sea from sea, so, too, humanity was losing those wilder energies we surmised in the cave-dweller or the hunters of mastodon, mammoth, and cave-tiger.   But it was all a dream—a dream, we suspect, about the earth as well as about humanity. While we indulged in these pleasing speculations on society, the scientists of our generation were placing beyond question or argument the doctrine of the indestructibility of energy and matter ; and we may be sure that while there is immortal life there must be immortal energies as its companions through time, and they will never be less powerful than they are to-day or were in the morning of the world.   There will be no weakening of that mighty God-begotten brotherhood of elemental powers ; and, while we cannot hope that by the wastage of time these powers will be feebler, we may hope that by an understanding of them we may get mastery over them.   The wild elephant of the woods, with a greater strength than man's, has yet been trained to be his servant, and that arcane power we call electricity, which, if it shoots out of its channel, shrivels up the body of man, is now our servant.   So we may hope, too, that the elemental energies in humanity itself, which break out in wars and Armageddons, will come under control.   We should not hope that man will ever be a less powerful being.   To hope that would be to wish for his degradation. We should wish him to become ever more and more powerful by understanding himself, and by the unity of the spiritual faculties and the elemental energies in him into one harmonious whole. At present he is feeble because he is, to use the scriptural illustration, a house divided against itself.

Our feebleness is due to the conflict of powers in us and our conflict with each other.   Get the two mightiest bulls in a herd, put them opposing each other in a narrow passage, and they, being of equal strength, will reduce each other to feebleness.   Neither will make headway.   Let them unite together in their charge, and what will oppose them ?   Men at conflict in their own hearts, opposing each other in the world, reduce themselves and each other to wretchedness. The race which could eliminate the factors which promote internal conflict in society and could organize human energies in harmony, would be powerful beyond our wildest dreams. Every now and then in world-history we come across instances of what organized humanity could accomplish. There are fragments of an architecture so majestic that they awe us as the high rocks of nature do, and they seem almost like portions of nature itself, and truly they are so, being portions of nature remade by man, who is also a nature energy of divine origin. Europe by its conflicts to-day is reducing itself to barbarism and powerlessness, and these conflicts arose out of the internal conflicts in society, for individuals and nations act outside themselves as they act inside themselves. The problem for Europe is to create a harmonious life, and it is the problem for us in Ireland, and we will have to work this out for ourselves. The creation of a harmonious life among a people must come from within. It can never come by the imposition of an external law imposed by another people. Never did master and slave work in true unison, no matter how benevolent the master or how yielding the slave, for there is in every man, no matter what his condition, a spark of divine life, and it will always be ready to stir him out of subjection, as the fires of earthquake lie below the cultivated plain. Man is a creature who has free will, and it

is by self-devised and self-checked efforts he
will attain his full human stature.   So the problem of creating an organic life in Ireland, a
harmony of our people, a union of their efforts
for the common good and for the manifestation
of whatever beauty, majesty, and spirituality is
in us, must be one we ourselves must solve for
ourselves.

   To be indifferent to the possibilities of human
life, to ignore the problem, is to turn our back on
heaven, which fashioned the spirit of man in its
image.   If the spirit of man has likeness to Deity,
it means that if it manifests itself fully in the world,
the world too becomes a shadowy likeness of
the heavens, and our civilizations will make a
harmony with the diviner spheres.   We give
still a service of lip belief to the Scriptures, yet
active faith we have not.   But they are true,
yesterday, to-day, and for ever ; and we have still
the root of the matter in us, for when any one
utters out of profound conviction his faith, there
are always multitudes ready to respond.   What
really prevents an organic unity in Ireland is the
economic individualism of our lives.   The science
of economics deals with the efforts of men to mine
out of nature the food, minerals, and materials
necessary to preserve life.   There is nothing more
certain than that where men work alone or only
with the aid of their families they are little higher
than the animals.   When they tend to unite
civilization begins.   Then arise the towers, the
temples, the cities, the achievements of the

architect and engineer.   The earth is tapped of
its arcane energies, the very air yields to us its
mysterious   powers.   We   control   the   etheric
waves and send the message of our deeds across
the ocean.   Yet in the midst of these vast external
manifestations of power, multitudes of men and
women live in squalor, isolated in their labours,
living in the slums of cities ; and this, if we
examine it, comes about because the organization
of human energies into a harmonious unity is
not complete.   There is really no lack of food,
clothing, building material, land.   Nature has
provided bountifully for more myriads than we
are likely to see peopling the earth.   But people
compete with each other and undersell each other,
and those who labour are mulcted of their due,
and instead of turning to the earth—the in-
exhaustible mother—and working unitedly for
the common weal, they continue that fierce competition and stultify each other's efforts and
reduce each other to wretchedness.   Humanity
is a house divided against itself.

Those who feel this to be true must gather
round any movement which gives a hope for the
future, which indicates a policy by which the
organic unity of society in Ireland might be
attained, and our people work harmoniously to
make beauty and health prevail in our civilization.
What each gives up to society in the making of a
civilization he gets back a thousandfold.   Now,
the co-operative movement alone of all movements
in Ireland has aspired to make an economic

solidarity in Ireland. Whatever the aims of other movements may be—and many of them have high ideals and are necessary for the spiritual and intellectual development of our people—there is none of them which has for aim the unity of economic life. They all leave untouched this problem—how are we to organize society so that people will not be in conflict with each other, will not nullify each other's efforts, but all will conspire together for unity, so that none shall be forgotten or oppressed or left out of our brotherhood? The policy I put forward is incomplete and imperfect, and it must necessarily be so, being mainly the work of one mind, and to complete it and perfect it there must be many minds and many workers fired by the ideal. But I have indicated in some completeness how the rural population could be co-operatively organized, federated together, and how the urban population could be organized and brought into a harmony of economic purpose with the folk of the country. Within the limits of object these suggestions amount to a policy for the nation.

If the tragic condition of the world leaves us unstirred, if we draw no lessons from it, if there is no fiery stirring of will in Ireland to make it a better place to live in, then indeed we may lose hope for our country. Let us remember the most scornful condemnation in Scripture was not given to the evil but to the indifferent : " Because thou art neither hot nor cold I will spew thee out of my mouth." Let us not be the Laodiceans

of Europe, listless and indifferent to human needs,
swallowing our whisky and our porter, stupefying
our souls, while our poor are sweated ; letting
the children of our cities die with more careless-
ness about life than the people of any other
European country, with sectarian organizations
crawling in secrecy like poisonous serpents
through the undergrowth of swamps and forests.
The co-operative movement is at least open and
ideal in its aims and objects.   It is national and
not sectional.   It seeks the triumph of no section
but the unity of our people, where unity alone is
possible.   Our intransigeants and extremists of
all parties are not hurt or wounded by their
adhesion to the co-operative ideal.   We may
make up our minds that the stubborn Irish
temperament will never be overcome, but it may
be won, and the movement which invites all
parties and creeds into its ranks and gives them the
largest opportunities of working together and
understanding each other, gives also the largest
hope of the gradual melting of old bitterness into
a common tolerance where what is best essentially
wins ; for all true triumphs are triumphs not
of force, but the conquest by a superior beauty of
what is less beautiful.   We should aim at a
society where people will be at harmony in their
economic life, will readily listen to different
opinions from their own, will not turn sour faces
on those who do not think as they do, but will,
by reason and sympathy, comprehend each other
and come at last, through sympathy and affection,

to a balancing of their diversities, as in that multitudinous diversity, which·is the universe, powers and dominions and elements are balanced, and are guided harmoniously by the Shepherd of the Ages.

THE END